THE FAMILY LAW LIBRARY FROM WILEY LAW PUBLICATIONS

W9-CPQ-914

SUBSCRIPTION NOTICE

This Wiley product is updated on a periodic basis with supplements to reflect important changes in the subject matter. If you purchased this product directly from John Wiley & Sons, Inc., we have already recorded your subscription for this update service.

If, however, you purchased this product from a bookstore and wish to receive (1) the current update at no additional charge, and (2) future updates and revised or related volumes billed separately with a 30-day examination review, please send your name, company name (if applicable), address, and the title of the product to:

Supplement Department
John Wiley & Sons, Inc.
One Wiley Drive
Somerset, NJ 08875
1-800-225-5945

BANKRUPTCY AND DIVORCE

SUPPORT AND PROPERTY DIVISION

THE HONORABLE JUDITH K. FITZGERALD

RAMONA M. ARENA, ESQUIRE

Wiley Law Publications

JOHN WILEY & SONS, INC.

New York • Chichester • Brisbane • Toronto • Singapore

Copyright © 1992 by John Wiley & Sons, Inc.

Library of Congress Cataloging-in-Publication Data

ISBN 0-471-55632-7

Printed in the United States of America

10 9 8 7 6 5 4 3 2 1

PREFACE

About two years ago it became evident to us that family law practitioners were becoming increasingly concerned about the effect on their clients when bankruptcy intervenes. We also began to see more bankruptcy cases that involved issues stemming from divorce proceedings. In the course of doing research, we realized that there are different points of view and legal analyses applicable to the variety of situations that develop when these two areas of the law clash.

This book covers the most common circumstances in which family law and bankruptcy practitioners may find themselves. It is intended to be a guide for the practitioner in either field. We hope that the reader will find it helpful.

The authors gratefully acknowledge the assistance of the law firm of Kabala & Geeseman of Pittsburgh, Pennsylvania, in the preparation of the section on pensions and retirement funds.

Last, but not least, we wish to give our heartfelt thanks to Catherine Dorsch Wreath, without whose assistance we could not have prepared the manuscript.

Pittsburgh, Pennsylvania
September 1991

JUDITH K. FITZGERALD
RAMONA M. ARENA

ABOUT THE AUTHORS

The Honorable Judith K. Fitzgerald graduated from the University of Pittsburgh School of Law in 1973. After over a decade litigating criminal and civil cases as an assistant United States attorney, she was appointed to the bench of the United States Bankruptcy Court for the Western District of Pennsylvania, where she has served since 1987. Judge Fitzgerald is a frequent lecturer and participant in many continuing professional education programs in matters including bankruptcy, family law, trial advocacy, ethics, evidence, and accounting.

Ramona M. Arena obtained her J.D. in 1981 and her LL.M. in 1982. She has authored articles for law reviews and seminars. A former teacher, she occasionally lectures on the subject of bankruptcy law. She joined the Bankruptcy Court for the Western District of Pennsylvania as a law clerk in 1987, after having engaged in private legal practice.

SUMMARY CONTENTS

DETAILED CONTENTS

CHAPTER 1

OVERVIEW

§ 1.1 Conflict Between Bankruptcy and Divorce

Bankruptcy laws were designed to give the honest but unfortunate debtor a fresh start. State divorce laws providing for property division and support obligations also have as their goal a fresh start for the parties involved. When bankruptcy laws and divorce settlements and orders meet, they frequently clash. Bankruptcy courts may interpret the bankruptcy law in a manner which puts the debtor's interests ahead of those of a dependent ex-spouse and children. Such a result often ignores the realities of a marital relationship, its dissolution, and the expenses involved, particularly those incurred in maintaining two households. It also disregards the fact that divorcing parties often structure their agreements in light of applicable tax consequences[1] or based on considerations of state law which permit modifications to be made in support provisions long after the initial support agreement has been finalized.

Congress seemed to recognize these realities when it declared support, alimony, and maintenance nondischargeable by enacting § 523(a)(5) of Title 11 of the United States Code. Congress envisioned that bankruptcy

---

[1] It must be noted that no tax analyses have been made. The focus of this book is on the question of support of dependents.

1

Title 11 of the United States Code. Congress envisioned that bankruptcy courts would decide the issue of whether a given obligation is actually in the nature of "support."[2] The divorce laws, certain tax provisions, and other laws concerning enforcement of support obligations indicate a clear intent to avoid turning the dependents into wards of the state or into bankruptcy debtors themselves.

The purpose of this book is to alert the family law practitioner to certain principles which may be applied by bankruptcy courts when faced with a domestic matter and to point out the various views taken by the federal courts on divorce issues in bankruptcy. The topics were selected to illustrate some of the factors which may affect a divorce client's obligation to pay pursuant to a marital dissolution agreement or order, or, conversely, the ability to collect on the obligation, when one spouse files a bankruptcy petition. The concentration will be on what constitutes support. Other considerations such as abstention by federal courts, the ability of state courts to enter contempt orders or to modify support orders post-petition, and the enforceability of those orders will be discussed. Awards of counsel fees and the drafting of premarital agreements will be mentioned as will other state law issues that often are affected once a bankruptcy is filed.[3]

§ 1.2   Basic Goals and Procedure in Bankruptcy

The Bankruptcy Code[4] has two primary goals: to provide a fresh start by discharging many debts of the honest but unfortunate debtor and to distribute assets for the benefit of creditors. A bankruptcy discharge has the effect of removing the personal liability of the debtor for any of the debts included in the discharge and prohibits any creditor from attempting to collect from the debtor the discharged debts.[5] Sometimes the distribution of the debtor's assets takes the form of a reorganization of the debtor through repayment of debts.[6] Sometimes it occurs through liquidation of

---

[2] The determination of support is said to be made under "federal common law" although, formerly, no such concept was recognized. Bankruptcy courts, therefore, are developing that body of law. *See* H.R. Rep. No. 595, 95th Cong., 1st Sess. 363 (1977); S. Rep. No. 989, 95th Cong., 2d Sess. 77–79 (1978).

[3] In the bankruptcy context, child support awards do not pose problems as extensive as those presented by property awards to spouses. *But see* Boyle v. Donovan, 724 F.2d 681 (8th Cir. 1984) (debtor's obligation to pay son's college and graduate school expenses found to be nondischargeable support obligation).

[4] Codified at 11 U.S.C. § 101 *et seq.* Note that all references to the Bankruptcy Code are to the 1978 Bankruptcy Reform Act as amended through 1991.

[5] 11 U.S.C. §§ 524, 727, 1141(d)(1), 1228, 1328.

[6] *See generally* Chapters 11, 12, and 13 of Title 11 U.S.C.

the debtor's assets.[7] Although there are instances in which a creditor can force a debtor into bankruptcy,[8] most cases are filed voluntarily by the debtor. A case is commenced when a debtor pays a filing fee[9] and submits to the court a bankruptcy petition, a statement of financial affairs, and a schedule of assets and liabilities.[10] An individual also must file a schedule of current income and current expenditures, a statement concerning executory contracts, and a statement concerning debtor's intentions with regard to secured debt.[11] Further, the debtor provides a written acknowledgment that he is aware and has been informed of the availability of relief under each of the four primary chapters (7, 11, 12, and 13) available to consumers under the Bankruptcy Code. Primarily, consumer debtors file for reorganization under Chapter 13 and for liquidation under Chapter 7. Chapter 12 applies only to certain farmers and Chapter 11 generally is utilized for corporate or business reorganizations, although it is used occasionally by individuals.

§ 1.3 Bankruptcy Estate

The filing of the petition creates an estate separate and distinct from the debtor which is subject to administration by the bankruptcy court.[12] The estate is composed of all interests of the debtor in property of any kind and wherever located that exist on the date of filing of the bankruptcy, regardless of the tenuous nature of the interests.[13] For example, an interest to which a debtor becomes entitled within 180 days *after* the bankruptcy is filed through a property settlement, as the result of an interlocutory or final divorce decree, or through bequest, devise, inheritance or life insurance policy or death benefit plan is property of the estate. A contingent right to payments based on a personal injury or breach of contract which occurred pre-petition is property of the estate, even though the debtor's right to payment is unliquidated.

A debtor is required to list all his assets and interests in property and all the claims against him and his property in the various schedules which he files.[14] This is so even though, in the final analysis, some enumerated

---

[7] *See generally* Chapter 7 of Title 11 U.S.C.

[8] 11 U.S.C. § 303.

[9] 28 U.S.C. § 1930.

[10] 11 U.S.C. § 301; Fed. R. Bankr. P. 1002, 11 U.S.C.

[11] *See* 11 U.S.C. § 521; Fed. R. Bankr. P. 1007, 11 U.S.C.

[12] *See* 11 U.S.C. § 541.

[13] 11 U.S.C. § 541(a).

[14] 11 U.S.C. § 521; Fed. R. Bankr. P. 1007, 11 U.S.C. *See also* Official Forms, Title 11 U.S.C.

interests may be determined by the court to be exempt or otherwise not subject to administration for the benefit of creditors. Property which a debtor claims as exempt in her schedules is property of the estate until the time for filing objections to the exemptions has passed or the court rules otherwise.[15]

§ 1.4 Exemptions

A debtor in a collection action is generally entitled to claim certain property as exempt from execution by a creditor under state law. Similarly, a debtor in bankruptcy is entitled to exempt certain interests in property from inclusion in the bankruptcy estate. The Bankruptcy Code itself enumerates federal exemptions in § 522(d). However, § 522 permits states to opt out of the federal exemption scheme and 36 states have done so. In those jurisdictions debtors may claim exemptions only under applicable state law. In the remainder of states debtors must choose either state or federal exemptions. The Bankruptcy Code prohibits a debtor from claiming both.[16] The debtor must include property claimed as exempt in his list of assets and must file a list of property claimed as exempt.

§ 1.5 Automatic Stay

The filing of the petition causes an injunction called the "automatic stay" to issue.[17] The automatic stay precludes almost all collection actions against the debtor and his property. As long as the case remains open and the property remains property of the estate, no action may be taken in contravention of the automatic stay unless a separate order is obtained from the bankruptcy court, the debtor is discharged in a Chapter 7 liquidation, or a plan is confirmed in the other chapters.[18] Actions taken in violation of the automatic stay are treated differently by the federal

---

[15] On July 8, 1991, the Court of Appeals for the Third Circuit ruled that exemptions claimed under § 522(b) are allowed unless a party in interest objects within 30 days of the § 341 creditors' meeting. Taylor v. Freeland & Kronz, 938 F.2d 420 (3d Cir. 1991). *But see In re* Bennett, 36 B.R. 893 (Bankr. W.D. Ky. 1984). *See also In re* Peterson, 920 F.2d 1389 (8th Cir. 1990); Munoz v. Dembs, 757 F.2d 777 (6th Cir. 1985).

[16] 11 U.S.C. § 522(b). *See* 3 Bankruptcy L. Ed. §§ 22:120–22:172 (1987) (survey of statutory "opt-out" provision); 7 Collier on Bankruptcy, *Exemptions* (15th ed. 1991) (collecting state exemption statutes).

[17] 11 U.S.C. § 362.

[18] 11 U.S.C. § 362(c).

courts. In some jurisdictions, those actions are void ab initio.[19] In others, such as the Eleventh and Fifth Circuits, they are voidable and subject to cure if the bankruptcy court can be persuaded to annul the stay.[20]

There are certain exceptions to the stay, one of which is the collection of alimony, maintenance, or support obligations from post-petition assets and from any property that is not property of the estate.[21] Property not subject to the stay usually includes the debtor's post-petition earnings and property acquired more than 180 days post-petition.[22] Further, as discussed in § 1.6, support, maintenance, and alimony payments are not dischargeable and, therefore, arrearages that occurred before the bankruptcy filing will remain due after bankruptcy.[23]

§ 1.6   Marital Estate

Property acquired during a marriage generally is owned by the spouses in the entireties or, in a few states, as community property. The concept of "marital property" comes into play when a divorce decree is entered in community property or common law states. Marital property has been explained as follows:

> Unlike community property marital property is not a method of ownership [in entireties states] but is merely a vehicle for achieving economic justice incident to divorce. Strictly speaking, "marital property" does not exist prior to the filing of the divorce complaint, and the enactment of the divorce code effected no change in the manner in which married people own property in Pennsylvania.[24]

The laws governing gifts, constructive trusts, and tracing of equitable title are also relevant but whether or not gifts or inheritances are part of the marital property depends on state law. The nine community property states are Louisiana, Texas, New Mexico, Arizona, California,

---

[19] Morgan Guaranty Trust Co. v. American Savs. & Loan Assoc., 804 F.2d 1487, 1490 (9th Cir. 1986); *In re* Stephen W. Grosse, P.C., 68 B.R. 847, 850 (Bankr. E.D. Pa. 1987). *See also In re* Celesti, Bankr. No. 87-03273 (Bankr. W.D. Pa., Oct. 25, 1989).

[20] Sikes v. Global Marine, Inc., 881 F.2d 176 (5th Cir. 1989); *In re* Albany Partners Ltd., 749 F.2d 670 (11th Cir. 1984).

[21] 11 U.S.C. § 362(b)(2). *Cf. In re* Adams, 12 B.R. 540 (Bankr. D. Utah 1981) (discussing what assets are available for support to non-debtor spouse following confirmation of Chapter 13 plan).

[22] 11 U.S.C. § 541(a)(5). *See* § 1.3.

[23] 11 U.S.C. § 523(a)(5).

[24] J. Wilder, J. Mahood, M. Greenblatt, Pennsylvania Family Law Practice and Procedure Handbook § 14-1 (2d ed. 1989) [hereinafter Wilder, Mahood & Greenblatt].

Washington, Idaho, Nevada and Wisconsin. Mississippi alone is known as a title theory state but joins the ranks of common law jurisdictions with respect to distribution of marital property except that its state courts may distribute only jointly held property in the event of divorce.[25]

Entireties estates are creatures of the common law based on the idea that husband and wife are one. Thus each owns the entire estate and upon the death of one spouse the other owns the property in fee simple. Entireties estates are commonly described as being composed of the unities of estate or title, possession, and control of the entire property.[26]

The source of a community estate in community property states is entirely statutory and the nature and extent of the interest depends on applicable state law. If the state law gives one spouse control over the other's separate property, that property becomes property of the bankruptcy estate. Whether the separate property is subject to administration under the bankruptcy laws probably requires a case-by-case analysis. For example, in common law jurisdictions the debtor's right to control the property would be an interest of the debtor in property and, therefore, by definition, property of the bankruptcy estate under § 541. However, the property would not be subject to administration under the Bankruptcy Code unless the debtor acquired, through the divorce proceedings, some ownership in it or the ability to dispose of it for his own benefit.

In community property states each spouse has an individual one-half interest in property, including the earnings of the other spouse.[27] If the marriage dissolves, however, the property is not necessarily divided equally, but instead may be divided relative to the needs of the parties.[28] California, New Mexico and Louisiana, however, do not permit unequal division of community property upon divorce.[29] Arizona, Idaho, Nevada, Texas, and Washington use equitable distribution principles to divide property upon divorce and Wisconsin treats the parties' property as community property during the marriage but subjects it to equitable distribution upon divorce.[30]

Upon divorce or separation in a community property state, the terms of the agreement or order dividing property will be relevant to the

---

[25] *See* Freed & Walker, *Family Law in the Fifty States: An Overview,* 21 Family L.Q. 367, 455–56 (1989).

[26] *See* Black's Law Dictionary 492 (5th ed. 1979).

[27] *Id.* at 254.

[28] *See In re* Nunnally, 506 F.2d 1024, 1026–27 (5th Cir.), *reh'g denied,* 509 F.2d 576 (5th Cir. 1975); Reppy, *Discharge In Bankruptcy of Awards of Money or Property at Divorce: Analyzing The Risk and Some Steps to Avoid It,* 15 Community Prop. J. 1, 3 (1988).

[29] Scheible, *Defining "Support" Under Bankruptcy Law: Revitalization of the "Necessaries" Doctrine,* 41 Vand. L. Rev. 1, 13 n.61 (1988).

[30] Wilder, Mahood & Greenblatt at § 14-1.

bankruptcy court's determination of what constitutes property of the bankruptcy estate.[31] If the bankruptcy is filed before the divorce court has concluded its division of community or entireties property, the bankruptcy court obtains exclusive jurisdiction over the property.[32] The property interests, however, are defined in accordance with state law.[33]

Typically, upon divorce in community property states the property either is divided equally or is apportioned in the degree to which each spouse contributed to its acquisition. In common law jurisdictions the division may be in any percentage depending on the support needs of the dependent spouse and children. Other factors, such as the following, also may play a role in how the judge in a common law jurisdiction divides property:

(1)   The length of the marriage.

(2)   Any prior marriage of either party.

(3)   The age, health, station, amount and sources of income, vocational skills, employability, estate, liabilities and needs of each of the parties.

(4)   The contribution by one party to the education, training, or increased earning power of the other party.

(5)   The opportunity of each party for future acquisitions of capital assets and income.

(6)   The sources of income of both parties, including but not limited to medical, retirement, insurance or other benefits.

(7)   The contribution or dissipation of each party in the acquisition, preservation, depreciation or appreciation of the marital property, including the contribution of a party as homemaker.

(8)   The value of the property set apart to each party.

(9)   The standard of living of the parties established during the marriage.

(10)   The economic circumstances of each party, including Federal, State and local tax ramifications, at the time the division of property is to become effective.

(11)   Whether the party will be serving as the custodian of any dependent minor children.[34]

In community property and common law jurisdictions problems may arise when there is an increase in the value of separately owned property during the course of marriage. In common law jurisdictions it may be that the increase in value would remain separate property, absent the applicability of equitable principles requiring a contrary result. For example, if

---

[31] 4 Collier on Bankruptcy § 541.15 (15th ed. 1991).

[32] *Id.*

[33] *But see* 11 U.S.C. §§ 547, 548 (transfers from debtor which are "preferential" or "fraudulent" may be set aside and transferred property made part of estate).

[34] Pa. Stat. Ann. tit. 23, § 401(d) (Purdon Supp. 1989) (repealed December 1990). *See* Pa. Stat. Ann. tit. 23, §§ 3323, 3501, 3502, 3503 (Purdon 1990).

the separate interest or increase in the value would have been marital property but for the interest holder's fraud, equity would not permit the innocent spouse to be deprived of his interest. Counsel must ascertain the local, state, and federal law and practice.

§ 1.7   Nondischargeability of Support Obligations

The nondischargeability of specific debts such as support must be distinguished from the concept of discharge of all unsecured obligations which is the general purpose of the bankruptcy laws. Objections to discharge are undertaken pursuant to § 727 and, if sustained, apply to all debts. When a discharge is denied, the creditors may proceed against the debtor and all his property as if a bankruptcy had never been filed. A creditor also may attack the dischargeability of one debt; that is, the debtor's right to be discharged from a particular obligation owed to that creditor, on grounds enumerated in § 523 of the Bankruptcy Code. Support obligations are nondischargeable by operation of law pursuant to § 523(a)(5), while the weight of current authority holds that a debt which is part of a property settlement is dischargeable.[35] Whether a particular obligation is actually in the nature of support is sometimes the subject of litigation in the bankruptcy courts. Counsel is cautioned that § 523(d) provides for an award of counsel fees to the debtor if a challenge to the dischargeability of a consumer debt is unsuccessful unless "special circumstances would make the award unjust." The authors are not aware of any cases which address the issue of whether an obligation created as the result of the dissolution of a marriage is a consumer debt.

Whether certain obligations imposed by state law in divorce proceedings and attendant property divisions are nondischargeable as alimony, maintenance, or support (hereafter collectively "support") is a problem with which federal bankruptcy and appellate courts continue to wrestle. The non-debtor spouse may need to litigate the nature of the debt in order to establish that it is nondischargeable. For example, when one spouse assumes a debt which can be considered as support even if it was incurred as part of a property settlement, actions to collect it might not be stayed, but, to avoid a contempt citation for violating the stay, the non-debtor spouse may want the protection of an order lifting the stay prior to

---

[35] *Compare* Shaver v. Shaver, 736 F.2d 1314 (9th Cir. 1984) (personal circumstances determine nature of obligation) *with In re* Burns, 21 B.R. 909 (Bankr. W.D. Okla. 1982) (underlying purpose of obligation determines its nature). 26.11 U.S.C. § 522(b). *See* 3 Bankruptcy L. Ed. § 22:120-172 (1987) for a survey of the statutory "opt-out" provision; 7 Collier on Bankruptcy, *Exemptions* (15th ed.) 1990 (collecting state exemption laws).

attempting collection. This is particularly true when it is not certain how the bankruptcy court will rule on the question of support or when there is a question as to whether estate property is involved.

When the question of dischargeability is raised because support is at issue, it should be noted that there is authority for the proposition that state and federal courts have concurrent jurisdiction to determine both whether an obligation is support and whether it is nondischargeable.[36] However, the determination of whether the obligation is support must be made using federal law. Parties may wish to include in marital dissolution agreements and decrees a provision that dischargeability of the obligations in event of a bankruptcy will be determined by the state or bankruptcy court. Before such a choice of forum clause is incorporated, counsel must examine carefully the rulings of the federal bankruptcy and appellate courts and the state courts in the jurisdiction in order to determine the likelihood of obtaining the desired result. It must be noted that the United States Supreme Court held in *Brown v. Felsen*[37] that the bankruptcy court is not bound to accept a state court ruling on dischargeability, but this was before the 1984 amendments to the Bankruptcy Code. *Brown v. Felsen* concerned § 17 of the Bankruptcy Act that required a court decision on the dischargeability of certain debts. Under the current Bankruptcy Code, only the bankruptcy court must determine the dischargeability of certain debts, but the dischargeability of support obligations is not among those. Section 523(c)(1) refers to questions of dischargeability of § 523(a)(2), (4), and (6) matters. Bankruptcy Rule 4007(c) refers to the time to file an objection to dischargeability for § 523(c) matters. There is no time limit for proceedings other than under § 523(c). Thus, the bankruptcy court probably would be required to accept a state court ruling on the dischargeability of a support obligation if collateral estoppel or res judicata elements were met.

§ 1.8   Enforceability of Other Types of Interests

Sometimes a dependent spouse obtains a lien on property awarded to the debtor in the divorce proceedings to secure payment. A divorce judgment which incorporates a property settlement may create the lien. Section 522(f)(1) permits avoidance of judicial liens which impair state or federal exemptions.[38] See **Chapter 4** concerning lien avoidance. Some courts permit this result regardless of whether the underlying obligation is in the

---

[36] *See, e.g., In re* Sailsbury, 13 Kan. App. 2d 740, 779 P.2d 878 (1989).

[37] 442 U.S. 127, 139–40 (1979).

[38] *See* 3 Collier on Bankruptcy ¶ 522.29, at 522–90, n.(a) (15th ed. 1991).

nature of support.[39] Other courts refuse to permit avoidance of consensual liens even though they fall within the definition of judicial liens.[40] Regardless of the treatment of the lien, the question of preferential or fraudulent transfers may arise under the Bankruptcy Code when a bankruptcy is filed close on the heels of a support or property division agreement or order and property is transferred pursuant thereto.[41] See **Chapter 4** concerning preferential and fraudulent transfers.

Obligations to pay to a dependent spouse portions of pensions or other retirement funds also may be discharged under some circumstances. The nature of the retirement benefit itself and the state court order distributing it between the spouses will affect the bankruptcy court's analysis.

Obligations arising from state court contempt orders for payment of money which are intended to enforce support obligations may be unenforceable or they may have been entered in violation of the automatic stay. The outcome depends on when in the course of the bankruptcy case the contempt order was issued and whether it required payment from estate assets. When a jail sentence is imposed, a different set of problems arises and is affected by whether it is necessary for the debtor to use estate assets to purge himself of the contempt in order to obtain release. Whether the bankruptcy courts should become involved in other aspects of enforcement of support orders or agreements is open to debate and will be discussed in **Chapters 2** and **7**.

§ 1.9   Type of Bankruptcy, Conversion, and Dismissal

The chapter under which the debtor chooses to file can have a significant effect on the amount paid to creditors. For example, in jurisdictions where certain pre-petition obligations of a debtor to an ex-spouse are discharged because they are determined to be in the nature of a property settlement and not support, a Chapter 11 or Chapter 13 could be of greater benefit to

---

[39] *See In re* Boyd, 26 B.R. 772 (Bankr. D. Minn. 1982), *rev'd on other grounds sub nom.* Boyd v. Robinson, 741 F.2d 1112 (8th Cir. 1984) (court did not consider whether underlying obligations might be support and found lien imposed on homestead to be avoidable judicial lien; Eighth Circuit reversed on basis of pre-existing interest theory). See **Chs. 3** and **4**.

[40] *In re* Maus, 48 B.R. 948 (Bankr. D. Kan. 1985), so held but was reversed on appeal, Maus v. Maus, 837 F.2d 935 (10th Cir. 1988), because the divorce decree provided that the debtor took the marital real estate free and clear of the spouse's interest. Borman v. Leiker, 886 F.2d 273 (10th Cir. 1989), distinguished *Maus* on the ground that the intent in *Borman* was to make the homestead the source of funds for payment under the divorce decree.

[41] 11 U.S.C. §§ 547, 548.

the non-debtor spouse because these chapters provide for payment plans pursuant to which a percentage of pre-petition obligations would be paid regardless of their nature. It is conceivable that a non-debtor spouse could move a court to dismiss a Chapter 7 case[42] or to convert it to a Chapter 11 in order to force payment.[43] However, the burden of proof is high and the logistics of pursuing such an action as well as the current improbability of success mandates that counsel consider carefully the advisability of such a course of action.

A case may not be converted to a Chapter 13 or 12 by the court unless the debtor requests it.[44] Bankruptcy courts may dismiss a bankruptcy petition rather than grant a discharge in appropriate cases. Section 707(b) specifically authorizes that action when the debts are primarily consumer debts and granting a discharge would constitute a substantial abuse of the Bankruptcy Code. However, a creditor may not petition the bankruptcy court for relief under this section. Section 707(a) authorizes dismissal for cause at the request of a creditor, whether or not the debts are primarily consumer debts. However, the burden of proof is high and a non-debtor spouse will rarely find § 707 a useful tool.

Because most consumer debtors file under Chapter 7 of the Bankruptcy Code, the main thrust of these remarks is directed to support and property division questions as they are affected under that chapter. The outcome of some issues may differ depending on the particular chapter selected by the debtor. In a Chapter 7, property in which there is equity over secured obligations and the debtor's exemptions is liquidated. A trustee selected by the United States Trustee's Office[45] or the creditors distributes this excess in accordance with statutorily mandated priorities.[46]

---

[42] 11 U.S.C. § 707(a).

[43] See 11 U.S.C. §§ 105, 706(b).

[44] 11 U.S.C. § 706(c).

[45] The United States Trustee's Office is a division of the United States Department of Justice. The United States Trustee is authorized to act in all judicial districts except those located in Alabama and North Carolina. It will be authorized in those districts when the district elects to be included in the system or on October 1, 2002. Judicial Improvements Act of 1990, Pub. L. No. 101-650, § 317(a), 104 Stat. 5115 (1991).

[46] See 11 U.S.C. § 726.

CHAPTER 2

WHAT IS SUPPORT?

§ 2.1 Relevant Factors

Whether obligations imposed by a divorce decree are support and therefore nondischargeable can vary from jurisdiction to jurisdiction. Some courts hold the obligations dischargeable even though they appear to have been intended for support. See §§ 2.2 and 2.3. Other courts, however, hold the obligations dischargeable simply because they are "debts" as that term is defined under the Bankruptcy Code without examining the economic realities of the situation.[1] One commentator suggests that determination of support should be examined in light of the necessaries doctrine.[2] Some cases examine the intent or effect of the award as well as the need for support and/or the form in which the award is made.[3] Factors such as whether the obligation to pay ceases on the death or remarriage of the former spouse can be critical.[4] Sometimes the parties' intent itself is determined by need.[5] All of these factors are relevant and, as a general rule, none should be given paramount importance.

The Bankruptcy Code provides that any and all interests of a debtor in property become property of the bankruptcy estate and that most debts

---

[1] *See* 11 U.S.C. § 101(5), (12) (1991).

[2] Scheible, *Defining "Support" Under Bankruptcy Law: Revitalization of the "Necessaries" Doctrine,* 41 Vand. L. Rev. (1988) [hereinafter Scheible, *Defining "Support" Under Bankruptcy Law*].

[3] *See, e.g.,* Forsdick v. Turgeon, 812 F.2d 801 (2d Cir. 1987); *In re* Hoivik, 79 B.R. 401 (Bankr. W.D. Wisc. 1987).

[4] *See In re* Hysock, 75 B.R. 113, 114 (Bankr. D. Del. 1987).

[5] *See, e.g., In re* Grijalva, 72 B.R. 334, 339 (S.D. W. Va. 1987) (regarding obligation to keep life insurance policy in effect, pay college expenses for children and ex-spouse's attorney's fees).

are dischargeable. Whether an obligation to pay a mortgage, to maintain life insurance or medical insurance or to pay debts, usually in the form of hold harmless agreements, is support and therefore nondischargeable can turn on the documents creating the obligation, extrinsic evidence, the parties' relative financial status, and the perception of the particular bankruptcy court deciding the issue. Although it is unlikely that a bankruptcy court would ignore state concepts entirely, in theory it may do so even though there are no federal domestic relations laws.

While the divorce action is pending, temporary support may be awarded so a dependent spouse can afford to prosecute the action.[6] The complexity of the issue of whether a delinquency or arrearage is support and therefore nondischargeable in a bankruptcy case may be compounded if no spousal support is awarded in the final decree. It is submitted that if the state court determined before the divorce that interim support was necessary, the mere fact that it was determined not to be necessary in the long run does not invalidate its status as support, particularly in light of the fact that § 523(a)(5) refers to "support" without qualification.[7]

In an effort to find a solution to the problem of determining what is support, one commentator suggests that parties should request the state court to add to each provision of an order which divides property, provides for support, or approves an agreement for same, that each specific obligation, right or interest is intended to be in the nature of support, alimony, or maintenance.[8] In jurisdictions which do not allow permanent alimony, it may be futile for the dependent spouse to include such provisions which, in any event, would not be binding on the bankruptcy court.

§ 2.2   Attorney's Fees

When the debtor consents or is ordered in a prebankruptcy divorce proceeding to pay a dependent spouse's attorney's fees or to pay debts incurred during the course of the marriage, courts often find the obligation to pay nondischargeable. The rationale is that (1) because of a lack of evidence of intent to make the fees or debt repayment part of a property settlement or (2) because the dependent spouse's financial, health, or other circumstances indicate that the provision was intended to assist in meeting living expenses, the obligation was "so intimately connected with the

---

[6] *See, e.g.,* Pa. Stat. Ann. tit. 23, § 502 (Purdon Supp. 1990).

[7] *See In re* Hoivik, 79 B.R. 401 (Bankr. W.D. Wis. 1987) (debtor did not contest nondischargeability of divorce judgment portion which required him to pay arrears of temporary support).

[8] Murphy, *The Dischargeability in Bankruptcy of Debts for Alimony and Property Settlements Arising From Divorce,* 14 Pepperdine L. Rev. 69, 79 (1986).

original order that [it] should be considered in the nature of alimony, maintenance or support."[9]

Courts sometimes view the obligation merely as a debt, especially if the obligation is payable directly to the attorney or the creditor. Others view it as having been assigned and therefore dischargeable under § 523(a)(5)(A).[10] Other courts hold the view that "undertakings by one spouse to pay the other's debts, including a debt to a lawyer for fees, can be 'support' for bankruptcy purposes. So can periodic payments . . . even if the [divorce] decree labels these payments a 'property settlement.'"[11]

The court in *In re Romano,* while acknowledging that "attorney's fees stand and fall with the primary debt," found no authority to support the proposition that the dischargeability of attorney's fees would depend on whether the fees were based on services rendered in connection with the property settlement or with the support provision.[12] The *Romano* court noted that the majority rule is that attorney's fees are support and non-dischargeable and that the debtor and ex-spouse had stipulated that the amounts were support.[13] It seems that a better test would be all the facts and circumstances, including the parties' intentions.[14] A review of the cases referred to in this section will provide the reader with a broad range of considerations, which, of course, are not all-inclusive. The factors may be as different as are the situations which require their consideration.

---

[9] *See In re* Pollock, 90 B.R. 747, 759 (Bankr. E.D. Pa. 1988). *See also* Scheible, *Defining "Support" Under Bankruptcy Law* at 33–34.

[10] *See* 11 U.S.C. § 523(a)(5)(A) (support obligation dischargeable when assigned except when assigned to certain governmental entities). *See also* Scheible, *Defining "Support" Under Bankruptcy Law* 39–46 and cases cited therein; Gold, *The Dischargeability of Divorce Obligations Under the Bankruptcy Code: Five Faulty Premises in the Application of Section 523(a)(5),* 39 Case W.L. Rev. 455, 484–86 (1988–89) [hereinafter Gold, *Dischargeability of Divorce Obligations*]. In a bankruptcy case involving an actual assignment based on Illinois law, the Court of Appeals for the Seventh Circuit recently ruled that a non-debtor custodial parent's interest in a judgment for past due child support is assignable. The debt, which had been assigned to the custodial parent's attorney, was allowed as a claim. *In re* Hosier, 875 F.2d 128 (7th Cir. 1989).

[11] *In re* Williams, 703 F.2d 1055, 1057 (8th Cir. 1983).

[12] 27 B.R. 36, 38 (Bankr. M.D. Fla. 1983).

[13] *But see In re* LaFleur, 11 B.R. 26, 29 (Bankr. D. Mass. 1981) (when attorney's fee award is part of contempt action brought for failure to pay child support, fees are support and are nondischargeable; all other attorney fee awards are dischargeable).

[14] *See In re* Williams, 703 F.2d 1055, 1057–58 (8th Cir. 1983). When the § 523(a)(5) exception to discharge was being drafted for the 1978 Bankruptcy Code, the National Conference of Bankruptcy Judges wanted to include a provision that debts "shall not be excepted from discharge merely to hold the spouse harmless on her obligation in any manner to pay the debt . . . ." *See* Gold, *Dischargeability of Divorce Obligations* at 463–64. It was thought that hold harmless clauses benefitted the creditors and not the dependent spouse (be it husband or wife). The limitation was rejected by Congress but counsel should be aware that its spirit is alive still.

It can be argued that an award of attorney's fees to a dependent spouse often represents support because without such an award a dependent spouse would be unable to obtain or pay for legal representation or to pursue the divorce through the judicial labyrinth. Some courts are cognizant of this.[15] Others simply take a technical view. For example, if the fee obligation is not labeled "support," it is a dischargeable debt.[16]

§ 2.3   Mortgage and Other Debt Obligations

Two of the problems that appear to be most common when one spouse files bankruptcy are those attendant to (1) the mortgage obligations when the marital residence is awarded to the non-debtor spouse and (2) obligations assumed by the debtor to pay debts other than the mortgage incurred during the marriage. In cases in which the dependent spouse with custody of the children receives the real estate and the debtor the obligation to pay the mortgage, or in cases in which the debtor is left with the obligation to pay certain other debts incurred during the marriage, a dispute often arises as to whether the payment obligations are in the nature of support or are part of the property division. Such obligations are often evidenced by a hold harmless clause in the underlying document and may be in the nature of support even if they appear under the label of "property settlement."

In *In re Hoivik,*[17] for instance, a mortgage obligation to the non-debtor spouse was found to be dischargeable. The court relied almost entirely on the language of one paragraph of the divorce judgment which stated "[t]hat as a complete and final property division . . ." the debtor assumed two mortgages on the marital residence. The court acknowledged that the non-debtor spouse was not working at the time of the judgment and that there was a disparity in income potentials.[18] However, the court concluded that the purpose of this provision and others related "directly to the preservation of equity in the property" awarded to the nondebtor and not to the balancing of the parties' income.[19] The effect on the dependents of the presence or absence of the payments was not examined. The non-debtor spouse had custody of the parties' three children and the mortgages and other obligations at issue were those for furniture payments, a

---

[15] Gold, *Dischargeability of Divorce Obligations* at 463–64.

[16] *See In re* Hoivik, 79 B.R. 401 (Bankr. W.D. Wis. 1987) (obligation to make certain payments held dischargeable because it followed a phrase which included the words "complete and final property division").

[17] 79 B.R. 401 (Bankr. W.D. Wis. 1987).

[18] *Id.* at 403–04.

[19] *Id.* at 404.

home improvement loan, and real estate taxes. It would appear that these obligations would have to be paid to keep a roof over the nondebtor spouse and the children. Other courts have found such obligations to be "clearly in the nature of support and maintenance and . . . therefore nondischargeable."[20]

One also must consider the fact that support obligations may be altered in some states upon evidence of changed circumstances and parties may wish to protect certain obligations from modification, if the state court will recognize the effort.[21] Furthermore, tax consequences often influence the characterization of obligations in the state court. However, most cases do not mention these factors.[22] Whether they are the subject of unexpressed consideration cannot be determined. Furthermore, Congress' intent that state law not control the definition of support in a bankruptcy context may be based, in part, on this realization. However, bankruptcy courts should not discount state law because there is no body of federal divorce or marital relations law.

In *In re Hysock*,[23] the court examined the format of the agreement in question and found that the debtor's obligation to pay a second mortgage was not support because (1) it was contained in the section dealing with property division rather than in two sections which dealt with support, (2) it did not terminate on the non-debtor spouse's death or remarriage, and (3) it did not "expressly or inferably [relate] to living expenses."[24] The non-debtor spouse did not list the payment as income on her tax return. The court also found that her net income, including child support of $55.00 per week for two children, exceeded the debtor's, although his gross income was approximately 33 percent greater than hers. The court apparently did not consider the fact that her income was spent on three people while debtor's, absent the payment obligations, was only for himself. The non-debtor spouse had been awarded the house and the furnishings and the debtor got the car. The court ignored the fact that without the house and furnishings, the non-debtor, who earned $606.00 per month gross and was a custodial parent with minor children, would be in dire straits. Because the debtor had not been represented by counsel the court applied general contract principles to construe the agreement strictly against the non-debtor whose attorney had drafted it. However, it

---

[20] *See In re* Allshouse, 34 B.R. 512, 514 (Bankr. W.D. Pa. 1983), and cases cited therein.

[21] *In re* Calhoun, 715 F.2d 1103, 1109–10 and nn.10–12 (6th Cir. 1983) (bankruptcy court examined changed circumstances in considering whether obligation was support).

[22] The authors are not aware of any cases which, in determining whether a prepetition obligation is support, rely on the fact that family law practitioners consider tax consequences in structuring support and property division agreements.

[23] 75 B.R. 113 (Bankr. D. Del. 1987).

[24] *Id.* at 114.

disregarded the family relationship and the economic reality of what resources are needed to support two children.

The court in *Hysock* also was influenced by the parties' present needs and circumstances. Other courts have found that present need is an inappropriate consideration in defining what was intended to constitute support.[25] Otherwise the bankruptcy court, in effect, becomes another branch of the state court and interposes its opinions, thus modifying state court decrees. This is impermissible for two reasons: (1) the congressional intent was that bankruptcy courts determine what obligations are in the nature of support, not that they formulate support orders, and (2) people who do not like the deal they made or were left with in a divorce proceeding will be encouraged to file bankruptcy in those jurisdictions which permit bankruptcy courts to alter state decrees, even though the support obligations may be modifiable in the state courts.[26]

A bankruptcy court's discharge of obligations in a divorce decree may or may not be useful as a factor supporting modification of a support obligation by a state court. In *Stolp v. Stolp*[27] a property settlement awarded to the non-debtor spouse which was to be paid in installments over a period of time was discharged in the debtor's bankruptcy case. On subsequent motion by the non-debtor spouse, the state trial court vacated the property settlement and awarded permanent maintenance. The state appellate court found the award to be an attempt to circumvent the discharge and further found that state law prohibited alteration of the initial divorce decree after the 90 day appeal period had passed. In contrast, in *In re Meyers*[28] the discharge of a debt in bankruptcy was not rejected as a relevant factor in increasing support payments to a spouse in state court.

§ 2.4 Bankruptcy Court's Role

Recognizing that the state courts have expertise in deciding family law matters, some non-debtor spouses seek relief from stay to allow the state

---

[25] These courts have held that state court modification procedures are the proper vehicles for the pursuit of modification of support obligations and not proceedings in bankruptcy court. *See In re* Gianakas, 917 F.2d 759 (3d Cir. 1990); Forsdick v. Turgeon, 812 F.2d 801 (2d Cir. 1987); *In re* Chedrick, 98 B.R. 731 (W.D. Pa. 1989). That is, the court must examine the parties' circumstances as they existed at the time of the divorce settlement or state court order. It is beyond the scope of this article to analyze whether an agreement between the parties to the contrary would be enforceable. Enforceability would depend on applicable state or federal law.

[26] See discussion of federal policy of nonintervention in state court affairs in **Ch. 9.**

[27] 383 N.W.2d 409 (Minn. Ct. App. 1986).

[28] 54 Wash. App. 233, 773 P.2d 118 (1989).

courts to finalize the divorce, support and property issues. In the Eastern District of Pennsylvania the bankruptcy court refused to grant relief from stay to a non-debtor spouse to permit her to pursue equitable distribution. In *In re Ziets*[29] the debtor filed bankruptcy after a report and recommendation had been submitted to the state court presiding over the divorce procedures and the debtor had filed exceptions to the report and recommendation. The court in *Ziets* could have granted the request for the limited purpose of permitting the equitable distribution to proceed to judgment but not to execution on the judgment. The bankruptcy court determined that because § 362(b)(2) of the Bankruptcy Code excepts from the automatic stay only the collection of support from non-estate property, other domestic relations matters are not excepted absent court order.[30]

The bankruptcy court stated that it would undertake equitable distribution itself, "cognizant of [its] duty to determine [debtor's] rights vis-a-vis the [non-debtor spouse] in accordance with the letter and spirit of the Pennsylvania Divorce Code."[31] The court cited several factors in reaching its conclusion, one of which was that the "balance of hardships" was in debtor's favor in that he would be required to litigate on two fronts, that is, bankruptcy and state court, and that equitable distribution would have an impact on his creditors. The court so decided, notwithstanding the fact that the divorce decree had been entered by the state court, the master's report and recommendation of equitable distribution were filed, and debtor's exceptions to the report were pending. The debtor and the spouse apparently did not contest the conclusion that all of the marital property was property of the bankruptcy estate. However § 541(a) of the Bankruptcy Code provides that property is estate property only to the extent of the debtor's interest in it. Because no state court judgment was entered on the report and recommendation of equitable distribution, the debtor's interest in the property was nearly identical to his pre-divorce interest, the distinguishing factor being that the entireties aspect of the interest was extinguished. Under the circumstances, however, the extent of the debtor's ultimate interest and therefore the extent to which it is estate property are not ascertainable until equitable distribution is complete.[32]

---

[29] 79 B.R. 222 (Bankr. E.D. Pa. 1987).

[30] *Id.* at 225.

[31] *Id.* at 227.

[32] The Bankruptcy Code permits sale of bankruptcy estate property even when a co-owner exists. The non-debtor receives a share of the sale proceeds in accordance with the extent of his ownership interest. 11 U.S.C. § 363. If the bankruptcy court sale takes place before the state court resolves property division issues, the non-debtor spouse's rights in the property are foreclosed but he receives payment. See **App. B**.

The bankruptcy court in *Ziets* feared that a state court decree would do away with all of the debtor's property interests to the detriment of his creditors.[33] However, the policy of the Bankruptcy Code is to give a debtor a fresh start, and the policy of the divorce laws is to do the same by providing economic parity to each spouse.[34] When family welfare is at issue, it is submitted that certain provisions of the Bankruptcy Code should be applied in a manner which differs from that in the typical debtor-creditor situation. That is, if there is a question as to whether the fresh start policy of the bankruptcy or divorce laws should take precedence, the policy of the divorce laws should prevail and doubts resolved in favor of finding an obligation to be in the nature of support, despite the liberal discharge policy of the Bankruptcy Code.

The Supreme Court of the United States articulated long ago that the fresh start provided under the bankruptcy laws should be subordinated to the duty of support.[35] There is nothing in the legislative history that indicates an intent to change these pronouncements. The bankruptcy laws were designed for the protection of debtors oppressed by financial over-extension. They were not created to undo or substitute for a state court's determination of the allocation of marital resources or to permit a debtor to be unjustly enriched by the discharge of his obligations to his ex-spouse which were created by, and the result of, the marriage and its dissolution. A non-debtor spouse is not in the same position as are creditors of the debtor. The spouse lent no money, did not contract for credit and incurred no debt to the debtor. The non-debtor spouse's involvement in the bankruptcy comes about not because of a debtor-creditor relationship but because of the marriage.

Decisions such as *Ziets* permit circumvention of state domestic relations laws and could force the non-debtor spouse into bankruptcy when he is burdened with the debtor's share of the marital obligations. If, as suggested earlier, the *Ziets* court had ordered relief from stay permitting the

---

[33] How such an event would occur was not clarified. One might envision a situation where there is equity over exemptions in the marital residence which might pass to the non-debtor spouse in the context of state court dissolution proceedings. It could be argued that this prejudices debtor's creditors no more than they were at the time the obligation to them was incurred inasmuch as the property could not have been used to satisfy debtor's separate debt during the marriage. If the debt were a joint debt, the creditors would not be prejudiced by permitting equitable distribution to proceed in state court because the debtor's obligation would be discharged through the bankruptcy and the creditors could proceed against the nondebtor spouse once the entireties impediment was removed.

[34] The *Ziets* court stated that the role of the automatic stay was as "protection for creditors of the debtor not seeking relief from it, as well as for the debtor himself." 79 B.R. at 224. *But see In re* Stivers, 31 B.R. 735 (Bankr. N.D. Cal. 1983) (stay protects debtor and estate, not junior lienholders).

[35] Wetmore v. Markoe, 196 U.S. 68 (1904); Dunbar v. Dunbar, 190 U.S. 340 (1903).

non-debtor spouse to pursue equitable distribution to judgment but forbidding execution pending further bankruptcy proceedings, the bankruptcy court would have had an opportunity to consider whether the obligation constituted support and to analyze what the effect would be on all parties in interest.[36]

Placing primary concern on the effect on creditors as the *Ziets* court did is misguided for three reasons. First and foremost, the governmental policy of protecting dependents is evident on both the state and federal levels. Second, the effect on creditors of state court property allocation would not necessarily be devastating because, until the parties are divorced, the co-owned property is not reachable by the creditors for payment of one spouse's individual obligations. Thus, in the bankruptcy context, the creditors would be no worse off if property division proceeded in state court. When property division cannot be effected until the divorce decree is entered, the creditors still are not prejudiced because state law governs whether such property is reachable. Creditors might be better off if the property division proceeded because the interest of the non-debtor co-owner would be removed and the debtor's separate nonexempt property would be subject to execution. Third, in most Chapter 7 cases there are no nonexempt assets available for distribution to creditors so the concern for creditors expressed by the *Ziets* court will arise only infrequently.

Counsel should also be aware of the somewhat different result reached by another judge of the Bankruptcy Court for the Eastern District of Pennsylvania. In *In re Murray*[37] relief from stay was granted to a non-debtor spouse to pursue support but exclusive jurisdiction in the bankruptcy court was retained over the nonexempt assets. As is evident from the discussion in this section, courts are dealing with the concept of "support" in a variety of ways as the law develops. It appears that decisions will be made on an ad hoc basis. Attorneys may find a creative approach

---

[36] The District Court for the Western District of Pennsylvania in *In re* Chedrick, 98 B.R. 731 (W.D. Pa. 1989), held that the only relevant inquiry in ascertaining support is the parties' intent on the date the agreement was entered into or the date of the state court decree and that the debtor's remedy is to petition the state court with jurisdiction over the divorce for modification. Inasmuch as many bankruptcy courts prohibit consideration of circumstances occurring after the date of the agreement, the state court order or the filing of the bankruptcy, the *Ziets* position bucks the trend. In 1990 the Court of Appeals for the Third Circuit decided *In re* Gianakas, 917 F.2d 759 (3d Cir. 1990), which also required that the examination must entail the function of the obligation at the time it was created. *Id.* at 763. *See* Boyle v. Donovan, 724 F.2d 681 (8th Cir. 1984). *Compare Ziets with In re* Hampton, 43 B.R. 633 (Bankr. M.D. Fla. 1984) (relief from stay was granted to permit collection of proceeds from sale of commercial property and bankruptcy court found resulting trust where debtor spouse held only bare legal title).

[37] 31 B.R. 499 (Bankr. E.D. Pa. 1983).

to be useful, but must remain cognizant of the fact that the bankruptcy court's perspective may differ from the attorneys'.[38]

---

[38] *See In re* Oswald, 883 F.2d 69 (4th Cir. 1989) (reversing and remanding without opinion, 90 B.R. 218 (Bankr. N.D.W. Va. 1988) (bankruptcy petition filed after divorce action commenced but before divorce decree did not require bankruptcy court to abstain from selling property in which nondebtor spouse held an entireties interest). The opinion of the Court of Appeals is unpublished but available through Westlaw. According to Fourth Circuit Rule, Rule 18, I.O.P. 363. 36.5, 28 U.S.C.A., citation of unpublished opinions is disfavored.

CHAPTER 3

PROPERTY SETTLEMENT: DEBT OR PROPERTY INTEREST

§ 3.1 Non-debtor Spouse's Ownership Interest

§ 3.2 Non-debtor Spouse's Interest: Trust Theory

§ 3.3 Arguing Property Interest Theories

§ 3.1 Non-debtor Spouse's Ownership Interest

It is questionable whether property settlements or payments ordered by a state court or agreed to by the parties in divorce actions in exchange for property constitute "debts," at least in the usual sense, even when there is no need for support. The Bankruptcy Code defines "debt" as "liability on a claim,"[1] and "claim," in general, as any "right to payment . . . or to an equitable remedy for breach of performance" regardless of the nature of the right.[2] Some courts view property division pursuant to a divorce as creating a debt which "may be discharged just like any other unsecured obligation without special status."[3]

For example, in *In re Goodnight*[4] a non-debtor spouse testified that the property division in an underlying divorce "was an exchange for relinquishing my [non-debtor's] interest and my claims that [debtor] would pay me this amount of money. . . . It was value exchanged for value."[5] The court concluded that the obligation was intended to equalize the division of the parties' assets. Thus the court held that the payments required were dischargeable because they represented a property settlement rather than support, even though it found specifically that the non-debtor spouse had

---

[1] 11 U.S.C. § 101(12).

[2] 11 U.S.C. § 101(5)(A), (B).

[3] *In re* Thomas, 47 B.R. 27, 34 (Bankr. S.D. Cal. 1984).

[4] 102 B.R. 799 (D. Kan. 1989).

[5] *Id.* at 802.

released her ownership interest in marital property in exchange for the debtor's promise to make the monthly payments. Under the *Goodnight* court's analysis the non-debtor spouse converted her property interest into a nullity by bargaining for payment of money.

Analyses such as that in *Goodnight* ignore what the authors believe is a critical factor—the ownership interest in the property held by the non-debtor. The usual assumption is that property, particularly homestead realty, acquired during a marriage is intended to be joint property, the exact nature of which, of course, depends on whether the property is in an entireties or community property state.[6] In either case each spouse has a vested ownership interest. When a divorce decree or agreement grants the debtor property that was once marital property and obligates the debtor to pay the former spouse for her interest, it would seem that this is not a debt in the traditional sense. The fact of the prior marriage distinguishes the situation from others in which there exists a co-owner. Furthermore, the nature of the ownership interest held by spouses and, therefore, ex-spouses, is vastly different from that held by other co-owners. State law creates the interest based on the mere fact of marriage.

Legislative history supports the proposition that a bankruptcy does not extinguish a marital property interest but merely reattaches it to another form of property so both spouses may receive economic justice. The Committee on the Judiciary of the House of Representatives, considering the problem posed when only one spouse files for bankruptcy during the course of the marriage and property is to be sold, stated:

> Interests in the nature of dower and curtesy will not prevent the property involved from becoming property of the estate, nor will it prevent sale of the property by the trustee. With respect to other co-ownership interest, such as tenancies by the entirety, joint tenancies, and tenancies in common, *the bill does not invalidate the rights, but provides a method by which the estate may realize on the value of the debtor's interest in the property* while protecting the other rights. The trustee is permitted to realize on

---

[6] It should be noted that some arrangements intended to provide security for a support or property settlement obligation may raise issues concerning what is property of the debtor's estate in bankruptcy. For example, in Porter v. Porter, 107 Wash. 2d 43, 726 P.2d 459 (1986), the parties' son was made the beneficiary of the father's life insurance policies, as security for support, under the terms of the divorce decree. The father remarried, created a trust for his son, but named the trust and the father's estate as beneficiaries of the policies which constituted the trust *res*. The father died and the Washington Supreme Court held that because the last premium payment had been made with money which was community property of the father and the second wife, the second wife could not be deprived of her half interest in the policy proceeds. *See Survey of Washington Law,* 23 Gonzaga L. Rev. 481, 483–86 (1988). How and whether a bankruptcy court could rectify this result is questionable because, for purposes of the Bankruptcy Code, an interest of the debtor in property is defined by state law.

the value of the property by being permitted to sell it without obtaining the consent or a waiver of rights by the spouse of the debtor or the co-owner, as may be required for a complete sale under applicable State law. The other interest is protected under H.R. 8200 by giving the spouse a right of first refusal at a sale of the property, and by requiring the trustee to pay over to the spouse the value of the spouse's interest in the property if the trustee sells the property to someone other than the spouse. Similar rules will govern certain sales of community property if both spouses are not preceeding [sic] under title 11.[7]

The non-debtor spouse should not be penalized with respect to his ownership interest simply because the other spouse files a bankruptcy. Because the *res* itself often cannot be physically divided on divorce, a money payment may be the only option. Thus the money the debtor is required to give to the non-debtor spouse in exchange for the property, although technically a debt, should be an unavoidable obligation and the non-debtor's claim to payment unassailable, much as in the case of secured transactions. In other words, the property interest arising from the divorce proceedings should not be extinguished even when it exists in the form of a right to payment.[8]

§ 3.2   Non-debtor Spouse's Interest: Trust Theory

Some courts and commentators have opined that a debtor who was awarded property in the divorce holds the property in trust for the dependent spouse. The debtor's interest, although property of the estate, is minimal in that it is not of the type which can be disposed of for the benefit of the creditors in a bankruptcy case. "[D]ivision [of marital property] is a separation of ownership rights."[9]

Which type of trust is appropriate is sometimes at issue. The Bankruptcy Court for the Middle District of Florida has held that a constructive trust is inappropriate because constructive trusts are to rectify fraud and arise only "at the time of the events which give rise to a duty to convey the property, . . . or, on the date of the order or judgment declaring

---

[7] Report of the Committee on the Judiciary, House of Representatives, To Accompany H.R. 8200, H.R. Rep. No. 95-595, 95th Cong., 1st Sess. (1977), *reprinted in* App. 2, Collier On Bankruptcy 177 (15th ed. 1989) (footnotes omitted; emphasis added).

[8] *See* Boyd v. Robinson, 741 F.2d 1112 (8th Cir. 1984).

[9] Scheible, *Defining "Support" Under Bankruptcy Law: Revitalization of the "Necessaries" Doctrine,* 41 Vand. L. Rev. 1, 13 n.61 (1988). The article also points out that marriage is an economic partnership and equitable distribution is intended to extinguish economic dependency. *Id.* at 11 n.54 (citing O'Brien v. O'Brien, 66 N.Y.2d 576, 587, 489 N.E.2d 712, 717, 498 N.Y.S.2d 743, 748 (1985)).

that a series of events has given rise to a constructive trust."[10] Citing Kansas law, the Court of Appeals for the Tenth Circuit is in agreement that a constructive trust can exist only when an element of wrongdoing including, but not limited to, fraud or constructive fraud is present.[11] The court apparently gave no weight to the fact that under Kansas law a constructive trust also is imposed to avoid one party's obtaining or holding property which rightfully belongs to another.[12]

"On the other hand, a resulting trust arises automatically out of a set of circumstances, to accomplish the presumed intent of the parties."[13] In *In re Hampton* the court applied Florida's special equity doctrine and found a resulting trust, thereby adopting a state court's marital dissolution award to a non-debtor spouse of the proceeds of sale of convenience stores purchased by the parties during the course of the marriage. The special equity doctrine's purpose was "to avoid the results of a statutory provision that prohibited an award of alimony to an adulterous wife even though she may have made exceptional contributions of money, property or services to the marriage."[14] Application of the special equity doctrine has been broadened and now "connotes the award of a vested property interest."[15] The court further noted that consideration of the relationship between the parties at the time the property was acquired could also evidence an intent that the business property be marital property. A review of the cases discussed in this section shows that such an analysis frequently is not made.

In re Teichman[16] is an example of an attempt to establish a trust by the use of § 523(a)(4) of the Bankruptcy Code which provides that debts for fraud or defalcation while acting in a fiduciary capacity are not dischargeable. However this section has been held to apply only when a fiduciary capacity existed at the time of default and then only if an express trust existed.[17] That is, the fiduciary duty has to be created before the wrongful act and not as a result of it. A constructive trust imposed after the default or a resulting trust does not fall under the terms of § 523(a)(4) and, therefore, the issue in these latter types of cases would not be dischargeability

---

[10] *In re* Hampton, 43 B.R. 633, 635–36 (Bankr. M.D. Fla. 1984).

[11] Maus v. Maus, 837 F.2d 935, 939 n.5 (10th Cir. 1988).

[12] *Id. Cf.*, Belisle v. Plunkett, 877 F.2d 512 (7th Cir. 1989), *cert. denied*, _____ U.S. _____, 110 S. Ct. 241 (1989) (as *bona fide* purchaser for value under 11 U.S.C. § 544(a)(3), trustee may bring into estate property which debtor holds in constructive trust for fraud victims).

[13] *In re* Hampton, 43 B.R. 633, 636 (Bankr. M.D. Fla. 1984).

[14] *Id.* at 635.

[15] *Id.*

[16] 774 F.2d 1395 (9th Cir. 1985).

[17] *Id.* at 1398, 1400; *In re* Thomas, 47 B.R. 27, 33 (Bankr. S.D. Cal. 1984).

per se, but ownership rights. Attention is directed to *In re Eichelberger*[18] where the court found that the language of the divorce decree created an express trust and thereby established a fiduciary relationship. The court concluded that the debtor's conduct constituted defalcation under 11 U.S.C. § 523(a)(4) and the debt was nondischargeable.[19]

§ 3.3   Arguing Property Interest Theories

Regardless of the theory used, the point remains that a state court division of marital property should not be set aside in bankruptcy because the debtor's obligation is one with respect to property which was owned equally by the other spouse.[20] However, the concepts of ownership and trust are not always discussed in the cases. Whether a particular court would accept either theory is open to question. However, there are cases and literature which support the pre-existing interest and the trust theories, and the practitioner should be aware of their existence and of contrary authority.

Practitioners should make bankruptcy courts aware of marital realities in general and the realities of their specific cases. The usual assumption is that property acquired during the marriage is intended to be joint property. In both common law and community property states each spouse has a vested ownership interest. Counsel should note, however, *In re Fisher.*[21] In that case the non-debtor spouse's rights in the debtor's property had vested upon institution of the divorce proceedings but were unperfected when the bankruptcy was filed. That is, the non-debtor had been awarded temporary maintenance but the state court had not determined permanent maintenance or property division. Under Colorado law, this meant that the non-debtor's interests in the marital property were unenforceable because, absent bankruptcy, a judgment creditor or bona fide purchaser would have been able to obtain clear title. Although the non-debtor spouse was precluded from enforcing her unperfected claim against specific

---

[18] 100 B.R. 861 (Bankr. S.D. Tex. 1989).

[19] At least one court has held that property held as the result of a statutory trust is not property of the debtor's estate. Begier v. IRS, 878 F.2d 762 (3d Cir. 1989), *aff'd,* _____ U.S. _____, 110 S. Ct. 2258 (1990) (trust fund withholding taxes pursuant to 26 U.S.C. § 7501 not property of estate).

[20] Reppy, *Discharge In Bankruptcy of Awards of Money or Property at Divorce: Analyzing the Risk and Some Steps to Avoid It,* 15 Community Prop. J. 1, 5 (1988) (obligation nondischargeable because non-debtor spouse was full owner or debtor was "mere agent or conduit to deliver" property already owned by the non-debtor spouse). *See also* 11 U.S.C. § 541(b)(1); Aetna Life Ins. Co. v. Bunt, 110 Wash. 2d 368, 754 P.2d 993 (1988) (under state exemption statutes support claimants are not creditors).

[21] 67 B.R. 666 (Bankr. D. Colo. 1986).

marital property, relief from stay was granted so she could pursue her right to be compensated for the value of her share of the property. Relief also was granted so the non-debtor could pursue a support claim.

The economic reality is that most couples own one or two major assets. The assets are usually encumbered by debts but the couple often has some equity. If a lump sum division of such property were required, the parties may not be able to complete the transaction if another loan of sufficient size could not be obtained. This is often the case because one spouse's income could not support the necessary obligation. Thus, the dissolution agreement or order saves the equity by stretching the division over time. This is not the traditional "debt" concept reached by the Bankruptcy Code. The obligation created is more akin to that existing in a trust. The debtor's interest is comparable to the concept of holding "bare legal title" with the beneficial interest in another, or to an indirect interest in assets similar to one owned by a partnership even though each general partner has an interest in the assets. In such situations the property involved is not considered to be property of the estate subject to administration by the bankruptcy courts.[22] Similarly, § 541 excludes property received through a property settlement or divorce decree if received more than 180 days after the bankruptcy filing. This section also excludes any power held by a debtor which can be exercised solely to benefit another.

It is submitted that a debtor whose divorce has left him with the obligation to pay for his spouse's former ownership in property is equivalent to a trustee and has no power in or right to use funds in a manner inconsistent with the support order or agreement, notwithstanding the provisions of the Bankruptcy Code. Although the approaches suggested in this Chapter are largely untested, it seems reasonable to conclude that Congress did not provide a separate category of nondischargeability for property divisions because it never considered that the non-debtor spouse's interest would be found to be property of the debtor's estate and subject to administration in the bankruptcy court. This analysis bears only on rights and interests of the former husband and wife, not of their creditors. Whatever rights to the property the creditors had before the divorce will not be prejudiced and will be accorded appropriate treatment in the bankruptcy context.

The recent decision of the United States Supreme Court in *Pennsylvania Department of Public Welfare v. Davenport*[23] bodes ill for the arguments advanced. In *Davenport* the Court held that criminal restitution obligations are dischargeable in Chapter 13 cases. The Court reasoned that because the definition of "debt" is "liability on a claim"[24] and

---

[22] 11 U.S.C. § 541.

[23] _____ U.S. _____, 110 S. Ct. 2126 (1990).

[24] 11 U.S.C. § 101(12).

"claim" is a "right to payment,"[25] "[t]he plain meaning of a 'right to payment' is nothing more nor less than an enforceable obligation, regardless of the objectives the State seeks to serve in imposing the obligation."[26] However, effective November 15, 1990, Congress amended § 1328 to provide that criminal restitution debts are nondischargeable.[27] In view of the Court's strict application of the definitions of debt and claim, it would appear overly optimistic to place too much stock in a belief that the Court would rule differently when a marital obligation which is not clearly support is considered in the context of a bankruptcy discharge.[28]

Although some courts conclude that a property division resulting from a divorce creates a trust or other type of property interest in the non-debtor spouse which cannot be attacked through the Bankruptcy Code, usually a money payment owing as a result of a pure property settlement is held to be a dischargeable debt. The non-debtor spouse, therefore, should consider obtaining, and perfecting, a mortgage or other consensual lien or security interest on the property to ensure payment. Then, if default occurs, the mortgage or security interest can be foreclosed upon once a discharge is entered or relief from stay is granted. Absent a perfected security interest, a dependent spouse can be left with nothing if the court finds that the obligation was not support.

There is authority for the proposition that § 506(d) of the Bankruptcy Code permits avoidance of a mortgage to the extent it exceeds the value of the property in conjunction with prior liens.[29] Moreover, nonconsensual liens and security interests often are avoidable in bankruptcy. The non-debtor spouse must consider these risks and treat them in the property agreement. See **Chapter 4** for a discussion of lien avoidance and fraudulent conveyances in connection with liens held by a non-debtor spouse.

---

[25] 11 U.S.C. § 101(5).

[26] *Davenport,* _____ U.S. at _____, 110 S. Ct. at 2131.

[27] 11 U.S.C. § 1328(a)(3). The amendment applies only to bankruptcy cases commenced after the effective date. Criminal Victims Protection Act of 1990, Pub. L. No. 101-581, § 4(b), 104 Stat. 2866 (1990).

[28] Four years before *Davenport* was decided the Supreme Court held that criminal restitution obligations are not dischargeable in Chapter 7 cases. Kelly v. Robinson, 479 U.S. 36, 50 (1986). The *Davenport* Court distinguished *Kelly* by noting that *Kelly* required an analysis of 11 U.S.C. § 523(a)(7), the section applicable to the nondischargeability of restitution "which explicitly tie[s] the application of that provision to the purpose of the compensation required." *Davenport,* 110 S. Ct. at 2131. The definition of claim, the Court pointed out, makes no reference to any purpose. Thus, in the Chapter 7 context, the obligation is nondischargeable. The Court stated that the discharge provisions applicable to Chapter 13 through 11 U.S.C. § 1328 exclude the § 523(a)(7) exception to discharge.

[29] *See* Gaglia v. First Fed. Sav. & Loan Ass'n, 889 F.2d 1304 (3d Cir. 1989).

CHAPTER 4

AVOIDANCE OF LIENS AND TRANSFERS

LIENS

§ 4.1   Avoidance of Judicial Liens

Section 522(f)(1) of the Bankruptcy Code permits a debtor to avoid a lien "on an interest of the debtor in property to the extent that such lien impairs an exemption to which the debtor would have been entitled under [state or federal law] if such lien is a judicial lien." When a lien arises by virtue of the parties' agreement and is judicially sanctioned in a divorce proceeding, bankruptcy courts take various views. One is that the lien is not avoidable because it is consensual and therefore in the nature of a security interest rather than a judicial lien.[1] Other courts hold that a lien required by a divorce decree is a judicial lien which may be avoided under § 522(f).

For example, in *Maus v. Maus*[2] the Court of Appeals for the Tenth Circuit held that a lien held by a non-debtor spouse "fixed pursuant to an . . . oral property settlement agreement set forth in the divorce decree" was a

---

[1] *See In re* Dunn, 10 B.R. 385 (Bankr. W.D. Okla. 1981).

[2] Maus v. Maus, 837 F.2d 935 (10th Cir. 1988).

31

judicial lien for the purpose of lien avoidance under § 522(f). This holding reversed the bankruptcy court, which held that the lien held by the non-debtor spouse was not a judicial lien because (1) it was created by a security interest, (2) it was consensual and (3) "[e]quity requires that a constructive trust be imposed on the debtor's homestead on behalf of this claimant which results in the claimant having an equitable mortgage."[3]

In contrast, the Court of Appeals for the Eighth Circuit has held that a lien against real estate awarded to one spouse upon a divorce is not avoidable by the debtor in bankruptcy, based on a theory of a pre-existing interest of the non-debtor spouse.[4] The pre-existing interest theory teaches that when property is acquired under a dissolution decree by one who subsequently becomes a bankruptcy debtor and when the property is subject to a non-debtor spouse's judicial lien which attached when title was transferred under the divorce decree, the lien is not avoidable.[5] That is, the non-debtor's interest in the property existed before the debtor obtained full title and before the non-debtor acquired the lien. The appellate court in *Maus* criticized the pre-existing interest theory, noting that when title is transferred to the debtor pursuant to a divorce proceeding, it usually is transferred outright and, therefore, the non-debtor's lien of necessity attaches to the debtor's interest in the property.[6] The point is valid as far as it goes but what the court apparently did not consider was that the dissolution award exchanges title in the *res* with the right to receive payments over time for that title. The purpose is not to extinguish the non-debtor's ownership interest without equivalent value in exchange. Adherence to a resulting trust theory in this instance would prevent the extinguishment of the non-debtor's interest.

In *In re Pederson*[7] the court avoided an ex-spouse's judicial lien on the debtor's homestead property because it impaired the debtor's exemption. In response to the non-debtor spouse's argument that the statutory scheme was unjust or unduly interfered with state divorce courts, the Court of Appeals for the Ninth Circuit directed her to appeal to Congress. The court

---

[3] *In re* Maus, 48 B.R. 948, 951 (Bankr. D. Kan. 1985), *rev'd,* Maus v. Maus, 837 F.2d 935 (10th Cir. 1988).

[4] Boyd v. Robinson, 741 F.2d 1112 (8th Cir. 1984). *See also* Zachary v. Zachary, 99 B.R. 916 (S.D. Ind. 1989). The Bankruptcy Court for the Southern District of Illinois has held that a lien could be avoided when it was created to secure a property settlement, rejecting the pre-existing interest theory. *In re* Boggess, 105 B.R. 470, 474 (Bankr. S.D. Ill. 1989).

[5] When relief from stay has been granted in the bankruptcy case to permit equitable distribution to proceed, the lien would not predate the bankruptcy and therefore this theory would not apply to the lien. However, the pre-existing interest itself could not be disputed. The divorce decree itself may effect the property transfer and lien or it may do so by incorporating an agreement of the parties.

[6] Maus, 837 F.2d at 939.

[7] 875 F.2d 781 (9th Cir. 1989).

concluded without analysis that this was a property settlement and not in the nature of support.

It is possible that the result in *Pederson* could have been avoided if the lien had been evidenced by a security agreement and financing statement and otherwise properly perfected under state law.[8] The Bankruptcy Code defines "judicial lien" as one "obtained by judgment, levy, sequestration, or other legal or equitable process or proceeding."[9] Thus, the liens at issue in the cases discussed fall within the definition and could be avoidable pursuant to § 522(f)(1) of the Bankruptcy Code, barring other considerations. Although a clarifying statutory amendment would resolve the matter, divorcing couples are not likely to be able to afford to present their cases to Congress or to hire a lobbyist to do so. Until then, the courts will continue to set the course of the law.[10]

§ 4.2   —Supreme Court Cases on Lien Avoidance in a Divorce Context

The decision of the United States Supreme Court in *Farrey v. Sanderfoot*[11] provides some guidance concerning avoidance of liens created by a divorce decree. In *Farrey* the non-debtor spouse obtained, through a divorce proceeding, a lien against the marital residence to secure the debtor's payment of the non-debtor's interest. The non-debtor also retained her record title, apparently pending payment. The debtor sought to avoid the lien under § 522(f) on the ground that it impaired his exemption. The opinion of the Court of Appeals for the Seventh Circuit establishes that there was no support issue and that the lien was imposed simply as part of a property settlement.[12] The Court of Appeals determined that any preexisting interest the non-debtor spouse had in the marital residence was extinguished by the divorce decree and therefore the judicial lien was avoidable because it impaired the debtor's exemptions.

The Supreme Court found that the lien did not attach to the non-debtor's interest. Rather, the lien was created simultaneously with the

---

[8] The issue of fraudulent conveyance or preferential transfer may arise when a security interest is taken. See §§ **4.5–4.6**.

[9] 11 U.S.C. § 101(36).

[10] On November 29, 1989, the Court of Appeals for the Third Circuit held that under 11 U.S.C. § 506(d) a debtor could avoid a mortgage to the extent it exceeds the value of the property. Gaglia v. First Fed. Sav. & Loan Ass'n, 889 F.2d 1304 (3d Cir. 1989). *But see* Dewsnup v. Timm, 908 F.2d 588 (10th Cir. 1990), *cert. granted,* 111 S. Ct. 949 (1991) (rejecting the *Gaglia* analysis as a misreading of literal wording of § 506(d)). *See also In re* Lange, 120 B.R. 132 (Bankr. 9th Cir. 1990).

[11] 111 S. Ct. 1825 (1991).

[12] *In re* Sanderfoot, 899 F.2d 598 (7th Cir. 1990), *rev'd,* Farrey v. Sanderfoot, 111 S. Ct. 1825 (1991).

parties' new interests created by the state court's divorce decree. The Court construed the state court order as transferring the non-debtor's interest to the debtor and securing payment by imposition of the lien. The Court pointed out that even if the divorce decree had simply restructured the parties' pre-existing interests, rather than creating new interests, the lien would have attached only to the non-debtor's pre-existing interest which the debtor never would have possessed free and clear. In other words, § 522(f) cannot be used "to avoid a lien on an interest acquired after the lien attached."[13]

At the arguments before the Supreme Court,[14] in *Farrey v. Sanderfoot,* in response to the question of whether a judicial lien was a security interest, it was noted that the Bankruptcy Code defines "security interest" as a lien which is created by agreement,[15] while a "judicial lien" is created by a "legal or equitable process or proceeding."[16] This raises the question of whether a judicial lien created by the *consent* of the parties in arranging their affairs in the course of a divorce is avoidable.

Section 522(f) refers to the "fixing of a lien on an interest of the debtor in property." The authors suggest that the debtor's pre-bankruptcy interest always was impaired from the moment he and his ex-spouse acquired the property during the marriage, in the sense that the debtor did not then have free rein to dispose of or encumber it without accounting for the non-debtor's interest. The impact, upon divorce, of the substitution of the lien for the marital encumbrance would seem to have no greater effect on the debtor's property interest than that which existed during the marriage. Arguably, the impact of the post-divorce lien is less because the debtor can pay what he owes on the lien and hold the property free and clear thereafter. During marriage it would be very difficult, if not impossible, to defeat a claim of the non-debtor spouse, particularly when legal title is held jointly.

The practitioner must be aware that the creation of new interests by the divorce decree in *Farrey* was a function of applicable state law.[17] The concurring opinion in *Farrey* notes that the avoidability of a lien created pursuant to a divorce will depend on when the property interest is created and when the lien attaches. In general, creation of property interests is governed by state law.

Farrey v. Sanderfoot arose in Wisconsin which adopted the Uniform Marital Property Act and, in conjunction therewith, enacted statutes presuming that all property owned by spouses is marital property.[18]

---

[13] Farrey, 111 S. Ct. at 1830.

[14] Summaries of the arguments appear in 59 U.S.L.W. 3665 (1991).

[15] 11 U.S.C. § 101(51).

[16] *Id.* at § 101(36).

[17] Farrey, 111 S. Ct. at 1830.

[18] *Id.* at _____, 111 S. Ct. at 1832 (Kennedy & Souter, J.J., concurring.)

Therefore, each spouse would have a prima facie pre-existing interest in all property upon division by agreement between the parties or state court order. If the non-debtor spouse obtained a lien on property which had been proven to be the debtor's separate property, thus defeating the presumption, arguably the debtor could assert § 522(f)(1) to avoid the lien because it attached to the debtor's property interest after he acquired it.

In entireties states the entireties interest is extinguished when a divorce decree is entered and the ex-spouses become tenants in common. When the non-debtor's interest is transferred to the debtor, with a lien in favor of the non-debtor, the lien would appear to be unavoidable, using the *Farrey* approach, because the debtor did not acquire an unencumbered interest. When the lien affixes could depend on the wording of the court order or the parties' agreement and/or on the state laws applicable to lien creation and attachment. Practitioners will have to thoroughly research applicable property and lien laws in order to obtain the advantages they seek for their clients through property division.

The Supreme Court's decision in *Owen v. Owen*[19] also provides some guidance concerning avoidance of liens in bankruptcy. In *Owen* the debtor sought to avoid a judicial lien under § 522(f). The lien came into existence before the debtor acquired the property, a condominium, in which he claimed a homestead exemption under Florida law. Florida has opted out of the federal exemptions. At the time the debtor acquired the property Florida law did not permit a homestead exemption in condominiums. However, one year after the debtor acquired the property, the law was amended to include condominiums as homestead property. Florida's homestead exemption precludes execution against homestead property except when the lien attached to the property before the property attained homestead status.[20] The debtor then filed a Chapter 7 bankruptcy and moved to avoid the lien.

The Court of Appeals for the Eleventh Circuit rejected the debtor's argument that the Bankruptcy Code permitted him to avoid the lien. In so ruling the court pointed out that the judgment attached before the homestead right.[21] The court reasoned that no impairment of the exemption existed because state law made the exemption specifically subject to the exception for liens which attached to the property before it obtained homestead status.

The Supreme Court held only that § 522(f) permits the avoidance of liens impairing state exemptions as well as federal exemptions. The matter was remanded because it had not been determined whether the lien had attached to the debtor's interest in the property or whether the lien

---

[19] 111 S. Ct. 1833 (1991).

[20] *Id.* at 1835.

[21] Owen v. Owen, 877 F.2d 44, 47 (11th Cir. 1989), *rev'd and remanded,* 111 S. Ct. 1833 (1991).

attachment predated the debtor's acquisition of the property. If the former situation occurred, the debtor could avoid the lien because § 522(f) permits the avoidance of "the fixing of a lien on an interest of the debtor in property." If the debtor acquired the property with the lien already attached, it is possible that the lien would be unavoidable. The Supreme Court remanded for the Court of Appeals to decide the issue.[22] Like *Farrey, Owen* indicates that state law, which determines when and how interests in property are created, will have a decisive impact on the question of whether a lien arising from a divorce proceeding is avoidable.

The *Owen* opinion is not limited specifically to judicial liens, although the issue before the court involved a judicial lien. Therefore § 522(f) may permit a debtor to avoid nonpossessory, nonpurchase money security interests that impair a debtor's state law exemptions when such security interests affix to the debtor's interest in property. Note, however, that avoidance of nonpossessory or nonpurchase money security interests under § 522(f) is limited to certain types of property, such as household goods and furnishings.[23] Cases such as *In re Pine,*[24] which interpreted Tennessee and Georgia exemption laws and held that § 522(f) could not be used to avoid nonpossessory, nonpurchase money security interests may have to be reanalyzed.[25] See **Chapter 3** for a discussion of arguments that a non-debtor spouse's interest in marital property should not be extinguished in favor of the debtor by virtue of the debtor's bankruptcy.

§ 4.3   Effect on Fifth Amendment Property Interests

An interesting concept is whether, in marital cases, avoidance of the lien under § 522(f)(1) violates the Fifth Amendment of the United States Constitution because it permits the non-debtor to be deprived of his property without even the compensation which had been ordered by the family court as the substitute for his ownership interest. The result of the lien avoidance mechanism, in essence, is that the non-debtor spouse, who lost the ownership in property and received the right to some other compensation in exchange, now loses even that compensation.

---

[22] The Supreme Court also raised the question whether the amendment of the Florida homestead exemption was a taking.

[23] 11 U.S.C. 522(f)(2).

[24] 717 F.2d 281 (6th Cir. 1983).

[25] *See In re* Bland, 793 F.2d 1172 (11th Cir. 1986) (interpreting Georgia exemption statute and holding that the same type of lien is subject to avoidance under § 522(f)). *See also In re* Snow, 899 F.2d 337 (4th Cir. 1990) (Virginia law); *In re* Leonard, 866 F.2d 335 (10th Cir. 1989) (Colorado law) which hold that § 522(f) may be used to avoid nonpossessory, nonpurchase money security interest when state law would permit exemption if no security interest existed.

In *Louisville Joint Stock Land Bank v. Radford,*[26] the United States Supreme Court, addressing the Frazier-Lemke Act of 1933, pointed out that "the effect of the Act . . . is not the discharge of . . . personal obligation. It is the taking of substantive rights in specific property acquired . . . prior to the Act."[27] Forty-seven years later, the Supreme Court considered the Bankruptcy Code in *United States v. Security Industrial Bank.*[28] The Court held that § 522(f)(2) could not be applied retroactively to destroy rights predating enactment of the Bankruptcy Code. The argument may be made that a similar constitutional prohibition exists with respect to pre-bankruptcy interests of a non-debtor spouse.[29] It must be noted that the Court of Appeals for the Third Circuit viewed *Radford* as an economic regulation case which the Supreme Court mischaracterized.[30]

§ 4.4   Protection Against Lien Avoidance

Except to the extent that the recent *Farrey* and *Owen* cases provide some guidance, there seem to be no clear cases which answer the question of whether a non-debtor spouse can be protected from a lien avoidance proceeding by virtue of creative drafting of property settlement agreements or orders. Some possibilities which do not appear in reported cases are suggested here, merely in an effort to stimulate ideas in this area.

Perhaps the problem of the avoidance of judicial liens in property settlement cases[31] could be resolved if defeasible fee interests were created by the state court in the spouse who, in exchange for realty, is made responsible for providing support or making payments under the property settlement terms. For example, the state court could award the real estate to the payor spouse "as long as" he continues to make the payments to the other. If a payment default occurs, the property would revert to the payee.[32]

Another possibility is to create a fee simple subject to a condition subsequent. In this situation, the payor would receive title on the condition that he continues to make the required payments to the other spouse in a timely manner. If he fails to do so, then the payee spouse may reenter and

---

[26] 295 U.S. 555 (1935).

[27] *Id.* at 589.

[28] 459 U.S. 70 (1982).

[29] For further discussion and case references *see* 3 Collier On Bankruptcy § 522.29 (15th ed. 1990).

[30] *In re* Ashe, 669 F.2d 105 (3d Cir.) *vacated and remanded,* 459 U.S. 1082 (1982), *aff'd,* 712 F.2d 864 (3d Cir. 1983), *cert. denied,* 465 U.S. 1024, *reh'g denied,* 466 U.S. 963 (1984).

[31] Note the distinction between property settlement and support.

[32] J. Cribbett, Principles of the Law of Property 42 (1975). Another construction could be "To payor until he ceases to make the payments." *Id.* at 43.

retake possession.[33] In these two situations it would seem that although the money payment obligation might be avoidable in a bankruptcy, the ownership interest would survive. Note that even though the payor spouse may hold title, the payee could be authorized to occupy the real estate.

A third alternative might entail creating a life estate in the payee so that if the payor defaulted, the payee would have an *in rem* action against the property. If the payor filed bankruptcy, the payee would be protected even if the arrangement constituted a property settlement because the payee would hold an in rem interest in the property, not merely an in personam claim against the payor debtor. The risks to the payee in this situation if the payor defaults in paying the mortgage, taxes, etc., as ordered, may include the fact that the property, once reacquired by the non-debtor, may be subject to the defaults in payments. However, depending on the situation, the damage created by such defaults could be minimized by quick action on the part of the payee. Even if a bankruptcy ensued after in rem proceedings began, the life estate holder would have a strong case to obtain relief from the automatic stay or for other relief to preserve the life interest. It should be noted that if the reversionary interest remained in the debtor, the non-debtor life estate holder's interest may be subject to an adversary sale,[34] from which his share of the proceeds should be paid even though the remainder of the funds would be distributed in accordance with the distribution scheme of the Bankruptcy Code.

Other techniques may be available to protect the non-debtor's property interest. Future cases may have to involve discussion of these issues.

AVOIDANCE OF TRANSFERS

§ 4.5 Fraudulent Conveyances

The Bankruptcy Code permits avoidance of certain transfers of the debtor's property.[35] For example, interests acquired in a divorce proceeding

---

[33] *Id.* at 43. Cribbett states that "the words 'on the condition that', 'on condition', or words setting up an affirmative right of reentry in any fashion indicate a fee simple subject to a condition subsequent." *Id.*

[34] *See In re* Nelson, 1991 WL 138846 (Bankr., W.D. Pa. 1991). (Non-debtor ex-spouse had the exclusive right to possession of the co-owned former marital residence as a result of a separation agreement. Trustee wanted to sell the property for the benefit of Chapter 7 creditors. The court found that the detriment to ex-spouse and children was not outweighed by benefits to the estate and refused the sale, citing 11 U.S.C. § 363(h)(3).)

[35] An interest acquired in a divorce may, in rare circumstances, be avoidable as a preferential transfer under § 547. Section 547 concerns a specific type of transfer commonly referred to as preferential. Preferential transfers are those that enable a creditor to receive more than it would otherwise and that are made to or for the benefit of a

by a non-debtor spouse may be deemed to be a fraudulent conveyance under § 548 of the Bankruptcy Code, regardless of intent to defraud or good faith. Section 548 permits the trustee, or a creditor when no trustee is appointed, to avoid what are deemed fraudulent transactions. This section generally tracks the Uniform Fraudulent Conveyance Act[36] and provides specifically that

> (a) The trustee may avoid any transfer of an interest of the debtor in property, or any obligation incurred by the debtor, that was made or incurred on or within one year before the date of the filing of the petition, if the debtor voluntarily or involuntarily—
>
> (1) made such transfer or incurred such obligation with actual intent to hinder, delay, or defraud any entity to which the debtor was or became, on or after the date that such transfer was made or such obligation was incurred, indebted; or
>
> (2)(A) received less than a reasonably equivalent value in exchange for such transfer or obligation; and
>
> (B)(i) was insolvent on the date that such transfer was made or such obligation was incurred, or became insolvent as a result of such transfer or obligation;

Note that § 548(a)(1) will allow a conveyance to be set aside if actual intent to hinder, delay, or defraud a creditor existed. Actual intent to defraud can be inferred from circumstances.[37] However, § 548(a)(2) permits the set-aside without proof of an intent to defraud if the elements of time, insufficient value received by the debtor, and his insolvency are established.

Transactions which seem fair to the spouses may be challenged in a bankruptcy as unfair to creditors. Because the marital residence often is the only asset of any value to creditors, divestment of one spouse's interest may provide an argument for insolvency in the bankruptcy context, particularly if it is linked to a finding that the transfer involved was not in the nature of support but was part of a property settlement. Section 548(c) provides:

> (c) Except to the extent that a transfer or obligation voidable under this section is voidable under section 544, 545 or 547 of this title, a transferee

---

creditor, for or on account of an antecedent debt, made while the debtor is insolvent, on or within ninety days or one year prepetition, depending on whether the transferee is an insider. Insiders under the Bankruptcy Code include a debtor's spouse, former spouse, and children. 11 U.S.C. § 101(31)(A). The instances in which a preference might exist between divorcing spouses are relatively rare and therefore the ramifications of § 547 are not addressed herein. However, the practitioner is cautioned to consider the possible antecedent nature of any debt treated in the course of the divorce.

[36] *See, e.g.,* Pa. Stat. Ann. Tit. 39, §§ 351–363.

[37] *See, e.g., In re* Purco, 76 B.R. 523 (Bankr. W.D. Pa. 1987).

or obligee of such a transfer or obligation that takes for value and in good faith has a lien on or may retain any interest transferred or may enforce any obligation incurred, as the case may be, to the extent that such transferee or obligee gave value to the debtor in exchange for such transfer or obligation.

However, "'value' . . . does not include an unperformed promise to furnish support to the debtor or to a relative of the debtor."[38] Thus, when the non-debtor spouse who owes support receives property in which there would have been equity for debtor's creditors absent the transfer, the fact of the support obligation will not be viewed as "value" in a § 548 action and the transfer could be set aside if the other elements of § 548 are satisfied. It is possible that an agreement that the non-debtor's release of his interest in other marital property constitutes "value" would be sufficient to defeat a § 548 action, but counsel advancing this argument in a bankruptcy case must have laid a solid factual foundation during the divorce proceeding.

State law provisions may complicate a § 548 analysis. For example, the Pennsylvania Divorce Code's definition of marital property includes "property which a party has sold, granted, conveyed or otherwise disposed of in good faith and for value prior to the date of final separation."[39] What constitutes "value" may depend on what valuation standard is used. Under the Bankruptcy Code market value is usually, but not always, the standard.[40]

§ 4.6   Trustee's Strong Arm Power

Interests acquired by a non-debtor spouse in a divorce proceeding may fall prey to a trustee's "strong-arm" powers under § 544. For example, if a transfer of real property is unrecorded, the trustee may avoid it pursuant to § 544(a)(3) of the Bankruptcy Code which provides:

(a) [t]he trustee shall have, as of the commencement of the case, and without regard to any knowledge of the trustee or of any creditor, the rights and powers of, or may avoid any transfer of property of the debtor or any obligation incurred by the debtor that is voidable by . . .

(3) a bona fide purchaser of real property, other than fixtures, from the debtor, against whom applicable law permits such transfer to be perfected, that obtains the status of a bona fide purchaser and has perfected

---

[38] 11 U.S.C. § 548(d)(2)(A).

[39] Pa. Stat. Ann., Tit. 23, § 401(e)(5).

[40] *See* Durrett v. Washington Nat'l Ins. Co., 621 F.2d 201 (5th Cir. 1980) (transfer for less than seventy percent of market value can be set aside).

such transfer at the time of the commencement of the case, whether or not such a purchaser exists.[41]

This provision is not inconsistent with state laws which embody the strong state interest in requiring recording of deeds to real estate and of security interests in personalty.[42]

Section 544(b) also expresses the trustee's "strong-arm" powers. Under § 544(b), the trustee may "avoid any transfer of an interest of the debtor in property or any obligation incurred by the debtor that is voidable under applicable law by a creditor holding an unsecured claim" which comports with § 502 and 502(e) of the Bankruptcy Code.[43] Under the Bankruptcy Code the trustee is made the hypothetical perfect creditor regardless of the facts and regardless of any personal knowledge the trustee may have.

In *In re Fisher*[44] the fact that the non-debtor spouse's rights in the debtor's property had vested upon institution of the divorce proceedings, but were unperfected when the bankruptcy was filed, meant that the interests were cut off. The court reached this conclusion because, absent bankruptcy, a judgment creditor or a bona fide purchaser would have been able to obtain clear title. Relief from stay was granted so that the non-debtor could pursue her share of marital property and support. In *Belisle v. Plunkett*[45] the Court of Appeals for the Seventh Circuit permitted the bankruptcy trustee to bring into the bankruptcy estate property which the debtor held in a constructive trust for victims of a prepetition fraud, even though the repayment obligation was held to be nondischargeable under § 523(a)(2) and (4).[46]

Although in the typical Chapter 7 bankruptcy an unsecured creditor is not able to reach an interest in real estate, the practitioner must always remember to consider the possible effect of § 544.[47] The law in this area is not well developed and these considerations may be of greater relevance when the property transferred was not the marital residence. Bankruptcy

---

[41] When the transfer has not been perfected but is made before the bankruptcy petition is filed, § 548, or possibly § 547, may apply. *See* 11 U.S.C. § 548(d)(1).

[42] Recordation serves as notice of interests in property. With respect to real estate, recordation protects the sanctity of transactions which depend on the ability to provide clear title. Note that even when the non-debtor spouse has obtained and properly perfected a security interest, the transfer may still be subject to challenge under § 547 or § 548.

[43] 11 U.S.C. § 544(b).

[44] 67 B.R. 666 (Bankr. D. Colo. 1986).

[45] 877 F.2d 512 (7th Cir. 1989), *cert. denied,* 110 S. Ct. 241 (1989).

[46] These sections concern obtaining various types of property through false pretenses, false representations, and fraud or for defalcation while acting in a fiduciary capacity.

[47] Generally, if there is equity over the mortgage and any applicable exemptions, judgment lien creditors and/or unsecured creditors would be entitled to share in the excess.

courts may be less likely to set aside the award of a marital residence to a dependent spouse and children, at least under § 548. If the bankruptcy court has any discretion pursuant to § 544, it is extremely limited because § 544(a) provides that "[t]he trustee *shall have*" the paramount rights enumerated in that section.[48] However, when business property has been awarded it may be easier to avoid the transfer, unless the practitioner can show that the award was intended to support the dependents.[49]

---

[48] 11 U.S.C. § 544(a) (emphasis added).

[49] *But see In re* Hampton, 43 B.R. 633 (Bankr. M.D. Fla. 1984) (proceeds of sale of business property awarded by state court to non-debtor spouse subject to resulting trust and not avoidable in bankruptcy).

CHAPTER 5

DISCHARGEABILITY OF ASSIGNED SUPPORT OBLIGATIONS

§ 5.1   Introduction

Section 523(a)(5)(A) of the Bankruptcy Code provides:

> (a) A discharge . . . does not discharge an individual debtor from any debt (5) to a spouse, former spouse, or child of the debtor, for alimony to, maintenance for, or support of such spouse or child, in connection with a separation agreement, divorce decree or other order of a court of record, determination made in accordance with state or territorial law by a governmental unit, or property settlement agreement, but not to the extent that (A) such debt is assigned to another entity, voluntarily, by operation of law, or otherwise (other than debts assigned pursuant to section 402(a)(26) of the Social Security Act, or any such debt which has been assigned to the Federal Government or to a State or any political subdivision of such State).

In order to create a valid assignment which will permit the assignee to sue on the claim as a real party in interest[1] there must be a transfer "of

---

[1] Certified Collectors, Inc. v. Lesnick, 116 Ariz. 601, 602, 570 P.2d 769, 770 (1977) (en banc).

the whole of any property . . . or of some right or interest therein."[2] Furthermore, the subject matter, the debt being assigned, has to be identifiable through a description provided.[3] "Mutuality of assent" is also necessary.[4] The parties must intend to vest the third party with a present right and the intent must be manifested.[5] When the debtor, either voluntarily or by virtue of a court order, has been saddled with the responsibility to pay a debt on behalf of a spouse, there is usually no intent to create a present interest in the creditor that ultimately receives the payment. The creditor's interest as it existed before the support obligation was created remains unchanged.[6] This is particularly true when the debt at issue is a joint obligation of the spouses. None of the interested parties' rights or liabilities changes except as between the spouses.[7] Even on those occasions when the debtor assumes responsibility for repayment of an individual debt of the non-debtor spouse, the intent is not to benefit the creditor but to benefit the dependent spouse or child. The intent is the same when the obligation is assumed voluntarily by the debtor and when the obligation is imposed on the debtor by court order.[8]

Before 1984 § 523(a)(5) simply provided that a debt that had been "assigned to another entity, voluntarily, by operation of law, or otherwise" would be dischargeable.[9] This was interpreted to mean that any obligation which had been assigned to a state welfare agency was dischargeable.[10] *In re Deblock*[11] is a little different from most other cases in that the ex-wife had obtained a judgment for child support arrearages which she assigned to a law firm for collection purposes. According to the bankruptcy court,

---

[2] *In re* Purman's Estate, 358 Pa. 187, 56 A.2d 86, 88 (1948).

[3] Certified Collectors v. Lesnick, 116 Ariz. at 603, 570 P.2d at 771.

[4] Hutsell v. Citizens' Nat'l Bank, 116 Tenn. 598, 64 S.W.2d 188 (1933).

[5] Harris v. Farquhar, 33 Pa. 369, 10 A.2d 10 (1940).

[6] The arguments and analyses in this section are based on an assumption that the obligation at issue is one in the nature of support and not a property settlement. References are to spousal support because the question of assignment in the reported cases does not appear to have arisen in child support cases to any great extent.

[7] *See, e.g.,* Stranathan v. Stowell, 15 B.R. 223, 226 (Bankr. D. Neb. 1981) (dicta).

[8] A creditor, such as the dependent spouse's attorney, may acquire an interest because of the divorce. That is, the other spouse may agree or be ordered by the state court to pay the dependent spouse's attorney's fee. In these cases it is sometimes the attorney who seeks to have the fee obligation declared nondischargeable. See § 5.4; *In re* Tessler, 44 B.R. 786 (Bankr. S.D. Cal. 1984); *In re* French, 9 B.R. 464 (Bankr. S.D. Cal. 1981); *In re* Knabe, 8 B.R. 53 (Bankr. S.D. Ind. 1980).

[9] 11 U.S.C. 523(a)(5)(A) (1981). *See* 3 Collier On Bankruptcy § 523.15 (15th ed. 1991).

[10] *In re* Deblock, 11 B.R. 51 (Bankr. N.D. Ohio 1981); *In re* French, 9 B.R. 464, 467 n.6 (Bankr. S.D. Cal. 1981); *In re* Wells, 8 B.R. 189 (Bankr. N.D. Ill. 1981); *In re* Knabe, 8 B.R. 53 (Bankr. S.D. Ind. 1980); *In re* Pelikant, 5 B.R. 404 (Bankr. N.D. Ill. 1980).

[11] 11 B.R. 51 (Bankr. N.D. Ohio 1981).

the assignment was made before the arrears judgment actually was obtained and the ex-wife was not indebted to the assignee.[12] The court interpreted the former configuration of § 523(a)(5)(A) to mean that only debts assigned to government agencies by virtue of receipt of welfare payments would be dischargeable. After the ex-husband filed bankruptcy the ex-wife filed a complaint in state court to void the assignment as impossible to perform and for lack of consideration. The bankruptcy court noted that obtaining a declaration that the assignment was null and void, although a "questionable practice," did not change the wife's "intention in making the assignment."[13] The authors submit that as long as the payment serves the function of support the intent of the assignor is irrelevant, regardless of the ultimate destination of the funds.

In 1984 Congress enacted the Bankruptcy Amendments and Federal Judgeship Act of 1984 (BAFJA).[14] The BAFJA amended § 523(a)(5) to make clear that support debts assigned as a condition of the non-debtor dependent's receipt of benefits through certain governmental programs, for example, Aid to Families with Dependent Children, would be nondischargeable.

§ 5.2   Case Law

Today bankruptcy courts as well as appellate courts are struggling with the question of whether an obligation to pay a third party on behalf of the non-debtor spouse, whether court imposed or achieved by agreement, is an assignment which renders the obligation dischargeable in bankruptcy. Without expressly identifying the issue as one of assignment, some early cases concluded that a payment to a third party, even if characterized as support by the parties or by the state court, was a dischargeable obligation.[15]

In *In re Daiker*[16] the court was faced with the issue of whether the debtor's obligations to pay, and to hold his ex-wife harmless for, three debts incurred jointly during the marriage were dischargeable. The expenditures had been made for furniture, medical services, and miscellaneous household items and some were debts related to transportation. The court held that unless the debt was payable directly to the non-debtor spouse it was dischargeable regardless of the fact that it may have been support

---

[12] 11 B.R. at 52.

[13] 11 B.R. at 53.

[14] Act of July 10, 1984, Pub. L. 98-353, 306, 98 Stat. 353.

[15] *See, e.g., In re* Daiker, 5 B.R. 348, 351 (Bankr. D. Minn. 1980).

[16] 5 B.R. 348 (Bankr. D. Minn. 1980).

otherwise.[17] The court also noted that if the amounts specifically designated as support were added to the wife's income and subtracted from the debtor's, their incomes were approximately equal. From this, the court concluded that the debt assumed by the debtor was part of a property settlement.

In support of its ruling the court cited the following excerpt from the legislative history of the 1978 enactment of the Code:

> Section 523(a)(5) is a compromise between the House Bill and the Senate Amendment. The provision excepts from discharge a debt owed to a spouse, former spouse or child of the debtor, in connection with a separation agreement, divorce decree, or property settlement agreement, for alimony to, maintenance for, or support of such spouse or child but not to the extent that the debt is assigned to another entity. If a debtor has assumed an obligation of the debtor's spouse to a third party in connection with the separation agreement, property settlement agreement, or divorce proceeding, such debt is dischargeable to the extent that the payment of the debt by the debtor is not actually in the nature of alimony, maintenance or support of debtor's spouse, former spouse, or child.[18]

It is submitted that the court strained the language of the applicable section of the Bankruptcy Code and the legislative history. As long as the bankruptcy court finds that the obligation actually serves the purpose of support or alimony or maintenance, the obligation is nondischargeable regardless of the arrangement by which its payment is effected. However, in some situations payments labelled as support may be determined not to serve the purpose of support. For example, a spouse who is receiving support payments could execute an assignment of the right to receive the payments in order to pay for luxuries. In this situation the paying spouse who then filed bankruptcy would probably be successful in seeking an order that the debt is dischargeable under § 523(a)(5)(A) because the obligation to pay does not appear to serve the function of supplying daily needs.

The Bankruptcy Court for the Western District of New York recognized this approach in 1984 in *In re Lewis*.[19] The court stated that

> Congress, beyond question, intended that all third party debts be discharged. However, if a debtor, explicitly or by implication, agrees to hold harmless and indemnify his or her spouse, former spouse, or child against such a third party debt, that undertaking would survive discharge if and

---

[17] *Id.* at 351.

[18] *Id.* at 351, n.2 (*citing* Congressional Record, 95th Cong., Vol. 124, No. 154, H. 11096 (Sept. 28, 1978)).

[19] 39 B.R. 842 (Bankr. W.D.N.Y. 1984).

only if the underlying liability were *actually in the nature of alimony, maintenance or support* (emphasis in original).[20]

The court, however, went on to say that "a promise to indemnify a joint third party debt, which debt is unrelated to past or present health, shelter or related support needs, would not survive."[21] The court did not define "related" but its bent can be inferred from its concern that "meaningful bankruptcy relief" should not be obstructed by a divorce[22] nor should the non-debtor achieve the effect of obtaining a discharge "unaccompanied by the pain and property losses attendant to bankruptcy."[23]

In 1982 the Court of Appeals for the Ninth Circuit in *Stout v. Prussel*[24] counted as a significant factor in the determination of dischargeability whether the payment was to be made directly to the spouse or to a third party. In 1983 *In re Edwards*[25] recited the same rule. However, the matter was before the court on the non-debtor's motion for summary judgment with respect to an objection to confirmation of the debtor's Chapter 13 plan. The court treated the objection as a complaint to determine dischargeability of the debtor's obligation to make mortgage payments. The court found that the divorce decree did not say whether the debtor was to make the payments to the non-debtor or to the mortgagee and so denied the motion for summary judgment. The court also discussed the fact that, on the state of the record before it, it could not determine whether the objection was in the nature of support or was intended to be part of the property division. However, the gist of the opinion is that the threshold issue was whether the payment was to be made to the non-debtor or to the mortgagee,[26] citing *Daiker* and *Stout v. Prussel*. If the payments went directly to the mortgagee, the court said, the debt would be dischargeable. Recently, less restrictive views seem to be gaining acceptance. Reported cases now often recognize that support and maintenance can include, for example, transportation, attorney's fees, mortgage payments, and hold harmless agreements.[27] It should be noted, however, that in situations such as those just illustrated, the non-debtor spouse remains liable to the creditor in the first instance and therefore has not obtained a discharge of the debt outside of bankruptcy.

---

[20] *Id.* at 845.

[21] *Id.*

[22] *Id.* at 845–46.

[23] *Id.* at 846.

[24] 691 F.2d 859, 861 (9th Cir. 1982).

[25] 31 B.R. 113 (Bankr. N.D. Ga. 1983).

[26] *Id.* at 114.

[27] *See generally In re* Gianakas, 917 F.2d 759, 763 (3d Cir. 1990).

Under *Lewis, Daiker, Stout v. Prussel,* and cases of that ilk, what is dischargeable is the debtor's support obligation. In *In re Horner*[28] the Bankruptcy Court for the Western District of Pennsylvania analyzed a situation in which the debtor was to make the non-debtor's car and credit card payments directly to the creditors. The bankruptcy court found that the payments were actually support and were necessitated by the debtor's prebankruptcy conduct involving the removal of all marital assets from the reach of the non-debtor. The debtor's conduct required the non-debtor to go into debt to provide for her daily needs. In rejecting the debtor's argument that his payment obligations were dischargeable, the court first defined assignment as entailing the transfer of the whole of a right or interest in property from one person to another.[29] The court also pointed out that § 523(a)(5)(A) of the Bankruptcy Code permits discharge of such a debt if it has been assigned. The Code defines debt as "liability on a claim."[30] However, the debtor's responsibility to pay support was not transferred.

The authors believe Congress's intent was to allow the discharge of an obligation to pay when the non-debtor recipient's claim to support is assigned. The Bankruptcy Code defines claim as a "right to payment."[31] If this is true, then Congress, in enacting § 523(a)(5), should have spoken to the assignment of the non-debtor's claim, rather than to the debtor's debt. However, Congress defined "debt" and "claim" and selected the use of the term "debt" as the nonassignable element. It is difficult to conceive of a situation in which the debt, i.e., the liability to pay support, would be assigned to another entity.

In *Horner* the state court's order did not effect an assignment of the non-debtor's right to support payments. If the debtor failed to make the payments, only the non-debtor could sue in state court to enforce the obligation. The creditors that ultimately received the money would have recourse against the non-debtor based only on the contracts between them. The creditors have no right to the non-debtor's claim to support payments, only to payment of their own claims, which claims exist solely against the non-debtor. Thus, some cases[32] did not reach the crux of the

---

[28] 125 B.R. 458 (Bankr. W.D. Pa. 1991). The opinion was authored by Judge Fitzgerald.

[29] *Id.* at 9–10 *citing* Kroeker v. State Farm Mut. Auto. Ins. Co., 466 S.W.2d 105 (Ct. App. Mo. 1971); *In re* Purman's Estate, 358 Pa. 187, 56 A.2d 86 (1948); Chasman v. Bremer, 206 Minn. 301, 288 N.W. 732 (1939); Minshall v. Sanders, 51 P.2d 940 (Okla. 1936); Love v. Clayton, 287 Pa. 205, 134 A. 422 (Pa. 1926).

[30] 11 U.S.C. 101(12).

[31] *Id.* 101(5).

[32] *See, e.g.,* Stout v. Prussel, 691 F.2d 859 (9th Cir. 1982); *In re* Daiker, 5 B.R. 348 (Bankr. D. Minn. 1980).

issue. Different analyses may be needed when the debtor's obligation arises through an order awarding support, rather than through a consensual agreement between the parties as discussed in the following section. See **Appendix A** for digests of cases.

§ 5.3   Third Party Beneficiary Analysis

There are several types of situations that give rise to a debtor's obligation to make payments on behalf of a dependent spouse. For purposes of this discussion it is assumed that the obligation is support and the only question is whether an assignment has been made which would trigger the dischargeability provisions of § 523(a)(5)(A) of the Bankruptcy Code. The support nature of the obligation is not vitiated by the fact that the non-debtor receives an indirect payment in the form of funds going directly to a creditor.[33]

Some courts have used third-party beneficiary analysis in determining the dischargeability of support obligations payable to third parties. A third-party beneficiary contract is one that is not only intended to benefit the third party but one that in fact does provide the third party with "a direct and not merely an incidental benefit of the contract."[34] Construing the *Restatement (Second) of Contracts,* the Pennsylvania Supreme Court stated in 1976 that one can be "an intended beneficiary only if he can reasonably rely on the contract as manifesting an intent to confer a right on him."[35] The court did not adopt the *Restatement* in that case even though it applied its principles.[36] The Second Circuit recently addressed the current status of third party beneficiary law in *Trans-Orient Marine Corp. v. Star Trading and Marine, Inc.*[37] The court stated that it is permitted to examine the circumstances as well as the agreement and that the third party need not be named in the contract in order to have an enforceable third party beneficiary contract. All that is necessary, said the court, is that the parties intended to benefit the third party and that the intent was expressed in the contract.

---

[33] *See* Stranathan v. Stowell, 15 B.R. 223, 225–26 (Bankr. D. Neb. 1981).

[34] Jardel Enter., Inc. v. Tri-Consultants, Inc., 770 P.2d 1301, 1302 (Colo. App. 1988) (reh'g denied 1989).

[35] Pennsylvania Liquor Control Bd. v. Rapistan, Inc., 472 Pa. 36, 45, 371 A.2d 178, 182 (1976) (reh'g denied).

[36] *See* Guy v. Liederbach, 501 Pa. 47, 58, 459 A.2d 744, 750 n.7 (1983).

[37] 925 F.2d 566 (2d Cir. 1991).

The *Restatement (Second) of Contracts* provides:

Section 302. Intended and Incidental Beneficiaries.

(1) Unless otherwise agreed between promisor and promisee, a beneficiary of a promise is an intended beneficiary if recognition of a right to performance in the beneficiary is appropriate to effectuate the intention of the parties and either (a) the performance of the promise will satisfy an obligation of the promisee to pay money to the beneficiary; or (b) the circumstances indicate that the promisee intends to give the beneficiary the benefit of the promise to performance.

(2) An incidental beneficiary is a beneficiary who is not an intended beneficiary.[38]

In order that a third party be an intended beneficiary there must first be a contract and "both reasonable and probable" reliance by the third party.[39] Not every third party who benefits from a contract will be entitled to maintain an action in it.[40] A third party beneficiary contract will exist if the non-debtor spouse, the promisee, cannot revoke or control the fulfillment of the promise.[41] Other factors to consider in a third-party beneficiary analysis include: (1) whether there has been a novation of the contract or a substitution of one debtor for another, (2) whether, if a debt is assumed, the creditors must consent; that is, what does applicable law provide with respect to debtors' ability to affect a creditor's right without the creditor's acquiescence,[42] and (3) whether the third party has acquired any rights against the debtor (promisor) or the non-debtor spouse (promisee) as determined by an examination of the contract language and the surrounding circumstances.[43] It is not enough to establish a third-party beneficiary contract that the third party knows of the contract nor that she may be detrimentally affected if the contract is not performed.[44] The third party must be "the real moving party in the transaction."[45]

When the obligation is one of support in a divorce case these factors often are not present and therefore a right in the third party to enforce payment from the debtor may not be appropriate "to effectuate the intention

---

[38] Restatement (Second) of Contracts § 302 (1979) (quoted in Guy v. Liederbach, 501 Pa. 47, 59, 459 A.2d 744, 751 (1983)).

[39] Restatement (Second) Contracts § 302 (1981).

[40] 17A C.J.S. *Extent and Limits of Rule* _____ § 519(4)(a), at 961–62 (1963).

[41] *Id.* at 963.

[42] *Id.* at 963.

[43] *Id.* § 519(4)(c), at 971–73.

[44] *Id.* at 977.

[45] *Id.*

of the parties."[46] One construction could be that a third-party beneficiary contract does not exist when the primary benefit is intended to and does exist for the non-debtor spouse. Thus, even if performance by the debtor will satisfy the dependent spouse's obligation to the creditor,[47] the arrangement could be held to fail as a third party beneficiary contract because the benefit to the creditor is incidental to the support obligation. However, in some situations there are arguments based on third party beneficiary theory which may be useful in upholding the nondischargeability of a support obligation.

§ 5.4   —In re Spong

In *In re Spong*[48] the debtor's obligation to pay his wife's attorney's fees incurred in the prosecution of the divorce arose in settlement of a contested divorce proceeding. In the bankruptcy proceeding, the facts established that a stipulation between husband and wife, which subsequently was incorporated into the final judgment of divorce, obligated the husband to pay a portion of the wife's attorney's fees. After the husband filed a bankruptcy petition, the wife's attorney filed a complaint on his own behalf to have the obligation declared nondischargeable. The bankruptcy court found the debt to be dischargeable because it was not payable directly to the wife, even though it was in the nature of alimony, support or maintenance[49] and the district court affirmed.

The Court of Appeals for the Second Circuit reversed the district court.[50] It first noted the existence of a duty to provide support in the form of the necessities of life and pointed out that an award of attorney's fees may be such a necessity if it is essential to the spouse's ability to maintain or defend a "matrimonial action."[51] The court next rejected the construction of § 523(a)(5) in cases such as *In re Daiker*[52] requiring the payments to be made directly to the spouse. The *Spong* court observed that the substance of the liability must be the controlling factor.[53]

The court acknowledged the existence of other cases such as *In re Deblock*[54] that had propounded that the assigned debts which were

---

[46] Restatement (Second) of Contracts § 302(1).

[47] *Id.* at 302(1)(a).

[48] 661 F.2d 6 (2d Cir. 1981).

[49] *In re* Spong, 3 B.R. 619, 622 (Bankr. W.D.N.Y. 1980), *rev'd,* 661 F.2d 6 (2d Cir. 1981).

[50] 661 F.2d at 11.

[51] *Id.* at 9.

[52] 5 B.R. 348 (Bankr. D. Minn. 1980).

[53] 661 F.2d at 9. *Accord In re* Calhoun, 715 F.2d 1103, 1106–07 (6th Cir. 1983).

[54] 11 B.R. 51 (Bankr. N.D. Ohio 1981).

dischargeable in bankruptcy were only those assigned to governmental agencies. The court further recognized that § 523(a)(5) could be interpreted to mean that any support obligation which had been assigned was dischargeable but stated that even if this were so the nondischargeable nature of this particular debt was not affected because it was akin to a third party beneficiary contract and was not an assignment.[55]

The case is interesting in at least two particulars: the identity of the parties and the theory used to support the holding. As stated above, the wife's attorney, not the wife herself, was the plaintiff who sought to have the obligation to pay his fees held nondischargeable.[56] The court agreed that he was a proper party on the ground that the arrangement between the spouses created a third party beneficiary contract under which benefits flowed to both the wife as promisee and to the attorney as the third party beneficiary. The court noted that in a third party beneficiary contract either the promisee or the third party could enforce the contract.[57] In so holding the court rejected the argument that the debt was dischargeable because it had been assigned.[58]

Spong is a rather unique case in that the plaintiff, the attorney who represented the wife in the divorce action, presumably had participated in the drafting of the settlement agreement which required the debtor to pay his fee.[59] Apparently it was not disputed that the wife was unable to pay her attorney's fees because of her poor financial condition.

§ 5.5   —Limits of Third Party Beneficiary Theory

Again, a third party beneficiary contract is one that is not only intended to benefit the third party but one that in fact provides the third party with a direct, and not merely incidental, benefit of the contract.[60] *Spong* involved a debt which resulted from the pendency of the divorce proceeding and, perhaps, must be distinguished from those cases in which the obligation assumed by the debtor does not arise from the divorce proceeding

---

[55] 661 F.2d at 10.

[56] The plaintiff in other cases where the debt was held nondischargeable was often the dependent spouse's attorney. *See, e.g., In re* French, 9 B.R. 464 (Bankr. S.D. Cal. 1981); *In re* Knabe, 8 B.R. 53 (Bankr. S.D. Ind. 1980).

[57] 661 F.2d at 10–11.

[58] In acknowledging the line of cases concerning assignment the court assumed, without deciding, that the prohibition against the discharge of assigned debts, as it was then in effect, concerned only assignments to state welfare agencies. See § **5.1.**

[59] Other cases in which the attorney was the plaintiff include *In re* Catlow, 663 F.2d 960 (9th Cir. 1981); *In re* Tessler, 44 B.R. 786 (Bankr. S.D. Cal. 1984).

[60] Jardel Enter., Inc. v. Tri-Consultants, Inc., 770 P.2d 1301, 1302 (Colo. Ct. App. 1988) (*reh'g denied* 1989).

itself. In a *Spong* situation the attorney-creditor is directly involved in and has notice of the transaction which gives rise to the debt.

When the third party creditor is not involved in the proceeding in which the debtor becomes obligated to pay the creditor on behalf of the non-debtor, either through a consensual assumption or court imposed obligation, and when the debt in question was incurred during the marriage as opposed to during the divorce, the benefit to the creditor is purely fortuitous. The primary purpose of the debtor's assumption of the payment obligation in this latter situation is to benefit the dependent non-debtor spouse. When the payment also constitutes or is actually in the nature of support, the purpose is to provide the necessities of life to the non-debtor dependent. This is so even though the payment may be made directly to a creditor. For example, when a debtor assumes the mortgage on the dependent spouse's residence the assumption of the debt is an act which enables the non-debtor to obtain or keep shelter.

Third party beneficiary contracts also have been found to exist if performance of the contract satisfies an obligation owed by one party to the beneficiary.[61] Thus, even when the creditor is not involved in the negotiation of the settlement, it could be argued that a third party beneficiary contract exists because, although the primary intent is to benefit the dependent spouse by paying off a debt for which that spouse otherwise would be liable, the agreement has the added benefit to the creditor of making it whole. The intent to benefit the creditor, if it exists at all, is clearly incidental.

The authors submit that when the primary benefit is to the non-debtor in the form of support the obligation should not be dischargeable. Therefore, courts should apply a primary benefit analysis as part of the determination of whether payments which a debtor makes to a third party constitute support, maintenance or alimony. In order to assess to whom the primary benefit is directed, the intent of the parties at the time the obligation is created is a helpful factor in making the threshold determination necessary to an ultimate conclusion that the obligation is support. Of course, the actual function of the debt is the controlling factor. If the obligation benefits the spouse by providing support, the obligation should be nondischargeable. If the purpose is primarily to take care of the creditor, the debt should be dischargeable because it would not be actually in the nature of support. The determination of primary benefit cannot ignore the support aspect of the payment. For instance, one could argue that when the creditor and the non-debtor are equally benefitted and the intent appears to be to benefit both entities, the support nature of the obligation should be accorded greater weight and result in the obligation being held

---

[61] *Id.*

nondischargeable. This should be the result regardless of whether the obligation arises by consent, agreement or court order.

One other point must be made concerning the use of the third party beneficiary contract analysis when the debtor assumes a debt owed solely by the dependent non-debtor spouse. If the facts of the case establish that the debtor's assumption of the debt served the function of support, under the suggested approach, there is no need to analyze the situation further. The debt is support and is nondischargeable. However, if one wishes to go beyond this simplistic statement, it is evident that no new debt has been created via the assumption and the creditor's position has not changed. In a pure third party beneficiary contract, for example, a life insurance contract, the third party acquires previously nonexistent rights by virtue of the contract and can sue to enforce them. In the typical bankruptcy scenario, however, the creditor could not sue if the debtor defaults. Only the non-debtor spouse to whom the debtor owes the obligation could do so. Moreover, unless there is a fact pattern similar to *Spong* wherein the dependent spouse's creditor is actually a part of the transaction giving rise to the debt, the creditor probably has no knowledge of the supporting spouse's newly assumed obligation to pay.

It would appear virtually impossible to utilize a third party beneficiary contract analysis in a case involving a court order. First, there is no contract. The obligations to repay are imposed on one spouse or the other, often without their consent, through a judicial proceeding. Second, when a court orders a spouse to pay support, only the dependent spouse has a claim against the debtor and the debtor is liable only to the spouse on that support claim. Upon a default by the debtor the creditor would have no standing to sue to collect because it does not own the right of support. It is that claim to support which created the debtor's obligation to remit to the creditor, but it was done for the benefit of the non-debtor dependent. The creditor is a stranger to the support obligation between the debtor and the dependent spouse.

In *State Farm Mutual Automobile Insurance Co. v. Foundation Reserve Insurance Co.*, an insurance subrogation case, two individuals were found not to own the right being enforced and not to have the power to discharge the defendant from the obligation.[62] That is, the creditor had no actual or substantial interest in the subject matter—no "legal or equitable right to, title or interest"—no "present, substantial interest as distinguished from a contingent interest or mere expectancy."[63] Furthermore, in a support context, the creditor could not be a real party in interest because it is neither

---

[62] 78 N.M. 359, 364, 431 P.2d 737, 742 (1967).

[63] Morgan v. King, 312 Ky. 792, 795, 229 S.W.2d 976, 978 (1950). *See also* Bowers v. Bailey, 237 Iowa 295, 300, 21 N.W.2d 773, 776 (1946).

benefitted nor injured by the court's pronouncement.[64] Its enforcement rights remain intact as they existed prior to the family court's orders.

§ 5.6   —Joint Debts

When the debt is a joint obligation and the debtor has agreed or has been ordered to hold the dependent spouse harmless, the legislative history of the 1978 enactment provides that an obligation assumed by one spouse in connection with a separation or property agreement or divorce proceeding is nondischargeable as long as it is actually in the nature of support.[65] This history was detailed in *In re French,*[66] a bankruptcy case from the Southern District of California. The court stated:

> A review of the legislative history of Section 523 . . . demonstrates . . . [t]he continuing theme in the legislative history . . . that a joint obligation to a third party "assumed" by the debtor, in one way or another, is nondischargeable if it is in the nature of alimony or support and maintenance. In the early legislative comments this point was made clear by reference to "an agreement by the debtor to hold the debtor's spouse harmless on joint debts, to the extent that the agreement is in payment of alimony, maintenance, or support. . . ."
>
> H.Rep. No. 95-595, 95th Cong., 1st Sess. 364 (1977) ("House Report"), U.S. Code Cong. & Admin. News 1978, 5787, 5963, 6320. *See also* S. Rep. No. 95-989, 95th Cong., 2d Sess. 79 (1978), U.S. Code Cong. & Admin. News 1978, 5787, 5865. Such an agreement was envisioned as creating a nondischargeable obligation even though the debt was owed to a third party.
>
> In the concluding legislative remarks on this subject, the intent of Congress takes on a slightly different cast, but the effect remained the same. For example, in the joint explanatory statement covering the compromise legislation arrived at by the House and Senate it is said that:
>
> Section 523(a)(5) is a compromise between the House bill and the Senate amendment. The provision excepts from discharge a debt owed to a spouse, former spouse or child of the debtor, in connection with a separation agreement, divorce decree, or property settlement agreement, for alimony to, maintenance for, or support of such spouse or child but not to the extent that the debt is assigned to another entity. *If the debtor has assumed an obligation of the debtor's spouse to a third party in connection with a separation agreement,*

---

[64] *See* Parnell v. Nationwide Mut. Ins. Co., 263 N.C. 445, 448, 139 S.E.2d 723, 726 (1965).

[65] 124 Cong. Rec. H. 11096 (daily ed. Sept. 28, 1978) (remarks of Rep. Edwards) (cited in *In re* French, 9 B.R. 464, 467 (Bankr. S.D. Cal. 1981)).

[66] 9 B.R. 464 (Bankr. S.D. Cal. 1981).

property settlement agreement, or divorce proceeding, such debt is dis-
chargeable to the extent that payment of the debt by the debtor is not
actually in the nature of alimony, maintenance, or support of debtor's
spouse, former spouse, or child.

124 Cong. Rec. H11096 (daily ed. Sept. 28, 1978) (remarks of Rep. Edwards) (emphasis added). *See also* 124 Cong. Rec. S17412 (daily ed. Oct. 6,
1978) (remarks of Sen. De Concini).[67]

If, before bankruptcy, both spouses owed the creditor on their joint
debt, the creditor had a claim against both spouses. Although a bankruptcy will discharge the debtor from his obligation to pay, it does not create a right to payment in the creditor which previously had not existed. A
contract for a joint debt includes both spouses and their creditor as parties
and creates the expectation of and right to rely on performance by all of
the parties. Thus, the third-party beneficiary contract analysis would not
apply to joint debts because the original contract included both spouses
and their creditor as parties and created the expectation of and right to
rely on performance by and between all of the contracting parties. Enforcement rights remain intact as they existed prior to the family court's
orders.

§ 5.7   What Is an Assignment
Under § 523(a)(5)(A)?

Courts have taken some extraordinary avenues in an effort to avoid declaring third party payments dischargeable in bankruptcy. *In re Silansky*[68] is
an opinion by the Court of Appeals for the Fourth Circuit and is the result
of a combination of a lawyer's creativity and what may be the court's attempt to achieve what it perceived to be a fair result. In *Silansky* each
spouse filed a separate Chapter 7 petition after divorcing. The wife's petition had listed as an asset of her estate a judgment against the husband in
favor of her attorneys for fees accrued during the divorce proceedings. The
judgment was entered as part of the divorce decree. Pursuant to the husband's complaint to determine the dischargeability of the debt, filed in his
own bankruptcy case, the Court of Appeals for the Fourth Circuit held
that there had been no assignment to the trustee by operation of law by
virtue of the wife having listed the obligation as an asset of her estate. Because there was no assignment, the debt was nondischargeable.

This holding was based on a conclusion that the debt was not owed directly to the wife and that the divorce judgment ordering the husband to

---

[67] *Id.* at 467.
[68] 897 F.2d 743 (4th Cir. 1990).

pay the fees was not a property right of the wife. Because bankruptcy estates include only property interests, the wife had no interest which could be assigned to the trustee and the fact that she listed the support obligation as an asset was not controlling. The court did not address the support nature of the judgment in favor of the wife's attorney but because it found the debt nondischargeable, it may be inferred that this is what the finding of nondischargeability entailed. However, it is arguable that a right to receive support payments is a property right of some type. In fact, the Bankruptcy Code itself includes rights to receive alimony, support or maintenance as "property [which] may be exempted"[69] when the debtor is the spouse receiving the support payments.

The *Silansky* court rejected the present benefit test stated in *Stranathan v. Stowell*[70] because *Stranathan* had not applied the test to attorney's fees.[71] The *Silansky* court, however, overlooked the fact that a requirement that one spouse pay the other's attorney's fees could provide a direct benefit to the dependent spouse which could be actually in the nature of support. That is, it may be that if the dependent spouse had to pay the attorney's fees, that spouse would be unable to pursue the entitlement to support through the legal labyrinth and/or there would be insufficient funds to provide for the necessities of daily living. In those circumstances, the payment of the fees provides a present benefit which is support.

In *In re Fields,* a child support debt was held to be dischargeable in the ex-husband's bankruptcy case when the ex-wife filed her own Chapter 7 petition.[72] In that case the trustee in the ex-wife's case brought an action to collect child support arrearages. The court held that by filing the Chapter 7, the ex-wife's right to receive the support was assigned to the bankruptcy trustee by operation of law and, therefore, the husband's obligation to pay child support was discharged under § 523(a)(5)(A). The court cited *Stranathan v. Stowell*[73] for the proposition that the ex-wife must receive a present benefit from the payment of the debt.[74] Because the filing of the ex-wife's bankruptcy transferred all right, title and interest in her property to the bankruptcy trustee, the trustee would receive the benefit of the payments and would apply the payments for the benefit of creditors.[75] The bankruptcy court was reversed on appeal by the district

---

[69] 11 U.S.C. 522(d)(10)(D). The exemption is allowed only "to the extent reasonably necessary for the support of the debtor and any dependent of the debtor." *Id.*

[70] 15 B.R. 223 (D. Neb. 1981).

[71] *In re* Silansky, 897 F.2d at 745.

[72] 23 B.R. 134 (Bankr. D. Colo. 1982).

[73] 15 B.R. 223 (Bankr. D. Neb. 1981).

[74] *In re* Fields, 23 B.R. at 136.

[75] *Id.* at 136–37.

court in Colorado in *Zimmerman v. Starnes*.[76] Under applicable law, "the right to support belongs to the child, who is the real party in interest when a parent seeks to enforce that right."[77] The child's rights are independent of the parents'. The court further pointed out that the ex-wife's creditors could not have enforced her interest in receiving the support payments outside of bankruptcy and, therefore, could not do so after a bankruptcy was filed.

In the bankruptcy court proceeding the ex-husband alleged that the child had not been residing with the ex-wife nor had the ex-wife been providing for the child. However, to whom the money should be going would be a matter for the state court to address. Whether or not the ex-husband's allegations were true would be relevant to the bankruptcy case only, for example, if the ex-wife had misappropriated the money which was to be used to support the child. In such a situation, a representative of the child could file a claim in the bankruptcy case and seek to have the ex-wife's liability to the child for repayment of the misappropriated funds declared to be nondischargeable. First, however, there would have to be a determination that the wife actually had misappropriated the funds. Whether or not the bankruptcy court would make this determination itself or would grant relief from stay to permit the action to be filed in the state court may depend on the prevailing philosophy in the jurisdiction and on the views of the judges involved at the time. An alternative for the child may be to seek to have the debt declared nondischargeable under § 523(a)(4) which provides that a debt "for fraud or defalcation while acting in a fiduciary capacity" shall not be discharged.

As discussed in § 5.6, the Congressional Record shows that Congress intended to discharge debts assumed by one spouse to a third party on behalf of a dependent spouse only if they were not "actually in the nature of alimony, maintenance or support of debtor's spouse, former spouse, or child" and did not serve a support function.[78] The line of reasoning followed in *Silansky*, therefore, is unnecessary to avoid the effect of § 523(a)(5)(A). A direct approach serves the purpose and is more palatable. The Bankruptcy Court for the Southern District of California seems to have recognized this in *In re French*.[79] In that case the attorney who was to be paid directly by the debtor for fees incurred in representing debtor's ex-wife in divorce proceeding sought to have the obligation declared nondischargeable. In so

---

[76] 35 B.R. 1018 (D. Colo. 1984).

[77] *Id.* at 1021. The court applied California law, apparently because the divorce decree was entered in California but found that under either California or Colorado law, the right to child support arrearages belonged to the child, not the ex-wife. *Id.* at 1019, 1022.

[78] 124 Cong. Rec. H. 11096 (daily ed. Sept. 28, 1978) (remarks of Rep. Edwards). See § 5.6.

[79] 9 B.R. 464 (Bankr. S.D. Cal. 1981). See § 5.6.

ordering, the bankruptcy court noted legislative history which provides, in pertinent part:

> If the debtor has assumed an obligation of the debtor's spouse to a third party in connection with a separation agreement, property settlement agreement, or divorce proceeding, such debt is dischargeable to the extent that payment of the debt by the debtor is not actually in the nature of alimony, maintenance, or support of debtor's spouse, former spouse, or child.[80]

In several of the cases cited in this section, the dependent spouse's attorney was the plaintiff. In jurisdictions which take a narrow view of what constitutes support, it would seem wiser for the non-debtor spouse for whose benefit the award of attorney's fees was made to have the state court award the payment to her and then, if a bankruptcy ensues, to institute the complaint to determine dischargeability in the bankruptcy court. The attorney representing the non-debtor first must be able to make a strong factual showing of the need for support, and of the nature and function of the debt as support.[81] When the debt is support, it is owed to the dependent spouse, not to the attorney—or to any other creditor, for that matter. Particularly in those jurisdictions which may still be troubled when payment is not made directly to the spouse, a suit with the wife as the plaintiff would seem to avoid at least some of the potential pitfalls.

§ 5.8   Unusual Situations

In re Seibert[82] is an example of an unusual situation involving the question of dischargeability of a debt arising from a paternity action. In that case Wade Seibert and Deanne Schneider cohabited. When Deanne became pregnant she received funds from the county social service department under the Aid to Families with Dependent Children Program. To obtain this assistance she had to assign to the agency her rights and those of her child to collect from Wade any medical expenses that the county paid under the program. The rights were duly assigned. The county then instituted a paternity action against Wade and obtained judgment against him to collect the medical expenses associated with the birth of the child as well as court costs related to the paternity action. Because Wade and

---

[80] 9 B.R. at 467 (quoting 124 Cong. Rec. H. 11096 (daily ed. Sept. 28, 1978) (remarks of Rep. Edwards)).

[81] Some jurisdictions permit only the circumstances at the time the obligation was incurred to be examined. *See, e.g., In re* Gianakas, 917 F.2d 759, 763 (3d Cir. 1990). Others allow an assessment of the present financial status and needs of the ex-spouses. *See, e.g., In re* Calhoun, 715 F.2d 1103, 1009–10 and nn.10–12 (6th Cir. 1983). The practitioner must know the law in the relevant circuit or district.

[82] 914 F.2d 102 (7th Cir. 1990).

Deanne were planning to be married, the institution of a repayment schedule was delayed to allow them time to have a wedding ceremony.

After they were married and before the repayment schedule could be formalized they filed a joint Chapter 7 seeking to discharge the debt to the county. The Court of Appeals for the Seventh Circuit framed the issue as whether the expenses of pregnancy were a debt owed to a child for child support.[83] The court concluded that the medical expenses were part of the paternity obligation owed to the child because they "necessarily and directly" benefitted the child.[84] The court cited legislative history of the Social Security statute which provides that child support obligations assigned to states as a condition of eligibility for Aid to Families with Dependent Children and medical assistance are nondischargeable.[85] In finding that the pregnancy and confinement expenses were owed to the child the court opined that the expenses would not have been incurred but for the pregnancy and that they directly benefitted the child. The opinion noted that Deanne would not have been eligible for assistance if she had not been pregnant and, because it was the child's welfare that was at stake, the debt to the county was nondischargeable. Section 523(a)(5)(A), however, provides for the nondischargeability of such assignments if they are "to the Federal Government or to a State or any political subdivision of such State." This raises the question whether the Aid to Families with Dependent Children program is such an entity.[86]

In *In re Rios* an attorney sought to obtain fees from a former client.[87] Rios hired DuBroff to represent her in a palimony suit. Before the complaint was filed Rios discovered she was pregnant so the first action taken was one to establish paternity. A petition to obtain support from the father of the child was dismissed without prejudice because Rios failed to appear at the hearing. Subsequently Rios hired another attorney to reopen the support matter. DuBroff then sued Rios to recover the attorney's fees owed from the prior actions, asserting that Rios and her new attorney's action prevented DuBroff from obtaining a court order directing Rios's ex-lover to pay the fees. Rios filed bankruptcy and DuBroff filed a complaint to have her claim for her fees declared nondischargeable. The court pointed out that DuBroff's claim was dischargeable because Rios's debt to her attorney was not a support debt owed to a spouse, former spouse or child of the debtor as required by § 523(a)(5). In fact, the debt was not owed to a spouse, former spouse, or child of the debtor at all and it was

---

[83] *Id.* at 105.

[84] *Id.* at 106.

[85] *Id.* at 106 (referring to 42 U.S.C. 656(b)).

[86] An analysis of what agencies fit within the limits of § 523(a)(5)(A) is beyond the scope of this chapter.

[87] 901 F.2d 71 (7th Cir. 1990).

not incurred to provide child support but to ease the debtor's burden.[88] In addition, there was no order of court or extrajudicial contract requiring support payments and so again § 523(a)(5) would not apply to prevent the discharge of the debt. One conclusion that may be extrapolated from the court's decision is that the attorney could not use § 523(a)(5) because she had no standing under the literal language of that provision. Therefore, DuBroff was an unsecured claimant.

In summary, it must be noted that there may be authority in the case law for any position a practitioner may wish to take concerning what constitutes an "assigned debt" for purposes of § 523(a)(5)(A). A thoughtful analysis must be undertaken to determine the nature of the debt at issue, i.e., did it serve as part of a support plan utilized by the state court to allow the nondebtor dependent to obtain and maintain daily necessities? If so, the support function should have primary weight in the ultimate decision as to whether the debt is dischargeable, even if the debtor makes the payment directly to a third party creditor rather than to the non-debtor dependent.

---

[88] *Id.* at 72.

CHAPTER 6

PENSIONS AND RETIREMENT FUNDS

§ 6.1   Spendthrift Trusts

Several issues arise in bankruptcy court with regard to a state court's award of retirement benefits to a non-debtor spouse. If the award is held to be alimony, maintenance or support, it will be nondischargeable and must be paid. If, however, it is determined to be in the nature of a property distribution, and the bankruptcy court does not adhere to a trust theory, it will be dischargeable.[1]

A more basic problem, however, is whether the retirement funds, hereafter referred to as pensions, are included as property of the estate, and therefore subject to administration by the bankruptcy court.[2] Although the debtor is required to disclose his interest in a spendthrift trust, such assets are specifically excluded from property of the estate.[3] Whether the specific pension in question is treated under state law as a spendthrift trust will determine whether it can be administered through the bankruptcy court. If it does not qualify under state law as a spendthrift trust, the pension comes into the bankruptcy estate for administration as does any other asset of the debtor.[4] The cases illustrate that the nature of a

---

[1] *See In re* Lelak, 38 B.R. 164 (Bankr. S.D. Ohio 1984).

[2] *See generally* Note, *Pension Awards in Divorce and Bankruptcy,* 88 Colum. L. Rev. 194 (1988).

[3] 11 U.S.C. § 541(c).

[4] *See In re* Goff, 706 F.2d 574 (5th Cir. 1983); *In re* Herndon, 102 B.R. 893 (Bankr. M.D. Ga. 1989); *In re* Sawdy, 49 B.R. 383 (Bankr. W.D. Pa. 1985); *In re* Di Piazza, 29 B.R. 916 (Bankr. N.D. Ill. 1983).

spendthrift trust is determined under state law. If a debtor is able to withdraw funds voluntarily at any time, even though withdrawal creates certain adverse tax consequences, the pension will not constitute a spendthrift trust. If the pension comes into the bankruptcy estate, the debtor still may claim it as exempt to the extent allowable under the normal exemption provisions of state or federal law as applicable.[5]

Generally speaking, the requirements of a spendthrift trust are stringent. A spendthrift trust must not violate public policy and must contain an express provision which prohibits anticipatory alienation and attachment by creditors.[6] One state court has reasoned that it violates public policy when an individual creates a trust for his own benefit which places his assets beyond the reach of creditors even if it is a spendthrift trust.[7] Further the identities of the settlor and the trustee or other person who controls the plan are often important considerations in determining whether a plan qualifies as a spendthrift trust. Certain self-settled trusts can be spendthrift trusts under state law, although the fact of control by the settlor may be determined to violate the spendthrift nature.[8] Even employer-created plans will not qualify as spendthrift trusts to the extent that they allow a debtor to withdraw his contributions at will or to demand and receive a distribution from an employer contribution prior to retirement.[9] It should be noted that because a debtor exercises control over annuities, they have been treated as property of the estate.[10]

Section 541(c)(2) of the Bankruptcy Code further provides that certain restrictions on transfers of beneficial interests under applicable nonbankruptcy law are enforceable in bankruptcy even though the interest itself is property of the bankruptcy estate. Some cases discuss the meaning of the term "applicable nonbankruptcy law." The majority view is that the phrase refers to state spendthrift law.[11] This view is of significance to a non-debtor spouse because to the extent that pensions are determined not to be subject to distribution in bankruptcy, they are assets available for support or property division.[12]

---

[5] *See* 11 U.S.C. § 522(b), (d)(10)(E).

[6] *See, e.g.,* Wilson v. United States, 372 F.2d 232 (3d Cir. 1967).

[7] *In re* Mogride's Estate, 342 Pa. 308, 311, 20 A.2d 307, 309 (1941).

[8] *In re* Hysick, 90 B.R. 770 (Bankr. E.D. Pa. 1988).

[9] *In re* Babo, 81 B.R. 389, 391 (Bankr. W.D. Pa. 1988).

[10] *In re* Johnson, 724 F.2d 1138 (5th Cir. 1984). *See generally* T. Salerno, Bankruptcy Litigation & Practice: A Practitioner's Guide, § 4.3.1 (1990).

[11] *In re* Daniel, 771 F.2d 1352, 1360 (9th Cir. 1985), *cert. denied,* 475 U.S. 1016 (1986); *In re* Lichstrahl, 750 F.2d 1488, 1490 (11th Cir. 1985); *In re* Goff, 706 F.2d 574, 582 (5th Cir. 1983); *In re* Pettit, 61 B.R. 341, 344–45 (Bankr. W.D. Wash. 1986). *But see In re* Lucas, 924 F.2d 597 (6th Cir. 1991) (applicable nonbankruptcy law includes ERISA as well as state spendthrift law).

[12] Valuation for equitable distribution purposes is a problem which will face the state domestic relations courts, and is outside the scope of this book.

§ 6.2 ERISA Benefits

Most courts which have dealt with the question of whether ERISA (Employee Retirement Income Security Act of 1974) benefits qualify for exclusion from the bankruptcy estate have determined that such benefits are property of the estate.[13] One court, however, has concluded that a monthly pension payment from an ERISA-qualified plan which contained an anti-alienation clause on only 90 percent of the benefits constitutes a spendthrift trust under Indiana state law and is excluded from the property which will be administered in the bankruptcy estate. The *LeFeber* court stated that even the remaining 10 percent could have been subject only to a revocable assignment which, the court opined, "is no better than no assignment at all."[14] Because the 10 percent would not be irrevocably assigned, the transfer would be restricted and the restriction would be enforceable under both nonbankruptcy and bankruptcy law.

In 1988 in *Mackey v. Lanier Collections Agency & Service, Inc.,*[15] the Supreme Court noted that ERISA supersedes any and all state laws as they relate to employee benefit plans defined in the ERISA.[16] Therefore, the debtor's interest in ERISA-qualified funds comes into the bankruptcy estate and may be exempted only to the extent "reasonably necessary for the support of the debtor and any dependent of the debtor."[17] The funds may not be claimed as exempted under the state "opt out" statutes.[18]

---

[13] *See, e.g., In re* Graham, 726 F.2d 1268 (8th Cir. 1984).

[14] *In re* LeFeber, 906 F.2d 330, 331 (7th Cir. 1990).

[15] 486 U.S. 825 (1988).

[16] For a review of the cases and analyses of the doctrine of federal preemption through ERISA of state laws exempting a debtor's interest in qualified pension plans, see Fylstra & Artigue, *ERISA Preemption of State Pension—Plan Exemption Laws,* Norton Bankr. L. Adv. 6 (No. 10) (Oct. 1989).

[17] 11 U.S.C. § 522(d)(10)(E). Even if the payment is for support, it is not exemptible under § 522(d)(10)(E) if:

(i) such plan or contract was established by or under the auspices of an insider that employed the debtor at the time the debtor's rights under such plan or contract arose;

(ii) such payment is on account of age or length of service; and

(iii) such plan or contract does not qualify under section 401(a), 403(a), 403(b), 408, or 409 of the Internal Revenue Code of 1954 (26 U.S.C. 401(a), 403(a), 403(b), 408, or 409).

[18] *In re* Weeks, 106 B.R. 257 (Bankr. E.D. Okla. 1989); *In re* Sheppard, 106 B.R. 724 (Bankr. M.D. Fla. 1989). *But see In re* Volpe, 100 B.R. 840, 848 (Bankr. W.D. Tex. 1989) (distinguishing state laws which "have a reference to" ERISA from those which merely "make a reference to" ERISA and concluding that Texas exemption statute did not relate to ERISA and was not preempted, despite unanimous *Mackey* opinion by the United States Supreme Court.) *But see In re* Fritsvold, 115 B.R. 192 (Bankr. D. Minn. 1990) (ERISA preempts Minnesota exemption).

§ 6.3   Pensions and Retirement Accounts as Exempt Property

Whether the debtor chooses state or federal exemptions may determine whether retirement funds are reachable by either the non-debtor spouse or creditors. The exemptions differ state to state and federal to state. See § 1.4 for discussion of exemptions. Thus, the choice of state law may enable the debtor to protect a certain type of asset which he cannot exempt under federal law and vice-versa.

For example, in *In re Clark,*[19] a debtor who chose federal exemptions to protect his Keogh retirement plan was found not to be entitled to those exemptions under the Bankruptcy Code. In *Clark* the court noted that the underlying purpose of the Bankruptcy Code is to alleviate present, not long-term, need.[20] Thus, future payments and income derived from the Keogh after the filing of the bankruptcy petition were not exempt. The court recognized that under § 522(d)(10)(E) of the Bankruptcy Code, Keogh payments could be exempt to the extent reasonably necessary for support, but found that the debtor had no present right to receive payments from the plan and therefore did not qualify for the exemption. It should be noted that in *Clark,* the debtor did not contend that the pension plan was not property of the estate. Consequently, the issue of whether the plan itself was an asset not subject to administration for the benefit of creditors was not before the court.

Because participants can withdraw funds from an Individual Retirement Account (IRA) at any time, an IRA is considered to be property of the debtor's estate.[21] Moreover, the debtor is not entitled to exempt the entire account under 11 U.S.C. § 522(d)(10)(E), but only the amount reasonably necessary for support of the debtor or debtor's dependents.[22] Most states permit the IRAs to be reached by creditors.[23] Various state courts

---

[19] 711 F.2d 21 (3d Cir. 1983).

[20] *Id.* at 23.

[21] *See generally* Cohen & Morgan, *Reaching the Bankruptcy Debtor's Interest in Individual Retirement Plans,* 5 Compleat Law. 57 (1988); *In re* Atallah, 95 B.R. 910 (Bankr. E.D. Pa. 1989).

[22] *See In re* Pauquette, 38 B.R. 170 (Bankr. D. Vt. 1984).

[23] *See, e.g., In re* Kochell, 804 F.2d 84 (7th Cir. 1986) (concerning Wisconsin state law); *In re* Kitson, 43 B.R. 589 (Bankr. C.D. Ill. 1984) (concerning an Illinois state law); *In re* Lowe, 25 B.R. 86 (Bankr. S.C. 1982) (concerning South Carolina state law); *In re* Howerton, 21 B.R. 621 (Bankr. N.D. Tex. 1982) (concerning Texas state law); *In re* Mace, 4 BCD 94 (Bankr. Or. 1978) (concerning Oregon state law). For contrary authority, *see, e.g., In re* Sopkin, 57 B.R. 43, 46 (Bankr. S.C. 1985) (concerning the same South Carolina state law above mentioned); *In re* Worthington, 28 B.R. 736 (Bankr. Ky. 1986) (concerning Kentucky state law). *See also In re* Matthews, 65 B.R. 24 (Bankr. N.D. Iowa 1986); Roemelmeyer v. Gefen, 35 B.R. 368 (Bankr. S.D. Fla. 1984). The choice of

have construed the IRA to be a participant controlled savings account with tax benefits into which deposits and from which withdrawals (on payment of a tax penalty) can be made at will. In the bankruptcy context, IRAs have been treated differently from annuities and pensions, both of which contemplate periodic payments rather than deposits and withdrawals at will.[24] An IRA generally is not considered to be an employee benefit plan.[25] Some states treat IRAs as exempt in whole or in part, however.[26] The practitioner is cautioned to analyze the specific statutes involved before planning exemptions in IRAs.

§ 6.4 Military Retirement Pay

Military retirement pay is a frequent topic of discussion. Several cases are noteworthy, beginning with two opinions of the United States Supreme Court. In 1981 the United States Supreme Court decided *McCarty v. McCarty*.[27] In that case the Court determined that the federal statutes which govern military retirement pay prevented state courts from treating that pay as community property. In response, in 1982 Congress enacted § 1408 of Title 10 United States Code, the Uniformed Services Former Spouses' Protection Act, which enables state courts to treat as community property "disposable retired or retainer pay." The Act also enabled the federal government to make direct community property payments of up to 50 percent of disposable retired or retainer pay to former spouses who qualified when they obtained a state court order granting such pay.

Although not a bankruptcy case, *Mansell v. Mansell*[28] construed the terms of the Act literally and determined that the state court has the ability to treat not more than 50 percent of the total disposable retirement pay as community property available to the former spouse. The state court's order in *Mansell* awarded 50 percent of the total, rather than "disposable,"[29] retirement pay to the wife as community property under California law. The Supreme Court has construed the Act strictly, and

---

IRA plan (*i.e.,* investment in insurance, stock, certificates of deposit, etc.) may affect whether creditors are able to reach the asset under certain state laws.

[24] *See, e.g., In re* Peeler, 37 B.R. 517 (Bankr. M.D. Tenn. 1989); *In re* Talbert, 15 B.R. 536 (Bankr. W.D. La. 1981).

[25] *See, e.g., In re* Laxson, 102 B.R. 85 (Bankr. N.D. Tex. 1989).

[26] 42 Pa. Cons. Stat. Ann. § 8124(b)(1)(viii); Marine Midland Bank v. Surfbelt, Inc., 532 F. Supp. 728 (W.D. Pa. 1982); *In re* Sopkin, 57 B.R. 43 (Bankr. S.C. 1985).

[27] 453 U.S. 210 (1981).

[28] 490 U.S. 581 (1989).

[29] "Disposable" income is that which is subject to discretionary spending after payment of, for example, mortgages, utilities and other firm, regular commitments.

practitioners may wish to calculate the amount of the retirement benefit which is disposable in planning support or equitable division orders.[30] In *In re MacMeeken,*[31] a property settlement case, the United States District Court for the District of Kansas examined the Act and the *Mansell* case and concluded that the 50 percent limitation applied only to direct payments by the federal government to the ex-spouse and did not limit the authority of the state court to award, in a divorce proceeding, more than 50 percent of the pay.[32]

Other federal courts have faced issues concerning the effect of a bankruptcy on state court orders dividing military retirement between the spouses. In *In re Thomas,*[33] the court determined that the debtor's failure to pay pursuant to a state court order awarding 45 percent of his gross military retirement pay to the wife constituted a conversion by him of her property. The court defined "conversion" to be the "wrongful assumption of dominion over personal property by one person to the exclusion of possession by the owner and in repudiation of the owner's rights."[34] When the debtor failed to forward the wife's share of the retirement pay, even though under a direct court order to do so, he was found to be in deliberate and willful violation of the order. His obligation was held to be nondischargeable to the extent that he could not establish a good faith belief that it no longer existed.[35]

In *In re Chandler,*[36] a state court awarded the non-debtor spouse a portion of monthly Army retirement benefits as part of the divorce decree. The order provided that the benefits had become the "sole and separate property" of the non-debtor spouse and that the debtor held those benefits only as trustee for her. The debtor subsequently filed a bankruptcy under Chapter 7 and the court of appeals affirmed the bankruptcy court's decision that the debtor could not discharge that portion of the monthly

---

[30] *Mansell* also stands for the proposition that because the Act excludes from "disposable retired or retainer pay" any military retirement pay waived in order for the retiree to receive Veterans' disability benefits, the waived benefits may not be considered to be property which is divisible upon divorce.

[31] 117 B.R. 642 (D. Kan. 1990).

[32] The bankruptcy court had held that the state court award of the military retirement pay was a property settlement and applied the doctrine of collateral estoppel to that order. *Id.* The district court addressed only the state court's power to award military retirement pay under the Uniformed Services Former Spouses' Protection Act.

[33] 47 B.R. 27 (Bankr. S.D. Cal. 1984).

[34] *Id.* at 33.

[35] *Cf. In re* Mace, 82 B.R. 864, 868 (Bankr. S.D. Ohio 1987) (to find an obligation nondischargeable an intent to cause injury is unnecessary, only an intent to do the act and that the act necessarily leads to injury).

[36] 805 F.2d 555 (5th Cir. 1986) *reh'g and reh'g en banc denied,* 810 F.2d 198 (1987), *cert. denied* 481 U.S. 1049 (1989).

retirement benefit awarded to the wife. Thus, the *Thomas* and *Chandler* courts refused to allow the debtor to avoid paying the non-debtor spouse.

A somewhat different analysis was provided by the Court of Appeals for the Ninth Circuit in *In re Teichman*,[37] wherein the status of the debtor as a trustee for purposes of § 523(a)(4) was addressed. The court determined that an award of retirement benefits to the non-debtor spouse under a property settlement agreement executed in California did not create a trust because the debtor's only obligation was to see that the Air Force paid the non-debtor's share of benefits directly to her. The debtor had done so for a period of time but later instructed the Air Force to cease sending the retirement benefits to the non-debtor.

The court determined that the portion of the payments in arrears constituted a dischargeable debt but that the future payments were not dischargeable because they were not yet debts. This holding was premised on the fact that at the time of default the husband was not acting in a fiduciary capacity. As a result, the evidence did not establish a defalcation of duty because the debtor was not shown to be the trustee of the non-debtor's interest in property. Because the exception to discharge for breach of fiduciary duty provided in § 523(a)(4) is to be construed narrowly, the court determined that unless the parties clearly intended to create a fiduciary relationship at the time they entered into a property settlement, a discharge would not be denied. See § 6.5 concerning fiduciary duty. The court distinguished other cases on the theory that the particular property settlements therein expressly created trusts. However, in a concurring and dissenting opinion Judge Fletcher stated:

> This reasoning [of the majority] ignores the fact that the husband had complete control over the wife's property interest in the Air Force pension. This control was clearly manifested by the husband's direction to the Air Force to cease making payments directly to his former wife. Since the husband was invested with complete control of the pension and charged by the property settlement with insuring that the wife's portion be disbursed to her, it is hard to understand the majority's statement that no estate was conveyed to the husband as trustee.[38]

Other courts have focused on whether the obligation to make payment to the spouse is a debt at all. In *In re Manners*,[39] the court determined that a military pension benefit awarded as part of an equitable distribution of property did not constitute a debt because the pension benefits belonged to the non-debtor and the liability to pay them fell on the United States.

---

[37] 774 F.2d 1395 (9th Cir. 1985).

[38] *Id.* at 1400.

[39] 62 B.R. 656 (Bankr. D. Mont. 1986).

In *In re Hall*,[40] the court found that an award to the non-debtor of 38 percent of the debtor's military retirement pension was not a debt and was in the nature of support and, therefore, was nondischargeable in bankruptcy. The court's analysis is interesting:

> Even if Mrs. Hall's claim were to constitute a debt, as opposed to an interest in property, the debt would not be one owed by Thomas Hall to Mrs. Hall. For purposes of Title 11 of the U.S. Code, "debt" means liability on a claim. 11 U.S.C. § 101(11) (1982). Division of the pension indeed gave Mrs. Hall a "claim" to the funds. However, "liability" for that claim rests with the United States, not with Thomas Hall. Under the state court order and federal statute, the United States is responsible for making good Mrs. Hall's claim. Hall has no duty to make payments from the pension funds to his former wife. He has no power to terminate the Government's payments to her without ending as well the payments to himself. The rights and responsibilities created by the property division resulted in no debt between Mr. Hall and Mrs. Hall, as the term debt is defined in 11 U.S.C. § 101(11).[41]

This case illustrates that when the debtor is found not to be the obligor, there is no debt which can be discharged in bankruptcy.

Although there is no definitive test to determine what result will be achieved if a debtor attempts to discharge military retirement obligations to his former spouse, most courts seem to require the debtor to continue the payments and refuse to discharge the arrearages. Practitioners must examine the law in the jurisdiction in which the bankruptcy court sits to determine whether the general approach applies.

§ 6.5   Fiduciary Duty

Several cases have also analyzed whether the obligation to pay retirement funds to an ex-spouse creates a fiduciary duty. Debts for fraud or defalcation while acting in a fiduciary capacity are not dischargeable under § 523(a)(4).

In *In re Eichelberger*,[42] discharge of a debt created under a divorce decree was denied under § 523(a)(4). In *Eichelberger*, the non-debtor's interest in the debtor's pension had been made an express trust by the terms of

---

[40] 51 B.R. 1002 (Bankr. S.D. Ga. 1985).

[41] *Id.* at 1003.

[42] 100 B.R. 861 (Bankr. S.D. Tex. 1989). Defalcation can arise from the debtor's negligence or from a mere deficit caused by the debtor's misconduct. *Id.* at 866. It has even been held to arise by the simple failure to account for funds entrusted to a trustee. *See* Carey Lumber Co. v. Bell, 615 F.2d 370 (5th Cir. 1980); *In re* Borbidge, 90 B.R. 728 (Bankr. E.D. Pa. 1988), *aff'd* 114 B.R. 63 (E.D. Pa. 1990).

the parties' divorce decree. In the decree the non-debtor was awarded an undivided one-half interest in the accrued monthly pension which was to be segregated by the debtor into a separate account over which the non-debtor was to exercise all investment decisions and control. The debtor did not comply with the order and, in fact, never created the segregated account. When he filed for relief under Chapter 11 of the Bankruptcy Code, the non-debtor filed a complaint to determine the dischargeability of that debt and sought damages for violation of the terms of the divorce decree.[43]

The bankruptcy court noted that the debtor's "fiduciary capacity" for dischargeability purposes under § 523(a)(4) must arise from an express or technical trust created pursuant to state law. The court found that as long as a trust on specifically identifiable property is created under a state statute and specific fiduciary duties are mandated by the statute, the intent of the purported trustee to become a fiduciary is irrelevant for dischargeability purposes and is not required by the Bankruptcy Code. The bankruptcy court found that the state court's intent was to create either a technical or an express trust specifically to protect the non-debtor's community property interest in the debtor's pension plan. The effect was to separate legal title in the pension from the beneficial interest. The bankruptcy court noted:

> The need for imposing an express or technical trust via a divorce decree will arise only when the beneficial and legal interest in a particular piece of community property cannot be vested immediately in the spouse awarded the property. Such a trust by its very nature can only come into existence prior to any wrongdoing on the part of the trustee.[44]

In summary, so long as nothing in the underlying state law suggests the contrary, a negotiated or court ordered property settlement could be construed to be an express or technical trust whether or not the word "trust" is used in the decree or in the underlying settlement documents. However, based on existing case law, the safer course is to expressly create a trust in the separation or property settlement agreement or order.[45]

---

[43] As a general rule, some repayment would be proposed under the terms of a Chapter 11 plan. The opinion did not address any plan issues.

[44] Eichelberger, 100 B.R. at 865.

[45] For further information regarding debts which are nondischargeable by virtue of a fiduciary relationship, *see* 1 Cowan's Bankruptcy Law and Practice § 6.43 (1986). What is evident from the survey of cases conducted by Cowan is that not every pre-existing fiduciary relationship leads to nondischargeable debts. For instance, Addison v. Addison, 95 Ohio App. 191, 118 N.E.2d 225 (1953), held that the holders of joint tenancy funds were not fiduciaries subject to the nondischargeability provisions of § 523.

CHAPTER 7

ABSTENTION

§ 7.1 Types of Abstention

In some circumstances a non-debtor spouse may request the bankruptcy court to abstain from exercising its jurisdiction pending the outcome of certain state court proceedings. The United States Supreme Court has noted that abstention from the exercise of federal jurisdiction is "the exception, not the rule."[1] In *Ohio v. Wyandotte Chemicals Corp.* the Court noted that the Anglo-American common law tradition is that a court which possesses jurisdiction generally must exercise it.[2]

Although the general rule is easily stated, abstention has been the subject of litigation and frequent commentary.[3] There are three commonly accepted variations of the abstention doctrine. The first, the *Pullman* doctrine, originated in *Railroad Commission of Texas v. Pullman Co.*[4] In that case the United States Supreme Court noted the principle that a lower federal court should abstain when there is an unresolved or unsettled state law question which, if resolved by the state courts, may eliminate the need to reach the federal question in the case. In *Hughes v. Lipscher*[5] the Court of Appeals for the Third Circuit noted that although federal courts generally are bound to adjudicate cases within their jurisdiction, there are

---

[1] Colorado River Water Conservation Dist. v. United States, 424 U.S. 800, 813 (1976).

[2] 401 U.S. 493, 496–97 (1971). *See also* Cohens v. Virginia, 19 U.S. 264 (1821) (courts which have jurisdiction have no more right to decline its exercise than to assume jurisdiction when they have none.)

[3] *See, e.g.,* Friedman, *A Revisionist Theory of Abstention,* 88 Mich. L. Rev. 530, 531 n.2 (1989) (collecting articles).

[4] 312 U.S. 496 (1941).

[5] 906 F.2d 961 (3d Cir. 1990).

a few notable exceptions to this rule. In some cases where questions under both state law and the federal constitution are present, the policies of promoting comity with the state courts and ensuring the smooth functioning of the federal judiciary counsel the federal courts to stay their hands, at least initially. This is the abstention doctrine explicated in *Railroad Comm'n. of Texas v. Pullman Co.*, 312 U.S. 496 (1941).[6]

The second doctrine is referred to as *Younger* abstention. In *Younger v. Harris*[7] the Supreme Court determined that a federal court should not enjoin ongoing state criminal proceedings absent enumerated circumstances. The third doctrine was enunciated in *Colorado River Water Conservation District v. United States*,[8] in which the high court analyzed circumstances in which abstention is appropriate. The Court broadly defined these categories:

(a) Abstention is appropriate "in cases presenting a federal constitutional issue which might be mooted or presented in a different posture by a state court determination of pertinent state law."[9]

(b) where there have been presented difficult questions of state law bearing on policy problems of substantial public import whose importance transcends the result in the case then at bar.[10]

(c) where, absent bad faith, harassment, or a patently invalid state statute, federal jurisdiction has been invoked for the purpose of restraining state criminal proceedings . . . ; state nuisance proceedings antecedent to a criminal prosecution, which are directed at obtaining the closure of places exhibiting obscene films . . . ; or collection of state taxes.[11]

Stating with clarity the types of abstention applicable in a given case is not an easy task. The Supreme Court itself has recognized the difficulty with categorizing abstention cases. In *Pennzoil Co. v. Texaco, Inc.*,[12] the Court noted: "The various types of abstention are not rigid pigeonholes into which federal courts must try to fit cases. Rather, they reflect a complex of considerations designed to soften the tensions inherent in a system

---

[6] *Id.* at 964.

[7] 401 U.S. 37 (1971).

[8] 424 U.S. 800 (1976).

[9] *Id.* at 814 (citations omitted).

[10] *Id.* (citations omitted).

[11] *Id.* at 816 (citation omitted). *Compare* Colorado River Water Conservation Dist. v. United States *with* Burford v. Sun Oil Co., 319 U.S. 315, 333 n.29 (1943) (recognizing as a matter of equity the discretion to decline the exercise of jurisdiction when judicial restraint seems "required by considerations of general welfare").

[12] 481 U.S. 1 (1987).

that contemplates parallel judicial processes."[13] The Court of Appeals for the Third Circuit recently noted that abstention is both an extraordinary and narrow exception to federal court jurisdiction and is justified only in exceptional circumstances when resort to a state court proceeding serves an important countervailing interest.[14]

§ 7.2 Abstention in Bankruptcy Matters: Dismissal of the Case

Section 305 of the Bankruptcy Code governs abstention in bankruptcy cases. It provides:

(a) The court, after notice and a hearing, may dismiss a case under this title, or may suspend all proceedings in a case under this title, at any time if—

(1) the interests of creditors and the debtor would be better served by such dismissal or suspension; or

(2) (A) there is pending a foreign proceeding; and

(B) the factors specified in section 304(c) of this title warrant such dismissal or suspension.

(b) A foreign representative may seek dismissal or suspension under subsection (a)(2) of this section.

(c) An order under subsection (a) of this section dismissing a case or suspending all proceedings in a case, or a decision not so to dismiss or suspend, is not reviewable by appeal or otherwise by the court of appeals under section 158(d), 1291, or 1292 of this title or by the Supreme Court of the United States under section 1254 of this title.

The section was amended, effective December 1, 1990,[15] to specify that nonreviewability was effective against the court of appeals and the United States Supreme Court. That is, an order under § 305 is appealable only to the district court. Before the amendment, the section simply stated that a decision to abstain or dismiss was not reviewable "by appeal or otherwise."[16] Both before the 1990 amendment and now, Bankruptcy Rule 5011(b) provided that, absent an order to the contrary by the district court, the bankruptcy court would hear an abstention motion and file a

---

[13] *Id.* at 11 n.9.

[14] Biegenwald v. Fauver, 882 F.2d 748 (3d Cir. 1989).

[15] Judicial Improvements Act of 1990, Pub. L. 101-650, § 309, 104 Stat. 5113 (1990). Although this particular section does not state an effective date, the Act's effective date was December 1, 1990.

[16] 11 U.S.C. § 305 (1978).

report and recommendation with the district court for review.[17] There was no such provision governing dismissals, however.

In *Parklane Hosiery Co., Inc. v. Parklane/Atlanta Venture*[18] the Court of Appeals for the Eleventh Circuit, construing the older version of 11 U.S.C. § 305(c), affirmed an order of the district court withdrawing the reference in an involuntary bankruptcy. That is, the court of appeals approved the district court's revocation of the jurisdiction the district court had granted to the bankruptcy court with respect to that particular case. *Parklane Hosiery* also had filed a motion for abstention or, in the alternative, dismissal of the involuntary bankruptcy proceeding and argued that the bankruptcy court could not enter an order under 11 U.S.C. § 305 concerning abstention or dismissal because the section as then constituted did not provide for appellate review by an Article III court. Both the district court and the court of appeals agreed.

In essence, the court of appeals said such an order would terminate the jurisdiction of the district court without review by an Article III court. That is, it would place the jurisdiction of an Article III court within the discretion of an Article I court and would constitute an impermissible exercise of the judicial power of the United States by a non-Article III court. Neither the plurality opinion nor the concurring opinion discussed the impact of Bankruptcy Rule 5011(b) or the Advisory Committee note thereto which recognized that, with respect to abstention matters, the bankruptcy judge is to make a report and recommendation to the district judge who would make a de novo review.[19]

Because abstention provisions were reviewable, before 1990, by virtue of Rule 5011(b), it could be argued that the *Parklane Hosiery* rationale is viable only with respect to dismissal orders. However, § 305 of the Bankruptcy Code, as formerly constituted, said only that the decision was not appealable and it is axiomatic that a rule of procedure cannot change a substantive statutory provision. Still, one might argue that the rule was evidence of the purpose and function of § 305. In light of the 1990 amendments, the issue would appear to be moot.

§ 7.3   Abstention in Bankruptcy Matters: Mandatory versus Discretionary Abstention

Under the Bankruptcy Code abstention from the entire case is discretionary. Section 305(a)(1) of Title 11 of the United States Code provides that

---

[17] Fed. R. Bank. P. 5011(b), 11 U.S.C.

[18] 927 F.2d 532 (11th Cir. 1991).

[19] *See* 11 U.S.C. § 1334. *Cf.* Fed. R. Bankr. P. 9033, 11 U.S.C. (review by district court of noncore matters).

the bankruptcy court may dismiss the bankruptcy case or suspend all proceedings therein if the interests of creditors and the debtor would be served by such dismissal or suspension. Sections 305(a)(2)(A) and (B) provide that the court may abstain when an action which can be timely adjudicated actually has been commenced in a state forum, provided that abstention is otherwise warranted.

Section 1334(c) of Title 28 of the United States Code sets out the standards used by the district court in ruling on a motion for abstention. In essence, this section provides that the motion *may* be granted in the interest of justice or in the interest of comity with state courts or respect for state law, but *mandates* abstention when a timely filed motion is based upon a state law claim or state law cause of action which could not have been commenced in federal court but for the fact that the debtor filed a bankruptcy petition.[20] The courts tend to apply these standards so that if the action on which the bankruptcy court is asked to abstain lacks a connection with the bankruptcy itself, abstention will be granted. Abstention has been granted when a Securities and Exchange Commission (SEC) receivership was pending[21] and when pending state court receiverships were close to termination even though the distribution under state law had a different system of priority than that under the Bankruptcy Code.[22] Courts have refused to dismiss or suspend the bankruptcy case, however, when there was no provision for the claims of all of the creditors who would seek to obtain a distribution in the bankruptcy court.[23]

Mandatory abstention under 28 U.S.C. § 1334(c)(2) is limited to those cases in which there is no nonbankruptcy federal jurisdiction. To gain abstention on this basis, the underlying claim must be proven to be based upon a state law or upon an interest important to the state itself.[24] The abstention must be granted only "if an action is commenced" which can be timely adjudicated in the state court.[25] The time of commencement has been held to refer exclusively to a state court action commenced prior to the bankruptcy case.[26] Some cases have focused on whether the state court provides a forum in which the action can be timely adjudicated.[27]

---

[20] *See generally* T. Salerno, Bankruptcy Litigation and Practice: A Practitioner's Guide, §§ 3.27–3.31 (1990) (collecting cases).

[21] *In re* Michael S. Starbuck, Inc., 14 B.R. 134 (Bankr. S.D.N.Y. 1981).

[22] *In re* Sun World Broadcasters, Inc., 5 B.R. 719 (Bankr. M.D. Fla. 1980).

[23] *See, e.g., In re* Nina Merchandise Corp., 5 B.R. 743 (Bankr. S.D.N.Y. 1980).

[24] *In re* Futura Indus., Inc., 69 B.R. 831 (Bankr. E.D. Pa. 1987).

[25] 28 U.S.C. § 1334(c)(2).

[26] *See, e.g., In re* Boughton, 49 B.R. 312, 315 (Bankr. N.D. Ill. 1985). *Cf.* Ram Constr. Co. v. Port Auth., 49 B.R. 363 (W.D. Pa. 1985) (failure to allege prior commencement of state court action despite existence of arbitration clause insufficient to require abstention).

[27] *See, e.g.,* National Acceptance Co. v. Levin, 75 B.R. 457 (D. Ariz. 1987).

When the interest of creditors necessitates prompt action or the bankruptcy court wants control of the calendar of events, it sometimes retains jurisdiction.[28]

Determining when to abstain is as difficult in a bankruptcy matter as in any other. Abstention remains the exception, not the rule. A few courts have examined requests for abstention from the standpoint of how closely related to the bankruptcy the underlying substantive matter is. In *In re Arnold Print Works, Inc.*[29] the court indicated that abstention should not be granted routinely in matters which affect the heart of the bankruptcy case.[30]

One case sheds some light on considerations which may make abstention appropriate. In *In re Titan Energy, Inc.*[31] the court faced the issue of whether a bankruptcy court should abstain from hearing an action brought by the debtor's insurer to determine the scope of coverage under certain product liability policies. The bankruptcy court abstained. This decision was affirmed by the Court of Appeals for the Eighth Circuit because no applicable policy concern favored the exercise of jurisdiction by the bankruptcy court. One pertinent fact was that the debtor was in a Chapter 7 liquidation proceeding, although the case originally had been filed under Chapter 11 as a reorganization. The *Titan Energy* court specifically found that it

> may consider the current financial situation of the parties when considering abstention. Titan's shift from Chapter 11 to Chapter 7 proceedings relieves us of the *Johns Manville, Davis,* and *Tringali* courts' concern that allowing a related state court action to proceed will hinder debtor's return to business. Thus, abstention presents itself as a suitable option here, where it was not in those cases.[32]

The court further noted that the insurer's action sounded in state law and had a limited connection to the debtor's bankruptcy case. The action was brought by a non-debtor against another non-debtor and would have had impact upon the estate only if a number of contingencies occurred.

---

[28] Ronix Corp. v. City of Philadelphia, 82 B.R. 19 (Bankr. E.D. Pa. 1988); *In re* World Solar Corp., 81 B.R. 603 (Bankr. S.D. Cal. 1988); *In re* Republic Reader's Serv., Inc., 81 B.R. 422 (Bankr. S.D. Texas 1987); *In re* Baldwin United Corp., 52 B.R. 541 (Bankr. S.D. Ohio 1985).

[29] 815 F.2d 165 (1st Cir. 1987).

[30] An example would be something that affected the statutory distribution priority. *See also In re* Fietz, 852 F.2d 455, 457 (9th Cir. 1988) (citing Pacor, Inc. v. Higgins, 743 F.2d 984, 994 (3d Cir. 1984) for the proposition that bankruptcy courts have broad jurisdiction over any actions which may have an impact on administration of the bankruptcy estate).

[31] 837 F.2d 325, 330–34 (8th Cir. 1988).

[32] *Id.* at 331.

The court stated that the bankruptcy court need not exercise its jurisdiction "where the nexus between the related state court action and debtor's estate is so attenuated."[33] *Titan Energy* also stands for the proposition that abstention is appropriate "where the action could not have been commenced in federal court absent bankruptcy jurisdiction and the issues can be timely adjudicated in state court."[34]

§ 7.4   Divorce Considerations

Although the various statutory sections are worded in a manner that indicates that abstention, if ordered, would apply to the entire case, there are cases that speak to abstention with respect to separate matters within a bankruptcy case. In some cases the abstention decision seems to be based on the philosophy of the particular court or jurisdiction that is hearing the issue. In others the courts appear to be influenced by what they perceive as a party's bad faith.

In re Hursa[35] involved a non-debtor spouse's attempt to have the bankruptcy court abstain from deciding the trustee's motion to sell the marital residence. The non-debtor spouse preferred to have the state court proceed with equitable distribution. The bankruptcy court held that mandatory abstention applied based on the complexity of the issues under New Jersey property and marital law, the fact that there would be no federal jurisdiction but for the fact of the bankruptcy filing, and the fact that marital proceedings already had been filed in the state court which could decide the matter in a timely manner.[36]

In re Markizer[37] concerned an action to determine the dischargeability of a debt to an ex-spouse. The ex-spouse's answer to the dischargeability complaint included a counter claim which requested that the matter be returned to the state court for enforcement of a settlement agreement

---

[33] *Id.* at 333. *See also In re* Futura Indus., Inc., 69 B.R. 831 (Bankr. E.D. Pa. 1987) (suggesting that bankruptcy courts ought to weigh the degree to which the issue to be tried is related to the bankruptcy case and that where most of the criteria for mandatory abstention are met, careful consideration should be given to the propriety of exercising the court's discretion to abstain).

[34] 837 F.2d at 333.

[35] 87 B.R. 313 (Bankr. D. N.J. 1988).

[36] *Hursa* suggests that the only activity that had taken place in the state court before the bankruptcy was filed was the filing of the divorce complaint and an entry by the state court of an order that purported to hold the parties' marital residence as security for alimony and child support arrearages. 87 B.R. at 314–15. This order was entered after the bankruptcy was filed and was of no force and effect under § 362 of the Bankruptcy Code.

[37] 66 B.R. 1014 (Bankr. S.D. Fla. 1986).

entered into by the parties some time before the filing of the bankruptcy. The court interpreted this request as a motion for abstention. The court denied the request, holding that it had to examine the agreement and the circumstances surrounding its creation in order to determine whether it represented support or a property settlement and therefore whether the debt was dischargeable.

In *In re Taylor*[38] the ex-spouse sought to collect alimony payments in state court proceedings after the debtor had received a discharge in bankruptcy. The state court rejected the debtor's defense of the discharge and the bankruptcy court abstained from deciding the dischargeability matter when the debtor sought to remove it to the bankruptcy court. The bankruptcy court noted that the debtor had not sought its intercession until after the state court had rejected his defense that the obligation had been discharged. The bankruptcy court viewed the debtor's attempt to remove the issue to bankruptcy court as an attempt to retry the case and by-pass the state appellate process.[39]

The circumstances discussed above may provide easier questions for the bankruptcy court to resolve than do the types of abstention problems arising in the domestic relations area. Many divorcing couples have creditor problems which must be considered by the bankruptcy court. Thus, when a motion to abstain is filed, a balancing test must be utilized to determine the interests of all creditors, not just the interest of the non-debtor spouse. When there is not a significant likelihood of an impact on creditors other than insiders, bankruptcy courts have abstained from jurisdiction to allow the state court to resolve the disputes.[40] However, abstention is not to be granted as a matter of course just because the underlying matter arose in a domestic relations context.[41]

In an unpublished decision, the Court of Appeals for the Fourth Circuit recently decided that the pendency of a divorce action was not a sufficient ground on which to base abstention of the exercise of jurisdiction by the bankruptcy court.[42] The bankruptcy court had authorized a sale of entireties property, although only the husband had filed bankruptcy, before

---

[38] 49 B.R. 416 (Bankr. N.D. Tex. 1985).

[39] Debtor had obtained an ex parte temporary restraining order in the bankruptcy court enjoining the ex-spouse from pursuing her support collection attempts. The ex-spouse's motion to vacate the injunction was granted.

[40] *See, e.g., In re* Evans, 8 B.R. 568 (Bankr. M.D. Fla. 1981).

[41] Erspan v. Badgett, 647 F.2d 550 (5th Cir.), *reh'g en banc denied,* 659 F.2d 26 (5th Cir. 1981), *cert. denied,* 455 U.S. 945 (1982); *In re* Ziets, 79 B.R. 222, 226–27 (Bankr. E.D. Pa. 1987).

[42] *See In re* Oswald, 883 F.2d 69 (4th Cir. 1989), *reversing and remanding without opinion,* 90 B.R. 218 (Bankr. N.D.W. Va. 1988). The opinion of the Court of Appeals is unpublished but available through Westlaw. According to Fourth Circuit Rule 18, I.O.P. 363.36.5, 28 U.S.C.A., citation of unpublished opinions is disfavored.

the divorce was final. The district court reversed and ordered abstention to allow the state court to order equitable distribution. The court of appeals found that abstention would delay the prompt determination of the size of the bankruptcy estate and reversed the district court. It should be noted that the Bankruptcy Code specifically provides for sale of a non-debtor co-owner's interest in property[43] and, although the *Oswald* court did not discuss this provision of the Bankruptcy Code, it may have been a factor.

In a bankruptcy which seeks to discharge a marital obligation, the bankruptcy courts often deal with state law causes of action. The marital dispute addressed in *Ex parte Lumpkin*[44] and *Lumpkin v. Lumpkin*[45] is illustrative. The wife sued for divorce and its attendant property division in Alabama and the husband sued for the same relief in Georgia. The wife was awarded $700 a month for her interest in the family business and filed a petition against her husband demanding that he pay an arrearage in excess of $15,000 due on a property settlement awarded in Alabama. The Alabama court found the husband to be in contempt for failing to pay those arrearages. The Georgia court later domesticated the Alabama decree and reiterated the finding of contempt. The husband filed bankruptcy in Georgia and contended in a motion to enforce the stay that his wife was in violation of the automatic stay by pursuing domestication of the Alabama decree. The bankruptcy court dismissed the husband's motion, lifted the stay, and specifically abstained from exercising jurisdiction, finding that the parties could pursue their monetary and property disputes in another court of competent jurisdiction. Eventually, the courts in both Alabama and Georgia found the husband to be in contempt for failing to pay the arrearages and both decisions were affirmed on appeal.

Some non-debtor spouses seek to have jurisdiction returned to state court by way of a motion for relief from stay rather than for abstention. Generally, they have not fared well. The bankruptcy courts seem reluctant to release any matters involving property division which may affect a distribution to creditors. In *In re Murray*[46] the debtor filed bankruptcy after the divorce was granted but before the division of property was completed. The non-debtor spouse was granted relief from the automatic stay to pursue support. However, her request to have the state court Master partition the realty was denied and the bankruptcy court retained jurisdiction over the property so that it could be sold by the bankruptcy

---

[43] 11 U.S.C. § 363. *See In re* Brown, 33 B.R. 219 (Bankr. N.D. Ohio 1983), for a discussion of sales of co-owner interests.

[44] *Ex parte* Lumpkin, 469 So. 2d 649 (Ala. Civ. App. 1985).

[45] Lumpkin v. Lumpkin, 328 S.E.2d 389 (Ga. Ct. App. 1985).

[46] 31 B.R. 499 (Bankr. E.D. Pa. 1983).

trustee.[47] After sale, the non-debtor wife would receive whatever distribution was authorized by the Bankruptcy Code.[48]

A review of the cases substantiates that there are no clear standards set forth to deal with abstention matters in a bankruptcy which has domestic relations overtones. Abstention motions should be considered as mechanisms to have the non-debtor spouse's interests determined by the state courts. Practitioners must be aware, however, of the heavy burden imposed upon the movant to establish that abstention is warranted. It may be difficult to prove that the interests of justice or comity with the state warrant dismissal of the bankruptcy action via abstention, particularly when there are debts aside from the intra-marital obligations over which the state court cannot exercise jurisdiction in the divorce proceeding.[49] Those creditors will have an interest in the outcome of the bankruptcy.[50]

A lawyer representing a non-debtor spouse who wishes to convince the bankruptcy court to abstain may fare better if an action based upon a state law, nonbankruptcy claim was commenced in the state court before bankruptcy and the practitioner can establish that the state court action can be timely adjudicated. Under such circumstances there may be an argument for mandatory abstention. Most often, however, attorneys will find themselves looking to the discretionary abstention sections of the federal statutes. The standards for the application of discretionary abstention are more subjective than those concerning mandatory abstention.

The most direct method of advising the bankruptcy court of a desire to have it abstain is to present a motion for abstention. The practice of abstention is equitable in nature.[51] The equitable arguments which the practitioner may wish to raise may be brought forth more clearly in the context of a motion for abstention. Although the issue may be reached of necessity by the court in the context of another pleading, such as a motion to enforce the stay or a motion for relief from stay, these are not the proper procedural avenues.[52]

---

[47] See Napotnik v. Equibank & Parkvale Sav. Assoc., 679 F.2d 316 (3d Cir. 1982) (discussing effect of creditor levy against entireties property for satisfaction of joint debt).

[48] See also In re Ziets, 79 B.R. 222 (Bankr. E.D. Pa. 1987) (bankruptcy court retained jurisdiction to make equitable distribution). Whether the bankruptcy court should become involved in what is essentially equitable distribution is an open question worthy of examination.

[49] See 11 U.S.C. § 305(a)(2)(B) and § 304(c).

[50] See the analysis of abstention standards set forth in *Biegenwald v. Fauver,* 882 F.2d 748 (3d Cir. 1989).

[51] Bellotti v. Baird, 428 U.S. 132, 143 n.10 (1976).

[52] Arguably, the failure to raise abstention could amount to a waiver. However, federal courts have authority to consider the matter sua sponte. Bellotti v. Baird, 428 U.S. 132, 144 n.10 (1976); Hughes v. Lipscher, 906 F.2d 961 (3d Cir. 1990) (citing cases).

Bankruptcy courts are guided by what will "assure an economical and expeditious administration of the debtor's estate."[53] When faced with an abstention motion the court will consider factors such as "the availability of an adequate state remedy, the length of time the litigation has been pending, and the potential impact on the parties from the delay in seeking a state ruling."[54] Because the court exercises its discretion in ruling on abstention motions, the practitioner should marshal every equitable consideration in support of his position, whether advocating the exercise of abstention or the retention of jurisdiction by the bankruptcy court. Of course the practitioner also must consider and apply such standards as exist.

---

[53] Harley Hotels, Inc. v. Rain's Int'l Ltd., 57 B.R. 773, 782 (M.D. Pa. 1985).

[54] Hughes v. Lipscher, 906 F.2d at 964 (3d Cir. 1990).

CHAPTER 8

CONTEMPT

§ 8.1   Introduction

Contempt powers are an inherent feature of a court's ability to regulate the conduct of litigation and enforce court orders.[1] Thus, when a violation of a court order issued in a support or custody proceeding is construed as willful, the errant party traditionally has been subject to the state court's contempt powers.[2] In most states, the rules governing violations of support matters specify that contempt proceedings brought to enforce support orders are civil in nature. The procedures employed may differ with regard to how an alleged contemnor is notified of the charges against him, subjected to hearing, and adjudicated.

Typically, upon a finding of civil contempt, the state court will issue an order which must specify the conditions for purging the contempt and which may include incarceration. The purpose of a civil contempt is to compel performance. Therefore, the court must impose conditions which the contemnor is able to perform.[3] The order of contempt is final when sanctions are imposed and is appealable in the same manner as is any other final order in civil litigation.[4] The bankruptcy courts can become

---

[1] Commonwealth v. Garrison, 478 Pa. 356, 386 A.2d 971 (1978); Hopkinson v. Hopkinson, 323 Pa. Super. 404, 470 A.2d 981 (1984). Hopkinson was overruled in Sonder v. Sonder, 378 Pa. Super. 474, 549 A.2d 155 (1988), at least to the extent that it permitted a court to incarcerate for nonpayment of support required by an agreement which is not merged into a divorce decree.

[2] *See, e.g.,* Knaus v. Knaus, 387 Pa. 370, 127 A.2d 669 (1956).

[3] Barrett v. Barrett, 470 Pa. 253, 368 A.2d 616 (1977).

[4] *See* 28 U.S.C. 158(c). An appeal from a final order of a bankruptcy court must be taken within ten days of the date of entry of the order. Fed. R. Bankr. P. 8001(a), 11 U.S.C.

involved in a challenge to any phase of the state contempt process and/or to the conditions for purge.

§ 8.2 Contempt and Relief from Stay

Bankruptcy courts hear contempt motions alleging violations of the provisions of the Bankruptcy Code. Contempt proceedings arise in bankruptcy court in a number of ways. One of the most common is pursuant to § 362 of the Bankruptcy Code when the allegation is made that a person has violated the automatic stay. Bankruptcy judges have jurisdiction in those proceedings and most are not reluctant to impose sanctions for wilful violations of the automatic stay.[5]

Issues of contempt arise in bankruptcy court in domestic relations contexts. In *Matter of Brock*[6] the state court ordered the debtor to pay a debt to a finance company which had been an obligation of both spouses during the marriage. The debtor filed bankruptcy and defaulted in the payments. The bankruptcy court determined that the automatic stay prevented the wife from taking any collection action against the debtor. When the wife pursued her civil contempt remedy in state court, the bankruptcy court found her to be in wilful violation of the automatic stay. She was ordered to pay the amount owed to the finance company plus the husband's attorney's fees and court costs.[7]

The first matter to be addressed in the bankruptcy court is whether relief from stay should be granted to institute or continue a state court contempt proceeding. Courts vary in their interpretation of this matter. Some allow the contempt proceeding to go to judgment but not to execution on the judgment if the execution would have an impact on assets of the bankruptcy estate.[8]

If an order of contempt does not have an impact on the estate, it can be argued that bankruptcy courts should be reluctant to interfere with the

---

[5] 11 U.S.C. 362(h). *See, e.g.,* Hubbard v. Fleet Mortgage Co., 810 F.2d 778 (8th Cir. 1987), *reh'g & reh'g en banc denied*; *In re* Better Homes of Va., Inc., 804 F.2d 289 (4th Cir. 1986); *In re* Wagner, 74 B.R. 898 (Bankr. E.D. Pa. 1987).

[6] 58 B.R. 797 (Bankr. S.D. Ohio 1986).

[7] Section 362(h) of the Bankruptcy Code permits one injured by "any willful violation" of the automatic stay to recover damages. 11 U.S.C. 362(h). A specific intent to violate the automatic stay is not necessary to a finding of a willful violation. If one acts with knowledge of the stay and intended the action taken, that the action was taken in good faith does not defeat the characterization of the act as willful. *In re* Atlantic Business & Community Corp., 901 F.2d 325, 329 (3d Cir. 1990).

[8] *In re* Cornell, Bankr. No. 88-03455, Motion No. 89-4152 (Bankr. W.D. Pa. June 28, 1989) (on appeal). After the appeal was filed the bankruptcy court dismissed the case at debtor's request.

underlying state court proceeding. The remedy for the contemnor in such a case is an appeal through the state court processes.

In *U.S. Steel Corp. v. Musisko*[9] the court, tracing the origins of the Anti-Injunction Act, noted that "hostility towards infringement on state sovereignty prompted the first congress to vest only limited jurisdiction in the lower federal courts."[10] "The general rule remains today one of nonintervention. . . . Inappropriate intervention breeds friction, but federal restraint facilitates the smooth and orderly operation of the dual judicial structure."[11] Thus, the standard in Anti-Injunction Act proceedings generally is to allow the state court to proceed without intervention by the federal courts with appellate relief available to the litigants through the state litigation. Although the Act is not applicable in a bankruptcy context, the reasoning may have some import in particular cases.

Some courts refuse to grant relief from the stay even to pursue the contempt to judgment.[12] In those cases in which a contempt does have an impact on estate assets, the bankruptcy courts typically forbid any execution on the order of contempt. Because the bankruptcy court has exclusive jurisdiction over the disposition of assets, it reserves jurisdiction to determine the distribution of those assets according to the priorities of the Bankruptcy Code.[13] If there is any doubt whether the assets are property of the estate, counsel would be well advised to request the bankruptcy court to decide the issue.

If the state contempt order involves collection of support from property which is not property of the estate, the contempt action should not be barred by virtue of 11 U.S.C. § 362(b)(2).[14] However, even though there is no specific statutory exclusion for such proceedings, Sections 362(b)(4) and (b)(5) exclude from the stay most actions taken by a governmental unit in the enforcement of its police or regulatory authority. A judicial process such as contempt, which is founded upon a court's ability to enforce its orders, would seem to fall within such an exclusion as long as the enforcement would not affect property of the estate.[15] An attempt by a

---

[9] 885 F.2d 1170 (3d Cir. 1989).

[10] *Id.* at 1174.

[11] *Id.* at 1174–75.

[12] *In re* Cherry, 78 B.R. 65 (Bankr. E.D. Pa. 1987).

[13] 11 U.S.C. 726.

[14] *But see In re* Cherry, 78 B.R. 65 (Bankr. E.D. Pa. 1987) (declining to grant relief from stay because 362(b) does not specify civil contempt proceedings as a statutory exclusion from operation of the stay).

[15] *See* Schall v. Joyce, 885 F.2d 101, 108 (3d Cir. 1989) (quoting Juidice v. Vail, 430 U.S. 327, 335 n.12 (1977)) (analyzing various non-bankruptcy cases which have ordered federal court abstention in favor of state court civil contempt proceedings because the contempt power "'stands in aid of the authority of the judicial system, so that its orders and judgments are not rendered negatory'"). It is important for the practitioner to

non-debtor spouse to hold a debtor in criminal contempt in state court has been held to be outside the scope of the automatic stay and therefore not subject to sanctions.[16]

Consider, however, the case of *In re McGinty*.[17] In that case the non-debtor spouse's attorney had been informed by the debtor's attorney of the fact that the stay precluded pursuit of matters in the divorce action. The non-debtor's attorney persisted, however, in an action in state court to obtain additional support on behalf of the non-debtor spouse and for a determination by the state court that his fees were nondischargeable in the debtor's bankruptcy. The bankruptcy court sanctioned him but held that he could not be held in contempt on the ground that a contempt finding require knowing and wilful violation of a written court order.

To the contrary the court in *In re Sermersheim*[18] granted the debtor's complaint for contempt against the ex-spouse and her attorney. The conduct which led to an order for sanctions was the filing by the ex-spouse and her attorney of a motion with the state court seeking to have the debtor held in contempt for nonpayment of certain liabilities. The state court motion was filed after they had been informed of the bankruptcy. It probably did not help their case that the bankruptcy court found the debts at issue to be nondischargeable.

The court in *In re Smith*[19] refused to find the non-debtor in contempt, although she had violated the stay, on the ground that the issues involved were so complicated that all the judges and law clerks of the court had had input into the decision and the court opined that if the issues were so difficult for the experts in the field, a lay person could not be expected to be aware of all the angles to consider. In that case spouses had reached a property settlement which the non-debtor spouse sought to set aside after the bankruptcy discharge alleging that the debtor had never intended to abide by it but had always planned to obtain a bankruptcy discharge.

It appears from a review of the cases that a non-debtor will not be found in contempt if the infraction was minor or technical. On the other hand, if the non-debtor cannot approach the court with clean hands, so to speak, or if the debtor has not committed what could be termed egregious conduct, the non-debtor and that party's attorney may find themselves subject to sanctions.

---

remember that the existence of a bankruptcy calls into play many rules not applicable in a nonbankruptcy context.

[16] *In re* Altchek, 124 B.R. 944 (Bankr. S.D.N.Y. 1991).

[17] 119 B.R. 290 (Bankr. M.D. Fla. 1990).

[18] 97 B.R. 885 (Bankr. N.D. Ohio 1989).

[19] 81 B.R. 888 (Bankr. W.D. Mich. 1988).

§ 8.3   Contempt and Marathon

It must be noted that whether bankruptcy courts have statutory authority to exercise their own civil contempt powers, aside from violations of the stay, is a subject frequently discussed in the literature since the United States Supreme Court decided *Northern Pipeline Construction Co. v. Marathon Pipe Line Co.*[20] *Marathon* involved a proceeding based on a traditional contract action under state law and addressed only the question of whether a bankruptcy court, a non-Article III court, has the power to render final judgments and issue binding orders in those actions absent the consent of the litigants and subject only to ordinary appellate review. Nonetheless, as a result of *Marathon,* other attacks on the jurisdiction of the bankruptcy courts have been mounted.

At least one circuit court of appeals has decided, based on *Marathon,* that a bankruptcy court does not have contempt power because it is no longer considered a "court of the United States" but rather "a unit of the district court."[21] More recently the Courts of Appeals for the Third Circuit, in an unpublished opinion,[22] and for the Fourth Circuit, in a published opinion,[23] reached the contrary conclusion, holding that 11 U.S.C. § 105(a) of the Bankruptcy Code authorizes bankruptcy judges to exercise civil contempt powers. If the United States Supreme Court grants the request for certiorari in the Fourth Circuit case, it may resolve the conflict in the circuits.

Contributing to the confusion is Bankruptcy Rule 9020 which in pertinent part provides that bankruptcy judges may enter binding orders when the contempt is committed in the presence of the judge.[24] The Rule further provides that if the contemnor files a timely objection to an order of contempt, the bankruptcy judge must prepare findings of fact which the district court must review de novo.[25] The district court then enters the final order.[26] Rule 9020 also specifies the notice requirements for

---

[20] 458 U.S. 50 (1982).

[21] *In re* Sequoia Auto Brokers, Ltd., 827 F.2d 1281, 1288 & n.10 (9th Cir. 1987); 28 U.S.C. 151. *See also* 28 U.S.C. § 451.

[22] *In re* Grosse, 96 B.R. 29 (E.D. Pa. 1989), *aff'd without published opinion,* 879 F.2d 856, *cert. denied* _____ U.S. _____, 110 S. Ct. 501 (1989).

[23] *In re* Walters, 868 F.2d 665, 669 (4th Cir. 1989).

[24] Fed. R. Bankr. P. 9020, 11 U.S.C. See **App.** C.

[25] *Id.*

[26] Contempt power is not exclusive to Article III judges. The Congress, the Tax Court, courts-martial and territorial courts may exercise contempt powers. With regard to the Tax Court, see 26 U.S.C. 7456(c); Ryan v. Commissioner of Internal Revenue, 517 F.2d 13 (7th Cir.), *cert. denied,* 423 U.S. 892 (1975). With regard to courts-martial, *see* 10 U.S.C. 848. With regard to territorial courts, *see* Francis v. People of Virgin Islands,

contempts other than those committed in the presence of the bankruptcy judge. Written notice of the essential facts constituting the contempt, a designation as to whether the charge is civil or criminal contempt, and the date, time and place of the hearing must be given. Reasonable time must be given to prepare a defense and a finding of contempt may be made only after a hearing. If there is a right to a jury trial, Rule 9020(d) preserves that right in such instances.

---

11 F.2d 860, 864 (3d Cir. 1926), *cert. denied sub. nom.* Francis v. Williams, 273 U.S. 693, 47 S. Ct. 91 (1926); Fleming v. United States, 279 F. 613 (9th Cir.), *cert. dismissed,* 260 U.S. 752 (1922).

CHAPTER 9

PREMARITAL AGREEMENTS

§ 9.1   Premarital Agreements in General
§ 9.2   —Dischargeability in Bankruptcy

§ 9.1   Premarital Agreements in General

When the parties execute a premarital agreement it is more difficult to foresee problems concerning property and the need for support than it is when a postmarital agreement or decree is under consideration. A property division based on the presence or absence of the need for support as perceived at the time the premarital agreement is executed may not be reasonable at the time of divorce because of changed circumstances. However, to the extent that it is contemplated that one spouse shall support the other, what the parties see as necessary to carry out that intent should be specified as much as possible. There is still no guarantee that the agreement will protect the dependent spouse or children in the event of a divorce or bankruptcy. Premarital agreements often are enforced under state law if there is full disclosure, the distribution of property provided for in the agreement is fair, and the agreement was entered into voluntarily.[1] Some jurisdictions will enforce a premarital agreement even if the property division is unfair, provided that there was full disclosure in its execution.[2]

In 1990 the Supreme Court of Pennsylvania took just such an approach in the case of *Simeone v. Simeone.* The court held that as long as there is a full and fair disclosure of each party's financial position, the contract shall be enforceable whether or not its terms are reasonable.[3] In so holding, the

---

[1] R. Wilder, J. Mahood & M. Greenblatt, Pennsylvania Family Law Practice and Procedure Handbook 53 n.15.1 (2d ed. 1989).

[2] Freed & Walker, *Family Law in the Fifty States: An Overview,* 21 Family L.Q. 367, 379 (1989).

[3] 525 Pa. 392, 402, 581 A.2d 162, 166–67 (1990).

court recognized the purported abandonment of the paternalistic views which were the foundation for earlier opinions permitting an inquiry into the reasonableness of the terms of the agreement.[4] The court concluded that "[t]raditional principles of contract law provide perfectly adequate remedies where contracts are procured through fraud, misrepresentation, or duress."[5] Although hindsight may be employed in the face of changed circumstances in some jurisdictions,[6] the Pennsylvania Supreme Court pointed out that everyone knows that circumstances can change during the term of a contract of long duration.[7]

To the extent that the agreement would purport to waive child support it probably would be held to be unenforceable.[8] Also if the provision for child support was inadequate or unreasonable, the contract principles theory of *Simeone* would not apply because the child was not a party to the contract.

Following the *Simeone* decision, the Pennsylvania Superior Court decided *Karkaria v. Karkaria.*[9] The issue before the court was whether a prenuptial agreement which had been executed before the enactment of the Pennsylvania Divorce Code could limit or waive statutory economic rights. The court held that such an agreement would be presumed valid and enforceable unless the objecting spouse could show that the proponent spouse had failed to make a full and fair disclosure of financial worth at the time the agreement was executed. The court found such a ruling to be consistent with general contract principles and *Simeone.*

§ 9.2   —Dischargeability in Bankruptcy

Cases interpreting the dischargeability in bankruptcy of premarital support arrangements are scarce. The sole reported case is from the Western District of Kentucky.

In *In re Jackson,*[10] the debtor husband filed bankruptcy, apparently Chapter 7, after the divorce action had been initiated. He and the non-debtor

---

[4] 525 Pa. at 400, 581 A.2d at 165.

[5] *Id.*

[6] *See* Freed & Walker, *Family Law in the Fifty States: An Overview,* 21 Family L.Q. 367, 430–31 (1989); Scheible, *Defining "Support" Under Bankruptcy Law: Revitalization of the "Necessaries" Doctrine,* 41 Vand. L. Rev. 1, 14–15 and n.67–73 (1988). North Carolina is one of the states which has adopted the Uniform Premarital Agreement Act.

[7] Simeone v. Simeone, 581 A.2d at 166.

[8] *See* Scheible, *Defining "Support" Under Bankruptcy Law: Revitalization of the "Necessaries" Doctrine,* 41 Vand. L. Rev. 1, 15 n.74 (1988).

[9] _____ Pa. Super. _____, 592 A.2d 64 (1991).

[10] 27 B.R. 892 (Bankr. W.D. Ky. 1983).

spouse had executed a premarital agreement that provided that the debtor was to furnish his spouse "a decent support" as long as debtor lived. The agreement had no provisions that "would lead one to conclude that it was limited to a divorce or dissolution of the marriage of these parties."[11] The court found that the "premarital promise of lifetime support is 'in connection with' a separation agreement or divorce decree" and, therefore, it was not dischargeable under § 523(a)(5).[12]

The same principles that apply to finding postmarital agreements or orders nondischargeable as support apply to provisions in premarital agreements. There is no formula for an agreement that will guarantee the nondischargeability of what the parties to a premarital agreement may designate as support. As with postmarital situations, much depends on the facts and circumstances surrounding either the transaction or present circumstances, depending on the jurisdiction. An agreement that certain obligations are nondischargeable is unenforceable.[13]

---

[11] *Id.* at 892–93.

[12] *Id.* at 893. The bankruptcy court rejected the debtor's contention that the obligation was dischargeable because it arose as a matter of contract under the common law. The obligation arose "in connection with" a divorce decree and thereby was brought within the terms of § 523(a)(5) of the Bankruptcy Code.

[13] 11 U.S.C. § 727(a)(10). *See also* 11 U.S.C. § 524(c), (d).

APPENDIXES

A. Digests of State Cases

B. Selected Sections of the Bankruptcy Code, Title 11
   United States Code

C. Selected Rules of the Federal Rules of Bankruptcy Procedure

D. Selected Sections of Title 28 United States Code

E. Sample Pleadings

APPENDIX A

DIGESTS OF STATE CASES

The cases are included for general interest purposes and are not intended by the authors or editors to represent correct or incorrect approaches.

Alabama

Ex Parte Henderson, 574 So. 2d 830 (Ala. Civ. App. 1990)

The court ruled that the automatic bankruptcy stay, in a bankruptcy proceeding filed after support had been awarded pendente lite, did not bar the wife from proceeding with a petition for rule nisi to enforce the support against assets which are not estate property. In doing so, the court noted that support is an exception to discharge.

McDonald v. McDonald, 574 So. 2d 842 (Ala. Civ. App. 1990)

The appellate court rejected the trial court's interpretation of a divorce decree that had awarded the wife $25,000 as "a property settlement and as alimony in gross." Although the trial court had found that a portion of the award was nondischargeable support, the appellate court pointed out that alimony in gross is in the nature of a property settlement so that the entire amount was dischargeable in bankruptcy.

Arizona

Jordan v. Jordan, 166 Ariz. 408, 803 P.2d 129 (1990)

In an action to enforce an out-of-state support order, the court first ruled that the bankruptcy court's dismissal with prejudice of the wife's attempt to intervene in the bankruptcy proceeding was not an adjudication on the merits because it was based on timeliness. Therefore, the trial court was not barred by res judicata from determining that the support order was not discharged in the bankruptcy proceeding when the question is raised in the trial court in a timely fashion. However, the court was persuaded by the husband's argument that he should have been allowed to establish that the support award was actually a property settlement which might be discharged. In reaching this conclusion, the court observed that this was a permissible collateral attack on the out-of-state award.

Arkansas

Barker v. Barker, 271 Ark. 956, 611 S.W.2d 787 (1981)

Applying relevant provisions of the Bankruptcy Act of 1898, the court looked to state law to determine what constitutes alimony, maintenance, or support. Observing that if the debt is a division in property it is dischargeable, the court determined that here the debt for a bass boat and motor were support or maintenance and were not dischargeable. In reviewing the evidence and how financial obligations were interrelated, the court pointed out that the debt on the boat and motor were to the bank where the wife was employed. When the husband discharged the debt in bankruptcy, the bank required the wife to pay it and discharged her when she could not. The court affirmed the trial court's finding of contempt against the husband, noting that he filed bankruptcy one week after the wife filed a contempt action against him and the only debt he did not reaffirm was the one for the boat and motor.

California

In re Marriage of Henderson, 225 Cal. App. 3d 531, 275 Cal. Rptr. 226 (1990)

Although a creditor disputing the dischargeability of a debt under § 523(a)(2), (4), or (6) must file an objection in the bankruptcy court, a creditor whose debt is listed as nondischargeable under § 523(a)(1), (3), (5), (7), (8), or (9), may bring suit in any appropriate nonbankruptcy forum even after the conclusion of the bankruptcy proceeding. Here, the county family support division sought renewal of its judgment in state court following the bankruptcy discharge. The court rejected the father's argument that the fact that he listed the county as an unsecured creditor in the bankruptcy proceeding resulted in a determination that the debt was dischargeable and had been discharged.

Colorado

Barber v. Barber, 811 P.2d 451 (Colo. Ct. App. 1991)

The state court had concurrent jurisdiction to determine that the award of attorney fees to the wife and the fact that the obligation was not to be paid directly to the wife or child did not prevent it from being nondischargeable. Citing *In re Calhoun*, 715 F.2d 1103 (6th Cir. 1983), the court held that the attorney fees were not dischargeable. Furthermore, the automatic bankruptcy stay did not prevent enforcement of support and maintenance obligations.

Connecticut

Celentano v. Celentano, 1991 WL 85180 (Conn. Super. Ct. 1991)

Caveat: This is an unpublished decision which may have no precedential value under local rules. The court divided specific debts between the parties with the provision that each indemnify and hold the other harmless on the obligation assigned. The court further stated that this division was intended as support in lieu of lump sum alimony and could not be discharged in bankruptcy. However, the court also ruled that each party was responsible for other debts listed on the financial affidavits and did not include them as intended for support.

Edwards v. Edwards, 1991 WL 85185 (Conn. Super. Ct. 1991)

Caveat: This is an unpublished decision which may have no precedential value under local rules. The court stated that the allocation of debts contained in two paragraphs of its property division was intended as support and the obligations were not intended to be dischargeable in bankruptcy. Other liabilities divided between the parties were exempted from that provision.

Dietrichsen v. Dietrichsen, 1990 WL 283997 (Conn. Super. Ct. 1990)

Caveat: This is an unpublished decision which may have no precedential value under local rules. Ruling that the wife was not entitled to pursue a contempt proceeding after the husband discharged, in bankruptcy, marital debts for which he was supposed to hold her harmless, in bankruptcy, the court pointed out that the wife failed to object to the discharge in the bankruptcy proceeding and also that the hold harmless provisions of the state court judgment clearly were not alimony, support, or maintenance but were part of a dischargeable property settlement.

Delaware

Derby v. Derby, 1990 WL 143877 (Del. Fam. Ct. 1990)

Caveat: This is an unpublished decision which may have no precedential value under local rules. The court determined that the husband had abandoned the marital homes by ceasing payments on the liens against it when it had negative equity and he went through bankruptcy. Since that time the wife had expended substantial sums on arrears and maintenance, and appraisals indicated that there was now equity in the property. The court ordered the husband to convey all his rights in the property to the wife.

Georgia

Lewis v. Lewis, 258 Ga. 617, 373 S.E.2d 18 (1988)

The court affirmed the determination of the trial court, on remand from the bankruptcy court, that payments for 48 months, attorney fees, and payments on a home mortgage and automobile loan were in the nature of support and nondischargeable.

Lumpkin v. Lumpkin, 173 Ga. App. 755, 328 S.E.2d 389 (1985)

In an action enforcing an Alabama divorce decree, the court affirmed the contempt finding over the husband's assertion that the trial court should have decided whether the property settlement was dischargeable in his bankruptcy action. The court observed that the bankruptcy court had specifically declined to stay collection of the property settlement during the pendency of the bankruptcy proceeding so there was no basis for the trial court to have concerned itself with the issue of its dischargeability.

Clements v. Household Finance Corp., 165 Ga. App. 220, 299 S.E.2d 916 (1983)

In this action, Household Finance brought an action against the wife on a note executed by both the wife and the husband. The wife filed a third-party complaint against the husband alleging that he had agreed to pay the debt and hold her harmless as part of their divorce decree. The court rejected the husband's defense that he had discharged the obligation in bankruptcy to the extent of finding that the trial court erred in dismissing the third-party complaint. The court ruled that the fact of the bankruptcy court's filing did not bar the wife from seeking relief against the husband for a nondischargeable debt.

McLure v. McLure, 163 Ga. App. 469, 294 S.E.2d 693 (1982)

Stating that it is entirely conceivable that the purpose of a property settlement might be to provide for maintenance or support, the reviewing court remanded this matter to the trial court to determine whether the property settlement was in the nature of maintenance or support and whether the obligation was dischargeable in bankruptcy.

Illinois

LaShelle v. LaShelle, ____ Ill. App. 3d ____, 572 N.E.2d 1190 (1991)

Distinguishing between a duty to pay a debt and an assignment of the right to have a debt paid, the court held that the husband's duty to pay the second mortgage was in the nature of support because otherwise the wife and children would lose their home. In reaching this conclusion, the court considered the fact that the decree did not explicitly state whether the second mortgage debt was part of the property division or constituted maintenance or support. The court also considered other factors including whether the decree otherwise provided for payments to the ex-spouse; whether the hold-harmless provision was intended to balance the relative income of the parties; whether the hold-harmless provision was in the midst of the property provisions; and whether the hold-harmless provision described the method and type of payment.

Alltop v. Alltop, 203 Ill. App. 3d 605, 561 N.E.2d 394 (1990)

Although commencement or continuation of proceedings against a debtor who has filed a petition violates the Bankruptcy Code, proceedings to uphold the dignity of the court against contumacious behavior are not subject to the automatic bankruptcy stay. However, here the court found that the debtor did not obtain adequate notice of the contempt proceedings from the filing of a petition to show cause.

Cesaretti v. Cesaretti, 203 Ill. App. 3d 347, 561 N.E.2d 306 (1990)

In this case, the husband obtained a discharge in bankruptcy without his wife's knowledge during the marriage. In the subsequent divorce, the trial court awarded the wife a sum as and for adjustment of marital debts for which the husband had obtained the discharge. On appeal, the court rejected the husband's argument that this award violated the "fresh start" policy of the Bankruptcy Code. Rather, the court ruled that the discharge did not cover his obligations to the marriage.

Iowa

In re Marriage of Francis, 442 N.W.2d 59 (Iowa 1989)

In this marriage, the wife had supported the husband through medical school and internship. The court determined that the husband's increased earning potential was a marital asset which should be divided between the parties. The mechanism for the division was "reimbursement alimony" as distinct from "rehabilitative" or permanent alimony. The court specifically pointed out the tax advantages and the nondischargeable nature of reimbursement alimony as preferable to a property settlement.

Kansas

Marriage of Sailsbury, 13 Kan. App. 2d 740, 779 P.2d 878 (1989)

The state district court has concurrent jurisdiction with the bankruptcy court to determine whether obligations under a separation agreement are dischargeable in bankruptcy under 11 U.S.C. § 523(a). To resolve the question, the court must look beyond the language of the agreement to determine whether the obligation is in the nature of support, maintenance, or alimony. Four factors should be considered: (1) whether the agreement fails to otherwise provide for spousal support; (2) whether there are minor children or an imbalance of income; (3) whether the obligation is to be paid in installments over a substantial period of time; and (4) whether the obligation terminates upon death or remarriage. *Id.* at 881.

Kentucky

Low v. Low, 777 S.W.2d 936 (Ky. 1989)

Noting the strong nexus between a property award and maintenance, the court found an exception to the rule that lump sum maintenance awards are final. After the husband had obtained a discharge in bankruptcy on the note owed to the wife as a property settlement, the court concluded that a manifest inequity would result if it did not modify the maintenance. Accordingly, maintenance was modified.

Maryland

Rogers v. Rogers, 80 Md. App. 575, 565 A.2d 361 (1989)

Although the wife's counsel fees for the divorce had been discharged in bankruptcy, the court could order the husband to reimburse her for the amount borrowed before discharge to pay attorney fees. The court also noted that the wife had incurred additional attorney fees after her discharge.

Michigan

Kowatch v. Kowatch, 179 Mich. App. 163, 445 N.W.2d 808 (1989)

The court affirmed a finding of contempt against the husband for his failure to pay alimony. He argued that the award of alimony was essentially a property settlement and should have been discharged in his bankruptcy proceeding under 11 U.S.C. § 523(a)(5)(B). The award of alimony apparently had been the divorce court's mechanism for compensating the wife for the loss of her personal property through the husband's failure to make mortgage payments. The reviewing court found that the bankruptcy court had decided the issue on the merits and declined to review that court's determination.

Minnesota

Dougherty v. Dougherty, 1991 WL 75256 (Minn. Ct. App. 1991)

Caveat: This is an unpublished opinion and should not be cited except as provided by Minn. Stat. § 480A.08(3). Rejecting the husband's argument that the award of permanent maintenance was a property settlement which had been discharged by his bankruptcy, the court looked behind the judgment to determine the "true nature" of the obligation. The court considered whether the obligation was to be paid in installments; terminated upon death or remarriage; and how it was labelled. Additionally, the court considered whether the spouse needed support based upon relative health, education and employment history of the parties.

Schmidt v. Schmidt, 1991 WL 26061 (Minn. Ct. App. 1991)

Caveat: This is an unpublished opinion and should not be cited except as provided by Minn. Stat. § 480A.08(3). The original decree had awarded the wife a cash settlement of $119,250 in addition to the equity in the marital home plus temporary maintenance because the property division limited her need for permanent maintenance. However, the decree had also provided that maintenance would be modifiable if the wife did not receive the property. The husband discharged the $119,250 in bankruptcy and opposed modification of maintenance. The court ruled that the third court's findings were sufficient to support a modification and that the award of permanent maintenance was appropriate under these circumstances.

Nelson v. Nelson, 444 N.W.2d 302 (Minn. Ct. App. 1989)

The reviewing court affirmed the addition to the settlement order of a provision that it was intended that the husband's obligation to pay maintenance was not dischargeable in bankruptcy. The finding had been added at the wife's request because the husband's business was having financial difficulties.

Missouri

McGill v. McGill, 809 S.W.2d 434 (Mo. Ct. App. 1991)

Agreeing that the doctrine of claim preclusion had no application, the court held that collateral estoppel did and prevented the wife from seeking maintenance payments after the bankruptcy court had ruled that the ambiguous provisions in the decree did not entitle her to two payments of maintenance. She had had, the court found, a full and fair opportunity to litigate this issue in the bankruptcy court and had not appealed its ruling although the bankruptcy court had limited her claim to a single payment.

Classe v. Classe, 772 S.W.2d 386 (Mo. Ct. App. 1989)

Denial of the father's motion to modify child support was not a violation of the automatic bankruptcy stay provided in 11 U.S.C. § 362. The motion was not an action by another party to recover a debt or claim. Additionally, the child support obligation is not dischargeable under 11 U.S.C. § 523(a)(5).

Montana

In re Marriage of Jones, 242 Mont. 119, 788 P.2d 1351 (1990)

The wife filed a motion requesting maintenance after the husband filed a bankruptcy petition listing the property settlement to her as a dischargeable debt. After the bankruptcy court did discharge the property settlement, the state court awarded the wife maintenance. The award of maintenance was affirmed over the husband's argument that it was a penalty for using proper bankruptcy procedures for discharging the debt on the property settlement.

New Jersey

Siegal v. Siegal, 243 N.J. Super. 211, 578 A.2d 1269 (1990)

Characterizing the husband's bankruptcy petition as "a model of deviant frivolity," the court recognized that the bankruptcy filing had the effect of staying the payment of its equitable distribution award and considered the "novel question" whether it should increase the alimony award during pendency of the bankruptcy case. The court did increase the alimony award but rejected the wife's request, in the name of equity, for attorney fees for counsel representing her in the husband's bankruptcy although the court also stated that "to sanitize the [husband's] hands would require amputation."

New Mexico

Hopkins v. Hopkins, 109 N.M. 233, 784 P.2d 420 (1989)

The bankruptcy and state courts have concurrent jurisdiction to determine whether a debt arising from divorce is dischargeable, but the determination must be made under federal law. Under federal law, the failure of the wife to present the debt in the bankruptcy proceeding of which she had knowledge did not discharge the debt as an unlisted debt because debts for support are not governed by § 523(a)(3)(A). The wife has the burden of proving that the debt is in the nature of support and is non-dischargeable. The court determined that the divorce obligation of the husband to pay the second and third mortgages was in the nature of support and therefore not dischargeable.

New York

Hilsen v. Hilsen, 161 A.D.2d 459, 555 N.Y.S.2d 370 (1990)

Admitting to some uncertainty whether the equitable distribution award was part of a debtor's estate, the court ruled that the award was part of the maintenance award and, therefore, not subject to the automatic stay in bankruptcy proceedings. The court further ruled that the issue whether the equitable distribution award was a property settlement and dischargeable or a debt for maintenance or support and not dischargeable is a question for the bankruptcy court.

North Carolina

Long v. Long, 102 N.C. App. 18, 401 S.E.2d 401 (1991)

After the husband obtained a discharge in bankruptcy, the wife sought to enforce a separation agreement and property settlement. The trial court had dismissed the claim on the basis that the wife had not sought alimony in the divorce action. The appellate court reversed, ruling that an evidentiary hearing was required to determine whether the periodic payments provided for in the separation agreement were in the nature of support. If the payments are determined to be in the nature of support, then they could not be discharged by the husband's Chapter 7 bankruptcy. The court also noted that the trial court had concurrent jurisdiction with the federal court to determine the dischargeability of debts.

North Dakota

Hartman v. Hartman, 466 N.W.2d 155 (N.D. 1991)

The father sought modification of his child support obligation, asserting that since the award of support he had filed and completed a bankruptcy proceeding, which had not discharged all his debts. The court determined that, contrary to his assertions, the father's income was still adequate for his expenses and the support obligation. The court also noted that temporary loss of income or difficulty in making payments is not a material change in circumstances which would justify a modification of the support obligation. Therefore, the court refused to modify the support obligation.

Ohio

Conley v. Conley, 1991 WL 60687 (Ohio Ct. App. 1991)

Caveat: This is an unpublished opinion and should be used only in compliance with Ohio Supreme Court Rule 2. Noting that it is the non-debtor spouse's burden to show that a debt is not dischargeable in bankruptcy, the court determined that the issue of the husband's mortgage obligation had been fully litigated in the bankruptcy proceeding and that the wife was barred from relitigating it in state court. However, the court did affirm the award of alimony arrears as having been not discharged in the bankruptcy proceeding.

Brodnax v. Brodnax, 1990 WL 121867 (Ohio Ct. App. 1990)

Caveat: This is an unpublished opinion and should be used only in compliance with Ohio Supreme Court Rule 2. Reversing the trial court, the appellate court found that the husband's obligation to make payments for the car awarded to the wife was discharged in the husband's subsequent bankruptcy proceeding. In contrast to *Pearl v. Pearl*, 1990 WL 118855, the debt here was not in the nature of alimony and the agreed judgment and decree indicated that it was a simple allocation of debts and property. Therefore, the husband could not be held in contempt for failure to pay a discharged debt.

Pearl v. Pearl, 1990 WL 118855 (Ohio Ct. App. 1990)

Caveat: This is an unpublished opinion and should be used only in compliance with Ohio Supreme Court Rule 2. The court was unpersuaded by the husband's argument that it was error to determine dischargeability of a debt upon the wife's petition for contempt. Because the trial court correctly applied the factors in *In re Calhoun*, 715 F.2d 1103 (6th Cir. 1983), the court affirmed that the husband's mortgage obligation on the marital home was not dischargeable.

Williams v. Williams, 1990 WL 102412 (Ohio Ct. App. 1990)

Caveat: This is an unpublished opinion and should be used only in compliance with Ohio Supreme Court Rule 2. Determining that the appeal was from an order involving child support arrearage, the court found no conflict in enforcing the order over the husband's argument that the state court could not so order while he was involved in a bankruptcy proceeding.

Broadwater v. Broadwater, 1989 WL 109495 (Ohio Ct. App. 1989)

Caveat: This is an unpublished opinion and should be used only in compliance with Ohio Supreme Court Rule 2. The court looked to *In re Calhoun,* 715 F.2d 1103 (6th Cir. 1983), to determine whether an assignment of debts, subsequently discharged in bankruptcy, was in the nature of support. The *Calhoun* court considered three factors: (1) whether the parties or the court intended to create a support obligation; (2) whether the provision has the effect of providing support; and (3) whether the amount of support is so excessive as to be unreasonable. Here, the trial court had indicated the assignment of debts was alimony and not dischargeable and had considered all the *Calhoun* factors in making the original determination. The appellate court affirmed the finding of nondischargeability.

Neff v. Neff, 1989 WL 13531 (Ohio Ct. App. 1989)

Caveat: This is an unpublished opinion and should be used only in compliance with Ohio Supreme Court Rule 2. Although the husband in this case alleged that he was in personal bankruptcy and could not afford to pay the dramatically increasing health insurance premiums which the divorce decree that obligated him to continue for the wife, the court found that no proper evidence of the bankruptcy had been admitted and, therefore, the trial court could not have addressed the question of dischargeability of the insurance obligation.

Costantino v. Costantino, 1989 WL 3951 (Ohio Ct. App. 1989)

Caveat: This is an unpublished opinion and should be used only in compliance with Ohio Supreme Rule 2. In a ruling focusing on whether the trial court's refusal to find the husband in contempt was an appealable order, the appellate court had no problem with the determination that the assignment of the car loan to the husband had been in the nature of support.

Oklahoma

Robinson v. McDaniel, 795 P.2d 513 (Okla. 1990)

After a husband's obligation to pay taxes as provided for in divorce decree was discharged in bankruptcy, wife could not maintain contempt proceeding to force him to pay the taxes.

Oregon

In re Marriage of Sheldon, 82 Or. App. 621, 728 P.2d 946 (1986)

In this case, the mother sought to offset and cease payment of her child support obligations after the father discharged his obligation to her on a promissory note in bankruptcy on the ground that the father had agreed to the offest. The court found that Oregon law prohibited modification of child support installment payments which accrued before a motion to modify obligation is filed. The court also found no basis in the record to support the mother's contention that the father had agreed to such an arrangement.

In re Marriage of Hadley, 77 Or. App. 295, 713 P.2d 39 (1986)

In declining to terminate spousal support payments, the court found no substantial change in circumstances. The husband had obtained a discharge in bankruptcy of joint debts so that now creditors were seeking payment from the wife. The court apparently felt that this offset her increase in income and the fact that her living expenses were paid by the man with whom she now lived.

In re Marriage of Bauer, 44 Or. App. 265, 605 P.2d 750 (1980)

The husband's discharge in bankruptcy did not relieve him of his obligation to hold the wife harmless for certain debts pursuant to the divorce decree. The court rejected the husband's argument that this placed him in the position of an indemnitor, contrary to the 1978 Bankruptcy Code. The court pointed out that the Bankruptcy Code exempts from discharge any debt not listed or scheduled unless the creditor had notice or actual knowledge of the proceedings and the record here did not indicate that the wife had either.

In re Carrier, 40 Or. App. 407, 595 P.2d 827 (1979)

In an action for relief from a foreign judgment alleging discharge in bankruptcy, the court ruled that the obligation was in the nature of alimony because the decree treated it like other alimony provisions rather than like a division of marital assets. Hence, it was not discharged in bankruptcy. The wife had not filed a claim in the bankruptcy case nor had she contested, in the bankruptcy, the dischargeability of the obligation represented by the judgment. The case arose under the Bankruptcy Act of 1898.

Pennsylvania

Deichert v. Deichert, 402 Pa. Super. 415, 587 A.2d 319 (1991)

Noting that the bankruptcy and state courts have concurrent jurisdiction over whether a particular obligation is dischargeable in bankruptcy, the court stated that the basis of the inquiry into dischargeability must take into account all relevant economic and non-economic factors including the living standards of the parties. Also, the label given to the obligation, even "equitable distribution," is not dispositive of whether the nature of the obligation is actually support which cannot be discharged. The court determined that on the facts before it the husband was attempting to challenge the original award through the bankruptcy proceeding, although he had failed to preserve his right to do so under the appellate rules. In conclusion, the court ruled that (1) the award of the marital residence and furnishings were support; (2) the award of the car was maintenance; (3) the lien on the husband's medical building was to ensure compliance with alimony obligation and, therefore, was nondischargeable support; (4) the obligation to pay joint debts was support.

Buccino v. Buccino, 397 Pa. Super. 241, 580 A.2d 13 (1990)

State and federal courts have concurrent jurisdiction over whether a particular obligation is dischargeable in bankruptcy. Hence, once a state court has determined the issue, collateral estoppel applies to any attempt to relitigate the issue in federal court. In balancing the competing interests of giving a debtor a fresh start and protecting adequate financial maintenance of a debtor's children and ex-spouse, the court held that the rights of former spouses and children should be "liberally protected." The court looked at the intent of the divorce court at the time the obligations were established and considered a long list of factors to determine that the obligations in this case were in the nature of alimony to support the former spouse. The court also noted that it considered the financial position of the parties at the time of the divorce rather than the present financial position of the parties. To do otherwise, it stated, would result in an ongoing assessment of need.

Rhode Island

Hopkins v. Hopkins, 487 A.2d 500 (R.I. 1985)

Although the bankruptcy court and the state court have concurrent jurisdiction under 11 U.S.C. § 523(a) to determine dischargeability of debts to a spouse or child, the court determined that the bankruptcy court had discharged the husband's debts after a full evidentiary hearing in which the wife participated. However, the court concluded that because the wife's waiver of alimony had been based upon the husband's assumption of those debts that there had been a substantial change in circumstances justifying a modification of alimony.

Sirvano v. Sirvano, 424 A.2d 1047 (R.I. 1981)

In a case arising under the Bankruptcy Act of 1898, and examining federal law in the district, the court found that the automatic stay prevented the state court from pursuing contempt proceedings for alimony arrearages.

South Carolina

Pratt v. Pratt, 280 S.C. 276, 312 S.E.2d 577 (1984)

The bankruptcy court determination that the monthly payments were alimony and the lump sum was a property settlement was dispositive of the claims brought in this state court action to enforce property settlement agreement.

Tennessee

Spence v. Spence, 1990 WL 112361 (Tenn. Ct. App. 1990)

Caveat: This is an unpublished case and should be used in compliance with Court of Appeals Rules 11 and 12. Here, the judgment of divorce had awarded the wife the marital home subject to the first mortgage, for which she was to hold the husband harmless. The husband was obligated to pay the second and third mortgages, for which he was to hold the wife harmless. The husband filed bankruptcy, reaffirming all his debts except for the second and third mortgages and did not give notice of the bankruptcy petition to the wife. The court ascertained that the wife had foregone any claim for alimony in exchange for the husband's agreement to pay the second and third mortgages and that he had engaged in fraud and misrepresentation in seeking to discharge those obligations. Accordingly, the court rejected the husband's contention that his obligation had been discharged in bankruptcy.

Bridges-Allen v. Allen, 1990 WL 7470 (Tenn. Ct. App. 1990)

Caveat: This is an unpublished case and should be used only in compliance with Court of Appeals Rules 11 and 12. The appellate court held that the trial court had erred in changing the property division to alimony in solido when it learned that its order would be subject to discharge in bankruptcy. The reviewing court found that no request had been made for maintenance nor had there been evidence on the issue because wife's attorney stated that no alimony was sought and the husband believed that no alimony was sought.

In re Rigney, 1990 WL 20803 (Tenn. Crim. App. 1990)

Caveat: This is an unpublished case and should be used only in compliance with Rule 19 of the Rules of the Court of Criminal Appeals. The court determined that the husband's pre-petition failure to pay alimony resulted in a civil, rather than criminal, contempt and directed that any future appeals should be addressed to the Court of Appeals. The court did observe that the Chapter 13 bankruptcy filing appeared to be part of a pattern of bad faith shown by husband's failure to pay alimony and his leaving a better paying job.

Hall v. Hall, 772 S.W.2d 432 (Tenn. Ct. App. 1989)

The court vacated that portion of the final order which required the husband to hold the wife harmless from any indebtedness which was not covered by discharge through her Chapter 7 bankruptcy. Although the husband had dissipated the wife's assets so that she was forced to file for bankruptcy, there was no evidence of indebtedness or any particular debt which justified this requirement.

Washington

In re Marriage of Myers, 54 Wash. App. 233, 773 P.2d 118 (1989)

After the husband discharged in bankruptcy debts he was obligated to pay under the divorce decree and his creditors attempted to obtain payment from the wife, the court increased the wife's maintenance for the remainder of the period she was to receive maintenance. The court rejected that husband's argument that it should not consider evidence of his bankruptcy discharge because it created a material change in circumstances for the wife. Any questions of dischargeability must be addressed to the bankruptcy court.

West Virginia

Nichols v. Nichols, 391 S.E.2d 623 (W. Va. 1990)

Although 11 U.S.C. § 553 has been interpreted to allow setoff of mutual debts which arose before bankruptcy, it does not permit setoff of the husband's post-petition alimony debt to the wife against pre-petition debt owed him by the wife in connection with a note, when the wife is the bankruptcy debtor. The bankruptcy court granted the husband relief from stay to set off the wife's debt to him against the pre-petition unpaid alimony obligation. The husband could not assert the wife's debt to him, which had been discharged, as a setoff against his post-petition alimony obligation. In so doing, the bankruptcy court had explicitly stated that its order did not alter or affect the ongoing alimony obligation to pay alimony post-petition.

APPENDIX B

SELECTED SECTIONS OF THE BANKRUPTCY CODE, TITLE 11 UNITED STATES CODE

This appendix contains only some of the sections of the Bankruptcy Code related to the issues discussed in the text. The applicability of other sections of the Code and the Federal Rules of Bankruptcy Procedure must be considered before taking action in a bankruptcy matter. In addition, local bankruptcy rules must also be consulted.

§ 101. Definitions

In this title—

* * *

(4) "attorney" means attorney, professional law association, corporation, or partnership, authorized under applicable law to practice law;

(5) "claim" means—

(A) right to payment, whether or not such right is reduced to judgment, liquidated, unliquidated, fixed, contingent, matured, unmatured, disputed, undisputed, legal, equitable, secured, or unsecured; or

(B) right to an equitable remedy for breach of performance if such breach gives rise to a right to payment, whether or not such right to an equitable remedy is reduced to judgment, fixed, contingent, matured, unmatured, disputed, undisputed, secured, or unsecured;

* * *

(8) "consumer debt" means debt incurred by an individual primarily for a personal, family, or household purpose;

* * *

(10) "creditor" means—

(A) entity that has a claim against the debtor that arose at the time of or before the order for relief concerning the debtor;

(B) entity that has a claim against the estate of a kind specified in section 348(d), 502(f), 502(g), 502(h) or 502(i) of this title; or

(C) entity that has a community claim;

* * *

(12) "debt" means liability on a claim;

(13) "debtor" means person or municipality concerning which a case under this title has been commenced;

* * *

(31) "insider" includes—

(A) if the debtor is an individual—

(i) relative of the debtor or of a general partner of the debtor;

(ii) partnership in which the debtor is a general partner;

(iii) general partner of the debtor; or

(iv) corporation of which the debtor is a director, officer, or person in control;

(B) if the debtor is a corporation—

(i) director of the debtor;

(ii) officer of the debtor;

(iii) person in control of the debtor;

(iv) partnership in which the debtor is a general partner;

(v) general partner of the debtor; or

(vi) relative of a general partner, director, officer, or person in control of the debtor;

(C) if the debtor is a partnership—

(i) general partner in the debtor;

(ii) relative of a general partner in, general partner of, or person in control of the debtor;

(iii) partnership in which the debtor is a general partner;

(iv) general partner of the debtor; or

(v) person in control of the debtor;

(D) if the debtor is a municipality, elected official of the debtor or relative of an elected official of the debtor;

(E) affiliate, or insider of an affiliate as if such affiliate were the debtor; and

(F) managing agent of the debtor;

(32) "insolvent" means—

(A) with reference to an entity other than a partnership and a municipality, financial condition such that the sum of such entity's debts is greater than all of such entity's property, at a fair valuation, exclusive of—

(i) property transferred, concealed, or removed with intent to hinder, delay, or defraud such entity's creditors; and

(ii) property that may be exempted from property of the estate under section 522 of this title;

* * *

(36) "judicial lien" means lien obtained by judgment, levy, sequestration, or other legal or equitable process or proceeding;

(37) "lien" means charge against or interest in property to secure payment of a debt or performance of an obligation;

* * *

(41) "person" includes individual, partnership, and corporation, but does not include governmental unit, *Provided, however,* That any governmental unit that acquires an asset from a person as a result of operation of a loan guarantee agreement, or as receiver or liquidating agent of a person, will be considered a person for purposes of section 1102 of this title.

(42) "petition" means petition filed under section 301, 302, 303, or 304 of this title, as the case may be, commencing a case under this title;

(43) "purchaser" means transferee of a voluntary transfer, and includes immediate or mediate transferee of such a transferee;

* * *

(45) "relative" means individual related by affinity or consanguinity within the third degree as determined by the common law, or individual in a step or adoptive relationship within such third degree;

* * *

(50) "security agreement" means agreement that creates or provides for a security interest;

(51) "security interest" means lien created by an agreement;

* * *

(53) "statutory lien" means lien arising solely by force of a statute on specified circumstances or conditions, or lien of distress for rent, whether or not statutory, but does not include security interest or judicial lien, whether or not such interest or lien is provided by or is dependent on a statute and whether or not such interest or lien is made fully effective by statute;

(54) "transfer" means every mode, direct or indirect, absolute or conditional, voluntary or involuntary, of disposing of or parting with property or with an interest in property, including retention of title as a security interest and foreclosure of the debtor's equity of redemption;

* * *

§ 102. Rules of construction

In this title—

(1) "after notice and a hearing", or a similar phrase—

(A) means after such notice as is appropriate in the particular circumstances, and such opportunity for a hearing as is appropriate in the particular circumstances; but

(B) authorizes an act without an actual hearing if such notice is given properly and if—

(i) such a hearing is not requested timely by a party in interest; or

(ii) there is insufficient time for a hearing to be commenced before such act must be done, and the court authorizes such act;

(2) "claim against the debtor" includes claim against property of the debtor;

(3) "includes" and "including" are not limiting;

(4) "may not" is prohibitive, and not permissive;

(5) "or" is not exclusive;

(6) "order for relief" means entry of an order for relief;

(7) the singular includes the plural;

(8) a definition, contained in a section of this title that refers to another section of this title, does not, for the purpose of such reference, affect the meaning of a term used in such other section; and

(9) United States trustee includes a designee of the United States trustee.

* * *

§ 105. Power of court

(a) The court may issue any order, process, or judgment that is necessary or appropriate to carry out the provisions of this title. No provision of this title providing for the raising of an issue by a party in interest shall be construed to preclude the court from, sua sponte, taking any action or making any determination necessary or appropriate to enforce or implement court orders or rules, or to prevent an abuse of process.

(b) Notwithstanding subsection (a) of this section, a court may not appoint a receiver in a case under this title.

(c) The ability of any district judge or other officer or employee of a district court to exercise any of the authority or responsibilities conferred upon the court under this title shall be determined by reference to the provisions relating to such judge, officer, or employee set forth in title 28. This subsection shall not be interpreted to exclude bankruptcy judges and other officers or employees appointed pursuant to chapter 6 of title 28 from its operation.

* * *

§ 301. Voluntary cases

A voluntary case under a chapter of this title is commenced by the filing with the bankruptcy court of a petition under such chapter by an entity that may be a debtor under such chapter. The commencement of a voluntary case under a chapter of this title constitutes an order for relief under such chapter.

* * *

§ 302. Joint cases

(a) A joint case under a chapter of this title is commenced by the filing with the bankruptcy court of a single petition under such chapter by an individual that may be a debtor under such chapter and such individual's spouse. The commencement of a joint case under a chapter of this title constitutes an order for relief under such chapter.

(b) After the commencement of a joint case, the court shall determine the extent, if any, to which the debtors' estates shall be consolidated.

* * *

§ 303. Involuntary cases

(a) An involuntary case may be commenced only under chapter 7 or 11 of this title, and only against a person, except a farmer, family farmer, or a corporation that is not a moneyed, business, or commercial corporation, that may be a debtor under the chapter under which such case is commenced.

(b) An involuntary case against a person is commenced by the filing with the bankruptcy court of a petition under chapter 7 or 11 of this title—

(1) by three or more entities, each of which is either a holder of a claim against such person that is not contingent as to liability or the subject of a bona fide dispute, or an indenture trustee representing such a holder, if such claims aggregate at least $5,000 more than the value of any lien on property of the debtor securing such claims held by the holders of such claims;

(2) if there are fewer than 12 such holders, excluding any employee or insider of such person and any transferee of a transfer that is voidable under section 544, 545, 547, 548, 549, or 724(a) of this title, by one or more of such holders that hold in the aggregate at least $5,000 of such claims;

(3) if such person is a partnership—

(A) by fewer than all of the general partners in such partnership; or

(B) if relief has been ordered under this title with respect to all of the general partners in such partnership, by a general partner in such partnership, the trustee of such a general partner, or a holder of a claim against such partnership; or

(4)   by a foreign representative of the estate in a foreign proceeding concerning such person.

(c) After the filing of a petition under this section but before the case is dismissed or relief is ordered, a creditor holding an unsecured claim that is not contingent, other than a creditor filing under subsection (b) of this section, may join in the petition with the same effect as if such joining creditor were a petitioning creditor under subsection (b) of this section.

(d) The debtor, or a general partner in a partnership debtor that did not join in the petition, may file an answer to a petition under this section.

(e) After notice and a hearing, and for cause, the court may require the petitioners under this section to file a bond to indemnify the debtor for such amounts as the court may later allow under subsection (i) of this section.

(f) Notwithstanding section 363 of this title, except to the extent that the court orders otherwise, and until an order for relief in the case, any business of the debtor may continue to operate, and the debtor may continue to use, acquire, or dispose of property as if an involuntary case concerning the debtor had not been commenced.

(g) At any time after the commencement of an involuntary case under chapter 7 of this title but before an order for relief in the case, the court, on request of a party in interest, after notice to the debtor and a hearing, and if necessary to preserve the property of the estate or to prevent loss to the estate, may order the United States trustee to appoint an interim trustee under section 701 of this title to take possession of the property of the estate and to operate any business of the debtor. Before an order for relief, the debtor may regain possession of property in the possession of a trustee ordered appointed under this subsection if the debtor files such bond as the court requires, conditioned on the debtor's accounting for and delivering to the trustee, if there is an order for relief in the case, such property, or the value, as of the date the debtor regains possession, of such property.

(h) If the petition is not timely controverted, the court shall order relief against the debtor in an involuntary case under the chapter under which the petition was filed. Otherwise, after trial, the court shall order relief against the debtor in an involuntary case under the chapter under which the petition was filed, only if—

(1)　the debtor is generally not paying such debtor's debts as such debts become due unless such debts are the subject of a bona fide dispute; or

(2)　within 120 days before the date of the filing of the petition, a custodian, other than a trustee, receiver, or agent appointed or authorized to take charge of less than substantially all of the property of the debtor for the purpose of enforcing a lien against such property, was appointed or took possession.

(i)　If the court dismisses a petition under this section other than on consent of all petitioners and the debtor, and if the debtor does not waive the right to judgment under this subsection, the court may grant judgment—

(1)　against the petitioners and in favor of the debtor for—

(A)　costs; or

(B)　a reasonable attorney's fee, or

(2)　against any petitioner that filed the petition in bad faith, for—

(A)　any damages proximately caused by such filing; or

(B)　punitive damages.

(j)　Only after notice to all creditors and a hearing may the court dismiss a petition filed under this section—

(1)　on the motion of a petitioner;

(2)　on consent of all petitioners and the debtor; or

(3)　for want of prosecution.

(k)　Notwithstanding subsection (a) of this section, an involuntary case may be commenced against a foreign bank that is not engaged in such business in the United States only under chapter 7 of this title and only if a foreign proceeding concerning such bank is pending.

* * *

§ 362.　Automatic stay

(a)　Except as provided in subsection (b) of this section, a petition filed under section 301, 302, or 303 of this title, or an application filed under section 5(a)(3) of the Securities Investor Protection Act of 1970 (15 U.S.C. 78eee(a)(3)), operates as a stay, applicable to all entities, of—

(1)　the commencement or continuation, including the issuance or employment of process, of a judicial, administrative, or other action or proceeding against the debtor that was or could have been commenced before the commencement of the case under this title, or to recover a claim against the debtor that arose before the commencement of the case under this title;

(2) the enforcement, against the debtor or against property of the estate, of a judgment obtained before the commencement of the case under this title;

(3) any act to obtain possession of property of the estate or of property from the estate or to exercise control over property of the estate;

(4) any act to create, perfect, or enforce any lien against property of the estate;

(5) any act to create, perfect, or enforce against property of the debtor any lien to the extent that such lien secures a claim that arose before the commencement of the case under this title;

(6) any act to collect, assess, or recover a claim against the debtor that arose before the commencement of the case under this title;

(7) the setoff of any debt owing to the debtor that arose before the commencement of the case under this title against any claim against the debtor; and

(8) the commencement or continuation of a proceeding before the United States Tax Court concerning the debtor.

(b) The filing of a petition under section 301, 302, or 303 of this title, or of an application under section 5(a)(3) of the Securities Investor Protection Act of 1970 (15 U.S.C. 78eee(a)(3)), does not operate as a stay—

(1) under subsection (a) of this section, of the commencement or continuation of a criminal action or proceeding against the debtor;

(2) under subsection (a) of this section, of the collection of alimony, maintenance, or support from property that is not property of the estate;

(3) under subsection (a) of this section, of any act to perfect an interest in property to the extent that the trustee's rights and powers are subject to such perfection under section 546(b) of this title or to the extent that such act is accomplished within the period provided under section 547(e)(2)(A) of this title;

(4) under subsection (a)(1) of this section, of the commencement or continuation of an action or proceeding by a governmental unit to enforce such governmental unit's police or regulatory power;

(5) under subsection (a)(2) of this section, of the enforcement of a judgment, other than a money judgment, obtained in an action or proceeding by a governmental unit to enforce such governmental unit's police or regulatory power;

(6)   under subsection (a) of this section, of the setoff by a commodity broker, forward contract merchant, stockbroker, financial institutions, or securities clearing agency of any mutual debt and claim under or in connection with commodity contracts, as defined in section 761(4) of this title, forward contracts, or securities contracts, as defined in section 741(7) of this title, that constitutes the setoff of a claim against the debtor for a margin payment, as defined in section 101(34), 741(5), or 761(15) of this title, or settlement payment, as defined in section 101(35) or 741(8) of this title, arising out of commodity contracts, forward contracts, or securities contracts against cash, securities, or other property held by or due from such commodity broker, forward contract merchant, stockbroker, financial institutions, or securities clearing agency to margin, guarantee, secure, or settle commodity contracts, forward contracts, or securities contracts;

(7)   under subsection (a) of this section, of the setoff by a repo participant, of any mutual debt and claim under or in connection with repurchase agreements that constitutes the setoff of a claim against the debtor for a margin payment, as defined in section 741(5) or 761(15) of this title, or settlement payment, as defined in section 741(8) of this title, arising out of repurchase agreements against cash, securities, or other property held by or due from such repo participant to margin, guarantee, secure or settle repurchase agreements;

(8)   under subsection (a) of this section, of the commencement of any action by the Secretary of Housing and Urban Development to foreclose a mortgage or deed of trust in any case in which the mortgage or deed of trust held by the Secretary is insured or was formerly insured under the National Housing Act and covers property, or combinations of property, consisting of five or more living units;

(9)   under subsection (a) of this section, of the issuance to the debtor by a governmental unit of a notice of tax deficiency;

(10) under subsection (a) of this section, of any act by a lessor to the debtor under a lease of nonresidential real property that has terminated by the expiration of the stated term of the lease before the commencement of or during a case under this title to obtain possession of such property; or

(11) under subsection (a) of this section, of the presentment of a negotiable instrument and the giving of notice of and protesting dishonor of such an instrument;

(12) under subsection (a) of this section, after the date which is 90 days after the filing of such petition, of the commencement or continuation, and conclusion to the entry of final judgment, of an action

which involves a debtor subject to reorganization pursuant to chapter 11 of this title and which was brought by the Secretary of Transportation under the Ship Mortgage Act, 1920 (46 App. U.S.C. 911 et seq.) (including distribution of any proceeds of sale) to foreclose a preferred ship or fleet mortgage, or a security interest in or relating to a vessel or vessel under construction, held by the Secretary of Transportation under section 207 or title XI of the Merchant Marine Act, 1936 (46 App. U.S.C. 1117 and 1271 et seq., respectively), or under applicable State law;

(13) under subsection (a) of this section, after the date which is 90 days after the filing of such petition, of the commencement or continuation, and conclusion to the entry of final judgment, of an action which involves a debtor subject to reorganization pursuant to chapter 11 of this title and which was brought by the Secretary of Commerce under the Ship Mortgage Act, 1920 (46 App. U.S.C. 911 et seq.) (including distribution of any proceeds of sale) to foreclose a preferred ship or fleet mortgage in a vessel or a mortgage, deed of trust, or other security interest in a fishing facility held by the Secretary of Commerce under section 207 or title XI of the Merchant Marine Act, 1936 (46 App. U.S.C. 1117 and 1271 et seq., respectively);

(14) under subsection (a) of this section, of the setoff by a swap participant, of any mutual debt and claim under or in connection with any swap agreement that constitutes the setoff of a claim against the debtor for any payment due from the debtor under or in connection with any swap agreement against any payment due to the debtor from the swap participant under or in connection with any swap agreement or against cash, securities, or other property of the debtor held by or due from such swap participant to guarantee, secure or settle any swap agreement.

(14) under subsection (a) of this section, of any action by an accrediting agency regarding the accreditation status of the debtor as an educational institution;

(15) under subsection (a) of this section, of any action by a State licensing body regarding the licensure of the debtor as an educational institution; or

(16) under subsection (a) of this section, of any action by a guaranty agency, as defined in section 435(j) of the Higher Education Act of 1965 (20 U.S.C. 1001 et seq.) or the Secretary of Education regarding the eligibility of the debtor to participate in programs authorized under such Act.

The provisions of paragraphs (12) and (13) of this subsection shall apply with respect to any such petition filed on or before December 31, 1989.

(c) Except as provided in subsections (d), (e), and (f) of this section—

(1) the stay of an act against property of the estate under subsection (a) of this section continues until such property is no longer property of the estate; and

(2) the stay of any other act under subsection (a) of this section continues until the earliest of—

(A) the time the case is closed;

(B) the time the case is dismissed; or

(C) if the case is a case under chapter 7 of this title concerning an individual or a case under chapter 9, 11, 12, or 13 of this title, the time a discharge is granted or denied.

(d) On request of a party in interest and after notice and a hearing, the court shall grant relief from the stay provided under subsection (a) of this section, such as by terminating, annulling, modifying, or conditioning such stay—

(1) for cause, including the lack of adequate protection of an interest in property of such party in interest; or

(2) with respect to a stay of an act against property under subsection (a) of this section, if—

(A) the debtor does not have an equity in such property; and

(B) such property is not necessary to an effective reorganization.

(e) Thirty days after a request under subsection (d) of this section for relief from the stay of any act against property of the estate under subsection (a) of this section, such stay is terminated with respect to the party in interest making such request, unless the court, after notice and a hearing, orders such stay continued in effect pending the conclusion of, or as a result of, a final hearing and determination under subsection (d) of this section. A hearing under this subsection may be a preliminary hearing, or may be consolidated with the final hearing under subsection (d) of this section. The court shall order such stay continued in effect pending the conclusion of the final hearing under subsection (d) of this section if there is a reasonable likelihood that the party opposing relief from such stay will prevail at the conclusion of such final hearing. If the hearing under this subsection is a preliminary hearing, then such final hearing shall be commenced not later than thirty days after the conclusion of such preliminary hearing.

(f) Upon request of a party in interest, the court, with or without a hearing, shall grant such relief from the stay provided under subsection (a) of this section as is necessary to prevent irreparable damage to the interest of an entity in property, if such interest will suffer such damage before there is an opportunity for notice and a hearing under subsection (d) or (e) of this section.

(g) In any hearing under subsection (d) or (e) of this section concerning relief from the stay of any act under subsection (a) of this section—

(1) the party requesting such relief has the burden of proof on the issue of the debtor's equity in property; and

(2) the party opposing such relief has the burden of proof on all other issues.

(h) An individual injured by any willful violation of a stay provided by this section shall recover actual damages, including costs and attorneys' fees, and, in appropriate circumstances, may recover punitive damages.

* * *

§ 503. Allowance of administrative expenses

(a) An entity may file a request for payment of an administrative expense.

(b) After notice and a hearing, there shall be allowed administrative expenses, other than claims allowed under section 502(f) of this title, including—

(1)(A) the actual, necessary costs and expenses of preserving the estate, including wages, salaries, or commissions for services rendered after the commencement of the case;

(B) any tax—

(i) incurred by the estate, except a tax of a kind specified in section 507(a)(7) of this title; or

(ii) attributable to an excessive allowance of a tentative carryback adjustment that the estate received, whether the taxable year to which such adjustment relates ended before or after the commencement of the case; and

(C) any fine, penalty, or reduction in credit relating to a tax of a kind specified in subparagraph (B) of this paragraph;

(2) compensation and reimbursement awarded under section 330(a) of this title;

(3) the actual, necessary expenses, other than compensation and reimbursement specified in paragraph (4) of this subsection, incurred by—

(A) a creditor that files a petition under section 303 of this title;

(B) a creditor that recovers, after the court's approval, for the benefit of the estate any property transferred or concealed by the debtor;

(C) a creditor in connection with the prosecution of a criminal offense relating to the case or to the business or property of the debtor;

(D) a creditor, an indenture trustee, an equity security holder, or a committee representing creditors or equity security holders other than a committee appointed under section 1102 of this title, in making a substantial contribution in a case under chapter 9 or 11 of this title; or

(E) a custodian superseded under section 543 of this title, and compensation for the services of such custodian;

(4) reasonable compensation for professional services rendered by an attorney or an accountant of an entity whose expense is allowable under paragraph (3) of this subsection, based on the time, the nature, the extent, and the value of such services, and the cost of comparable services other than in a case under this title, and reimbursement for actual, necessary expenses incurred by such attorney or accountant;

(5) reasonable compensation for services rendered by an indenture trustee in making a substantial contribution in a case under chapter 9 or 11 of this title, based on the time, the nature, the extent, and the value of such services, and the cost of comparable services other than in a case under this title; and

(6) the fees and mileage payable under chapter 119 of title 28.

* * *

§ 507. Priorities

(a) The following expenses and claims have priority in the following order:

(1) First, administrative expenses allowed under section 503(b) of this title, and any fees and charges assessed against the estate under chapter 123 of title 28.

(2) Second, unsecured claims allowed under section 502(f) of this title.

(3) Third, allowed unsecured claims for wages, salaries, or commissions, including vacation, severance, and sick leave pay—

(A) earned by an individual within 90 days before the date of the filing of the petition or the date of the cessation of the debtor's business, whichever occurs first; but only

(B) to the extent of $2,000 for each such individual.

(4)   Fourth, allowed unsecured claims for contributions to an employee benefit plan—

(A) arising from services rendered within 180 days before the date of the filing of the petition or the date of the cessation of the debtor's business, whichever occurs first; but only

(B) for each such plan, to the extent of—

(i)   the number of employees covered by each such plan multiplied by $2,000; less

(ii) the aggregate amount paid to such employees under paragraph (3) of this subsection, plus the aggregate amount paid by the estate on behalf of such employees to any other employee benefit plan.

(5)   Fifth, allowed unsecured claims of persons—

(A) engaged in the production or raising of grain, as defined in section 557(b)(1) of this title, against a debtor who owns or operates a grain storage facility, as defined in section 557(b)(2) of this title, for grain or the proceeds of grain, or

(B) engaged as a United States fisherman against a debtor who has acquired fish or fish produce from a fisherman through a sale or conversion, and who is engaged in operating a fish produce storage or processing facility—

but only to the extent of $2,000 for each such individual.

(6)   Sixth, allowed unsecured claims of individuals, to the extent of $900 for each such individual, arising from the deposit, before the commencement of the case, of money in connection with the purchase, lease, or rental of property, or the purchase of services, for the personal, family, or household use of such individuals, that were not delivered or provided.

(7)   Seventh, allowed unsecured claims of governmental units; only to the extent that such claims are for—

(A) a tax on or measured by income or gross receipts—

(i)   for a taxable year ending on or before the date of the filing of the petition for which a return, if required, is last due, including extensions, after three years before the date of the filing of the petition;

(ii) assessed within 240 days, plus any time plus 30 days during which an offer in compromise with respect to such tax that was made within 240 days after such assessment was pending, before the date of the filing of the petition; or

(iii) other than a tax of a kind specified in section 523(a)(1)(B) or 523(a)(1)(C) of this title, not assessed before, but assessable, under applicable law or by agreement, after, the commencement of the case;

(B) a property tax assessed before the commencement of the case and last payable without penalty after one year before the date of the filing of the petition;

(C) a tax required to be collected or withheld and for which the debtor is liable in whatever capacity;

(D) an employment tax on a wage, salary, or commission of a kind specified in paragraph (3) of this subsection earned from the debtor before the date of the filing of the petition, whether or not actually paid before such date, for which a return is last due, under applicable law or under any extension, after three years before the date of the filing of the petition;

(E) an excise tax on—

(i) a transaction occurring before the date of the filing of the petition for which a return, if required, is last due, under applicable law or under any extension, after three years before the date of the filing of the petition; or

(ii) if a return is not required, a transaction occurring during the three years immediately preceding the date of the filing of the petition;

(F) a customs duty arising out of the importation of merchandise—

(i) entered for consumption within one year before the date of the filing of the petition;

(ii) covered by an entry liquidated or reliquidated within one year before the date of the filing of the petition; or

(iii) entered for consumption within four years before the date of the filing of the petition but unliquidated on such date, if the Secretary of the Treasury certifies that failure to liquidate such entry was due to an investigation pending on such date into assessment of antidumping or countervailing duties or fraud, or if information needed for the proper appraisement or classification of such merchandise was not available to the appropriate customs officer before such date; or

(G) a penalty related to a claim of a kind specified in this paragraph and in compensation for actual pecuniary loss.

(8) Eighth, allowed unsecured claims based upon any commitment by the debtor to the Federal Deposit Insurance Corporation, the Resolution Trust Corporation, the Director of the Office of Thrift Supervision, the Comptroller of the Currency, or the Board of Governors

of the Federal Reserve System, or their predecessors or successors, to maintain the capital of an insured depository institution.

(b) If the trustee, under section 362, 363, or 364 of this title, provides adequate protection of the interest of a holder of a claim secured by a lien on property of the debtor and if, notwithstanding such protection, such creditor has a claim allowable under subsection (a)(1) of this section arising from the stay of action against such property under section 362 of this title, from the use, sale, or lease of such property under section 363 of this title, or from the granting of a lien under section 364(d) of this title, then such creditor's claim under such subsection shall have priority over every other claim allowable under such subsection.

(c) For the purpose of subsection (a) of this section, a claim of a governmental unit arising from an erroneous refund or credit of a tax has the same priority as a claim for the tax to which such refund or credit relates.

(d) An entity that is subrogated to the rights of a holder of a claim of a kind specified in subsection (a)(3), (a)(4), (a)(5), or (a)(6) of this section is not subrogated to the right of the holder of such claim to priority under such subsection.

* * *

§ 521. Debtor's duties

The debtor shall—

(1) file a list of creditors, and unless the court orders otherwise, a schedule of assets and liabilities, a schedule of current income and current expenditures, and a statement of the debtor's financial affairs;

(2) if an individual debtor's schedule of assets and liabilities includes consumer debts which are secured by property of the estate—

(A) within thirty days after the date of the filing of a petition under chapter 7 of this title or on or before the date of the meeting of creditors, whichever is earlier, or within such additional time as the court, for cause, within such period fixes, the debtor shall file with the clerk a statement of his intention with respect to the retention or surrender of such property and, if applicable, specifying that such property is claimed as exempt, that the debtor intends to redeem such property, or that the debtor intends to reaffirm debts secured by such property;

(B) within forty-five days after the filing of a notice of intent under this section, or within such additional time as the court, for cause, within such forty-five day period fixes, the debtor shall perform his intention with respect to such property, as specified by subparagraph (A) of this paragraph; and

(C) nothing in subparagraphs (A) and (B) of this paragraph shall alter the debtor's or the trustee's rights with regard to such property under this title;

(3) if a trustee is serving in the case, cooperate with the trustee as necessary to enable the trustee to perform the trustee's duties under this title;

(4) if a trustee is serving in the case, surrender to the trustee all property of the estate and any recorded information, including books, documents, records, and papers, relating to property of the estate, whether or not immunity is granted under section 344 of this title; and

(5) appear at the hearing required under section 524(d) of this title.

Historical and Revision Notes

* * *

§ 522. Exemptions

(a) In this section—

(1) "dependent" includes spouse, whether or not actually dependent; and

(2) "value" means fair market value as of the date of the filing of the petition or, with respect to property that becomes property of the estate after such date, as of the date such property becomes property of the estate.

(b) Notwithstanding section 541 of this title, an individual debtor may exempt from property of the estate the property listed in either paragraph (1) or, in the alternative, paragraph (2) of this subsection. In joint cases filed under section 302 of this title and individual cases filed under section 301 or 303 of this title by or against debtors who are husband and wife, and whose estates are ordered to be jointly administered under Rule 1015(b) of the Bankruptcy Rules, one debtor may not elect to exempt property listed in paragraph (1) and the other debtor elect to exempt property listed in paragraph (2) of this subsection. If the parties cannot agree on the alternative to be elected, they shall be deemed to elect paragraph (1), where such election is permitted under the law of the jurisdiction where the case is filed. Such property is—

(1) property that is specified under subsection (d) of this section, unless the State law that is applicable to the debtor under paragraph (2)(A) of this subsection specifically does not so authorize; or, in the alternative,

(2)(A) any property that is exempt under Federal law, other than subsection (d) of this section, or State or local law that is applicable on the date of the filing of the petition at the place in which the debtor's domicile has been located for the 180 days immediately preceding the date of the filing of the petition, or for a longer portion of such 180-day period than in any other place; and

(B) any interest in property in which the debtor had, immediately before the commencement of the case, an interest as a tenant by the entirety or joint tenant to the extent that such interest as a tenant by the entirety or joint tenant is exempt from process under applicable non-bankruptcy law.

(c) Unless the case is dismissed, property exempted under this section is not liable during or after the case for any debt of the debtor that arose, or that is determined under section 502 of this title as if such debt had arisen, before the commencement of the case, except—

(1) a debt of a kind specified in section 523(a)(1) or 523(a)(5) of this title;

(2) a debt secured by a lien that is—

(A)(i) not avoided under subsection (f) or (g) of this section or under section 544, 545, 547, 548, 549, or 724(a) of this title; and

(ii) not void under section 506(d) of this title; or

(B) a tax lien, notice of which is properly filed; or

(3) a debt of a kind specified in section 523(a)(4) or 523(a)(6) of this title owed by an institution-affiliated party of an insured depository institution to a Federal depository institutions regulatory agency acting in its capacity as conservator, receiver, or liquidating agent for such institution.

(d) The following property may be exempted under subsection (b)(1) of this section:

(1) The debtor's aggregate interest, not to exceed $7,500 in value, in real property or personal property that the debtor or a dependent of the debtor uses as a residence, in a cooperative that owns property that the debtor or a dependent of the debtor uses as a residence, or in a burial plot for the debtor or a dependent of the debtor.

(2) The debtor's interest, not to exceed $1,200 in value, in one motor vehicle.

(3) The debtor's interest, not to exceed $200 in value in any particular item or $4,000 in aggregate value, in household furnishings, household goods, wearing apparel, appliances, books, animals, crops,

or musical instruments, that are held primarily for the personal, family, or household use of the debtor or a dependent of the debtor.

(4)   The debtor's aggregate interest, not to exceed $500 in value, in jewelry held primarily for the personal, family, or household use of the debtor or a dependent of the debtor.

(5)   The debtor's aggregate interest in any property, not to exceed in value $400 plus up to $3,750 of any unused amount of the exemption provided under paragraph (1) of this subsection.

(6)   The debtor's aggregate interest, not to exceed $750 in value, in any implements, professional books, or tools, of the trade of the debtor or the trade of a dependent of the debtor.

(7)   Any unmatured life insurance contract owned by the debtor, other than a credit life insurance contract.

(8)   The debtor's aggregate interest, not to exceed in value $4,000 less any amount of property of the estate transferred in the manner specified in section 542(d) of this title, in any accrued dividend or interest under, or loan value of, any unmatured life insurance contract owned by the debtor under which the insured is the debtor or an individual of whom the debtor is a dependent.

(9)   Professionally prescribed health aids for the debtor or a dependent of the debtor.

(10)   The debtor's right to receive—

(A)   a social security benefit, unemployment compensation, or a local public assistance benefit;

(B)   a veterans' benefit;

(C)   a disability, illness, or unemployment benefit;

(D)   alimony, support, or separate maintenance, to the extent reasonably necessary for the support of the debtor and any dependent of the debtor;

(E)   a payment under a stock bonus, pension, profitsharing, annuity, or similar plan or contract on account of illness, disability, death, age, or length of service, to the extent reasonably necessary for the support of the debtor and any dependent of the debtor, unless—

(i)   such plan or contract was established by or under the auspices of an insider that employed the debtor at the time the debtor's rights under such plan or contract arose;

(ii)   such payment is on account of age or length of service; and

(iii) such plan or contract does not qualify under section 401(a), 403(a), 403(b), 408, or 409 of the Internal Revenue Code of 1954 (26 U.S.C. 401(a), 403(a), 403(b), 408, or 409).

(11) The debtor's right to receive, or property that is traceable to—

(A) an award under a crime victim's reparation law;

(B) a payment on account of the wrongful death of an individual of whom the debtor was a dependent, to the extent reasonably necessary for the support of the debtor and any dependent of the debtor;

(C) a payment under a life insurance contract that insured the life of an individual of whom the debtor was a dependent on the date of such individual's death, to the extent reasonably necessary for the support of the debtor and any dependent of the debtor;

(D) a payment, not to exceed $7,500, on account of personal bodily injury, not including pain and suffering or compensation for actual pecuniary loss, of the debtor or an individual of whom the debtor is a dependent; or

(E) a payment in compensation of loss of future earnings of the debtor or an individual of whom the debtor is or was a dependent, to the extent reasonably necessary for the support of the debtor and any dependent of the debtor.

(e) A waiver of an exemption executed in favor of a creditor that holds an unsecured claim against the debtor is unenforceable in a case under this title with respect to such claim against property that the debtor may exempt under subsection (b) of this section. A waiver by the debtor of a power under subsection (f) or (h) of this section to avoid a transfer, under subsection (g) or (i) of this section to exempt property, or under subsection (i) of this section to recover property or to preserve a transfer, is unenforceable in a case under this title.

(f) Notwithstanding any waiver of exemptions, the debtor may avoid the fixing of a lien on an interest of the debtor in property to the extent that such lien impairs an exemption to which the debtor would have been entitled under subsection (b) of this section, if such lien is—

(1) a judicial lien; or

(2) a nonpossessory, nonpurchase-money security interest in any—

(A) household furnishings, household goods, wearing apparel, appliances, books, animals, crops, musical instruments, or jewelry that are held primarily for the personal, family, or household use of the debtor or a dependent of the debtor;

(B) implements, professional books, or tools, of the trade of the debtor or the trade of a dependent of the debtor; or

(C) professionally prescribed health aids for the debtor or a dependent of the debtor.

(g) Notwithstanding sections 550 and 551 of this title, the debtor may exempt under subsection (b) of this section property that the trustee recovers under section 510(c)(2), 542, 543, 550, 551, or 553 of this title, to the extent that the debtor could have exempted such property under subsection (b) of this section if such property had not been transferred, if—

(1)(A) such transfer was not a voluntary transfer of such property by the debtor; and

(B) the debtor did not conceal such property; or

(2) the debtor could have avoided such transfer under subsection (f)(2) of this section.

(h) The debtor may avoid a transfer of property of the debtor or recover a setoff to the extent that the debtor could have exempted such property under subsection (g)(1) of this section if the trustee had avoided such transfer, if—

(1) such transfer is avoidable by the trustee under section 544, 545, 547, 548, 549, or 724(a) of this title or recoverable by the trustee under section 553 of this title; and

(2) the trustee does not attempt to avoid such transfer.

(i)(1) If the debtor avoids a transfer or recovers a setoff under subsection (f) or (h) of this section, the debtor may recover in the manner prescribed by, and subject to the limitations of, section 550 of this title, the same as if the trustee had avoided such transfer, and may exempt any property so recovered under subsection (b) of this section.

(2) Notwithstanding section 551 of this title, a transfer avoided under section 544, 545, 547, 548, 549, or 724(a) of this title, under subsection (f) or (h) of this section, or property recovered under section 553 of this title, may be preserved for the benefit of the debtor to the extent that the debtor may exempt such property under subsection (g) of this section or paragraph (1) of this subsection.

(j) Notwithstanding subsections (g) and (i) of this section, the debtor may exempt a particular kind of property under subsections (g) and (i) of this section only to the extent that the debtor has exempted less property in value of such kind than that to which the debtor is entitled under subsection (b) of this section.

(k) Property that the debtor exempts under this section is not liable for payment of any administrative expense except—

(1) the aliquot share of the costs and expenses of avoiding a transfer of property that the debtor exempts under subsection (g) of this

section, or of recovery of such property, that is attributable to the value of the portion of such property exempted in relation to the value of the property recovered; and

(2) any costs and expenses of avoiding a transfer under subsection (f) or (h) of this section, or of recovery of property under subsection (i)(1) of this section, that the debtor has not paid.

(l) The debtor shall file a list of property that the debtor claims as exempt under subsection (b) of this section. If the debtor does not file such a list, a dependent of the debtor may file such a list, or may claim property as exempt from property of the estate on behalf of the debtor. Unless a party in interest objects, the property claimed as exempt on such list is exempt.

(m) Subject to the limitation in subsection (b), this section shall apply separately with respect to each debtor in a joint case.

* * *

§ 523. Exceptions to discharge

(a) A discharge under section 727, 1141, 1228(a), 1228(b), or 1328(b) of this title does not discharge an individual debtor from any debt—

(1) for a tax or a customs duty—

(A) of the kind and for the periods specified in section 507(a)(2) or 507(a)(7) of this title, whether or not a claim for such tax was filed or allowed;

(B) with respect to which a return, if required—

(i) was not filed; or

(ii) was filed after the date on which such return was last due, under applicable law or under any extension, and after two years before the date of the filing of the petition; or

(C) with respect to which the debtor made a fraudulent return or willfully attempted in any manner to evade or defeat such tax;

(2) for money, property, services, or an extension, renewal, or refinancing of credit, to the extent obtained by—

(A) false pretenses, a false representation, or actual fraud, other than a statement respecting the debtor's or an insider's financial condition;

(B) use of a statement in writing—

(i) that is materially false;

(ii) respecting the debtor's or an insider's financial condition;

(iii) on which the creditor to whom the debtor is liable for such money, property, services, or credit reasonably relied; and

(iv) that the debtor caused to be made or published with intent to deceive; or

(C) for purposes of subparagraph (A) of this paragraph, consumer debts owed to a single creditor and aggregating more than $500 for "luxury goods or services" incurred by an individual debtor on or within forty days before the order for relief under this title, or cash advances aggregating more than $1,000 that are extensions of consumer credit under an open end credit plan obtained by an individual debtor on or within twenty days before the order for relief under this title, are presumed to be nondischargeable; "luxury goods or services" do not include goods or services reasonably acquired for the support or maintenance of the debtor or a dependent of the debtor; an extension of consumer credit under an open end credit plan is to be defined for purposes of this subparagraph as it is defined in the Consumer Credit Protection Act (15 U.S.C. 1601 et seq.);

(3) neither listed nor scheduled under section 521(1) of this title, with the name, if known to the debtor, of the creditor to whom such debt is owed, in time to permit—

(A) if such debt is not of a kind specified in paragraph (2), (4), or (6) of this subsection, timely filing of a proof of claim, unless such creditor had notice or actual knowledge of the case in time for such timely filing; or

(B) if such debt is of a kind specified in paragraph (2), (4), or (6) of this subsection, timely filing of a proof of claim and timely request for a determination of dischargeability of such debt under one of such paragraphs, unless such creditor had notice or actual knowledge of the case in time for such timely filing and request;

(4) for fraud or defalcation while acting in a fiduciary capacity, embezzlement, or larceny;

(5) to a spouse, former spouse, or child of the debtor, for alimony to, maintenance for, or support of such spouse or child, in connection with a separation agreement, divorce decree or other order of a court of record, determination made in accordance with state or territorial law by a governmental unit, or property settlement agreement, but not to the extent that—

(A) such debt is assigned to another entity, voluntarily, by operation of law, or otherwise (other than debts assigned pursuant to section 402(a)(26) of the Social Security Act, or any such debt which has been assigned to the Federal Government or to a State or any political subdivision of such State); or

(B) such debt includes a liability designated as alimony, maintenance, or support, unless such liability is actually in the nature of alimony, maintenance, or support;

(6) for willful and malicious injury by the debtor to another entity or to the property of another entity;

(7) to the extent such debt is for a fine, penalty, or forfeiture payable to and for the benefit of a governmental unit, and is not compensation for actual pecuniary loss, other than a tax penalty—

(A) relating to a tax of a kind not specified in paragraph (1) of this subsection; or

(B) imposed with respect to a transaction or event that occurred before three years before the date of the filing of the petition;

(8) for an educational loan made, insured, or guaranteed by a governmental unit, or made under any program funded in whole or in part by a governmental unit or a nonprofit institution, unless—

(A) such loan first became due before five years (exclusive of any applicable suspension of the repayment period) before the date of the filing of the petition; or

(B) excepting such debt from discharge under this paragraph will impose an undue hardship on the debtor and the debtor's dependents;

(9) for death or personal injury caused by the debtor's operation of a motor vehicle if such operation was unlawful because the debtor was intoxicated from using alcohol, a drug, or another substance;

(10) that was or could have been listed or scheduled by the debtor in a prior case concerning the debtor under this title or under the Bankruptcy Act in which the debtor waived discharge, or was denied a discharge under section 727(a)(2), (3), (4), (5), (6), or (7) of this title, or under section 14c(1), (2), (3), (4), (6), or (7) of such Act;

(11) provided in any final judgment unreviewable order, or consent order or decree entered in any court of the United States or of any State, issued by a Federal depository institutions regulatory agency, or contained in any settlement agreement entered into by the debtor, arising from any act of fraud or defalcation while acting in a fiduciary capacity committed with respect to any depository institution or insured credit union; or

(12) for malicious or reckless failure to fulfill any commitment by the debtor to a Federal depository institutions regulatory agency to maintain the capital of an insured depository institution, except that this paragraph shall not extend any such commitment which would otherwise be terminated due to any act of such agency.

(b) Notwithstanding subsection (a) of this section, a debt that was excepted from discharge under subsection (a)(1), (a)(3), or (a)(8) of this section, under section 17a(1), 17a(3), or 17a(5) of the Bankruptcy Act, under section 439A of the Higher Education Act of 1965 (20 U.S.C. 1087-3), or under section 733(g) of the Public Health Service Act (42 U.S.C. 294f) in a prior case concerning the debtor under this title, or under the Bankruptcy Act, is dischargeable in a case under this title unless, by the terms of subsection (a) of this section, such debt is not dischargeable in the case under this title.

(c)(1) Except as provided in subsection (a)(3)(B) of this section, the debtor shall be discharged from a debt of a kind specified in paragraph (2), (4), or (6) of subsection (a) of this section, unless, on request of the creditor to whom such debt is owed, and after notice and a hearing, the court determines such debt to be excepted from discharge under paragraph (2), (4), or (6), as the case may be, of subsection (a) of this section.

(2) Paragraph (1) shall not apply in the case of a Federal depository institutions regulatory agency seeking, in its capacity as conservator, receiver, or liquidating agent for an insured depository institution, to recover a debt described in subsection (a)(2), (a)(4), (a)(6), or (a)(11) owed to such institution by an institution-affiliated party unless the receiver, conservator, or liquidating agent was appointed in time to reasonably comply, or for a Federal depository institutions regulatory agency acting in its corporate capacity as a successor to such receiver, conservator, or liquidating agent to reasonably comply, with subsection (a)(3)(B) as a creditor of such institution-affiliated party with respect to such debt.

(d) If a creditor requests a determination of dischargeability of a consumer debt under subsection (a)(2) of this section, and such debt is discharged, the court shall grant judgment in favor of the debtor for the costs of, and a reasonable attorney's fee for, the proceeding if the court finds that the position of the creditor was not substantially justified, except that the court shall not award such costs and fees if special circumstances would make the award unjust.

(e) Any institution-affiliated party of a depository institution or insured credit union shall be considered to be acting in a fiduciary capacity with respect to the purposes of subsection (a)(4) or (11).

* * *

§ 524. Effect of discharge

(a) A discharge in a case under this title—

(1) voids any judgment at any time obtained, to the extent that such judgment is a determination of the personal liability of the debtor

with respect to any debt discharged under section 727, 944, 1141, 1228, or 1328 of this title, whether or not discharge of such debt is waived;

(2) operates as an injunction against the commencement or continuation of an action, the employment of process, or an act, to collect, recover or offset any such debt as a personal liability of the debtor, whether or not discharge of such debt is waived; and

(3) operates as an injunction against the commencement or continuation of an action, the employment of process, or an act, to collect or recover from, or offset against, property of the debtor of the kind specified in section 541(a)(2) of this title that is acquired after the commencement of the case, on account of any allowable community claim, except a community claim that is excepted from discharge under section 523, 1228(a)(1), or 1328(c)(1) of this title, or that would be so excepted, determined in accordance with the provisions of sections 523(c) and 523(d) of this title, in a case concerning the debtor's spouse commenced on the date of the filing of the petition in the case concerning the debtor, whether or not discharge of the debt based on such community claim is waived.

(b) Subsection (a)(3) of this section does not apply if—

(1)(A) the debtor's spouse is a debtor in a case under this title, or a bankrupt or a debtor in a case under the Bankruptcy Act, commenced within six years of the date of the filing of the petition in the case concerning the debtor; and

(B) the court does not grant the debtor's spouse a discharge in such case concerning the debtor's spouse; or

(2)(A) the court would not grant the debtor's spouse a discharge in a case under chapter 7 of this title concerning such spouse commenced on the date of the filing of the petition in the case concerning the debtor; and

(B) a determination that the court would not so grant such discharge is made by the bankruptcy court within the time and in the manner provided for a determination under section 727 of this title of whether a debtor is granted a discharge.

(c) An agreement between a holder of a claim and the debtor, the consideration for which, in whole or in part, is based on a debt that is dischargeable in a case under this title is enforceable only to any extent enforceable under applicable nonbankruptcy law, whether or not discharge of such debt is waived, only if—

(1) such agreement was made before the granting of the discharge under section 727, 1141, 1228, or 1328 of this title;

(2) such agreement contains a clear and conspicuous statement which advises the debtor that the agreement may be rescinded at any time prior to discharge or within sixty days after such agreement is filed with the court, whichever occurs later, by giving notice of rescission to the holder of such claim;

(3) such agreement has been filed with the court and, if applicable, accompanied by a declaration or an affidavit of the attorney that represented the debtor during the course of negotiating an agreement under this subsection, which states that such agreement—

(A) represents a fully informed and voluntary agreement by the debtor; and

(B) does not impose an undue hardship on the debtor or a dependent of the debtor;

(4) the debtor has not rescinded such agreement at any time prior to discharge or within sixty days after such agreement is filed with the court, whichever occurs later, by giving notice of rescission to the holder of such claim;

(5) the provisions of subsection (d) of this section have been complied with; and

(6)(A) in a case concerning an individual who was not represented by an attorney during the course of negotiating an agreement under this subsection, the court approves such agreement as—

(i) not imposing an undue hardship on the debtor or a dependent of the debtor; and

(ii) in the best interest of the debtor.

(B) Subparagraph (A) shall not apply to the extent that such debt is a consumer debt secured by real property.

(d) In a case concerning an individual, when the court has determined whether to grant or not to grant a discharge under section 727, 1141, 1228, or 1328 of this title, the court may hold a hearing at which the debtor shall appear in person. At any such hearing, the court may inform the debtor that a discharge has been granted or the reason why a discharge has not been granted. If a discharge has been granted and if the debtor desires to make an agreement of the kind specified in subsection (c) of this section, then the court shall hold a hearing at which the debtor shall appear in person and at such hearing the court shall

(1) inform the debtor—

(A) that such an agreement is not required under this title, under nonbankruptcy law, or under any agreement not made in accordance with the provisions of subsection (c) of this section; and

(B) of the legal effect and consequences of—

(i) an agreement of the kind specified in subsection (c) of this section; and

(ii) a default under such an agreement;

(2) determine whether the agreement that the debtor desires to make complies with the requirements of subsection (c)(6) of this section, if the consideration for such agreement is based in whole or in part on a consumer debt that is not secured by real property of the debtor.

(e) Except as provided in subsection (a)(3) of this section, discharge of a debt of the debtor does not affect the liability of any other entity on, or the property of any other entity for, such debt.

(f) Nothing contained in subsection (c) or (d) of this section prevents a debtor from voluntarily repaying any debt.

* * *

§ 541. Property of the estate

(a) The commencement of a case under section 301, 302, or 303 of this title creates an estate. Such estate is comprised of all the following property, wherever located and by whomever held:

(1) Except as provided in subsections (b) and (c)(2) of this section, all legal or equitable interests of the debtor in property as of the commencement of the case.

(2) All interests of the debtor and the debtor's spouse in community property as of the commencement of the case that is—

(A) under the sole, equal or joint management and control of the debtor; or

(B) liable for an allowable claim against the debtor, or for both an allowable claim against the debtor and an allowable claim against the debtor's spouse, to the extent that such interest is so liable.

(3) Any interest in property that the trustee recovers under section 329(b), 363(n), 543, 550, 553, or 723 of this title.

(4) Any interest in property preserved for the benefit of or ordered transferred to the estate under section 510(c) or 551 of this title.

(5) Any interest in property that would have been property of the estate if such interest had been an interest of the debtor on the date of the filing of the petition, and that the debtor acquires or becomes entitled to acquire within 180 days after such date—

(A) by bequest, devise, or inheritance;

(B) as a result of a property settlement agreement with the debtor's spouse, or of an interlocutory or final divorce decree; or

(C) as a beneficiary of a life insurance policy or of a death benefit plan.

(6) Proceeds, product, offspring, rents, or profits of or from property of the estate, except such as are earnings from services performed by an individual debtor after the commencement of the case.

(7) Any interest in property that the estate acquires after the commencement of the case.

(b) Property of the estate does not include—

(1) any power that the debtor may exercise solely for the benefit of an entity other than the debtor;

(2) any interest of the debtor as a lessee under a lease of nonresidential real property that has terminated at the expiration of the stated term of such lease before the commencement of the case under this title, and ceases to include any interest of the debtor as a lessee under a lease of nonresidential real property that has terminated at the expiration of the stated term of such lease during the case; or

(3) any eligibility of the debtor to participate in programs authorized under the Higher Education Act of 1965 (20 U.S.C. 1001 et seq.; 42 U.S.C. 2751 et seq.), or any accreditation status or State licensure of the debtor as an educational institution.

(c)(1) Except as provided in paragraph (2) of this subsection, an interest of the debtor in property becomes property of the estate under subsection (a)(1), (a)(2), or (a)(5) of this section notwithstanding any provision in an agreement, transfer instrument, or applicable nonbankruptcy law—

(A) that restricts or conditions transfer of such interest by the debtor; or

(B) that is conditioned on the insolvency or financial condition of the debtor, on the commencement of a case under this title, or on the appointment of or taking possession by a trustee in a case under this title or a custodian before such commencement and that effects or gives an option to effect a forfeiture, modification, or termination of the debtor's interest in property.

(2) A restriction on the transfer of a beneficial interest of the debtor in a trust that is enforceable under applicable nonbankruptcy law is enforceable in a case under this title.

(d) Property in which the debtor holds, as of the commencement of the case, only legal title and not an equitable interest, such as a mortgage secured by real property, or an interest in such a mortgage, sold by the debtor but as to which the debtor retains legal title to service or supervise the servicing of such mortgage or interest, becomes property of the estate under subsection (a)(1) or (2) of this section only to the extent of the debtor's legal title to such property, but not to the extent of any equitable interest in such property that the debtor does not hold.

* * *

§ 544. Trustee as lien creditor and as successor to certain creditors and purchasers

(a) The trustee shall have, as of the commencement of the case, and without regard to any knowledge of the trustee or of any creditor, the rights and powers of, or may avoid any transfer of property of the debtor or any obligation incurred by the debtor that is voidable by—

(1) a creditor that extends credit to the debtor at the time of the commencement of the case, and that obtains, at such time and with respect to such credit, a judicial lien on all property on which a creditor on a simple contract could have obtained such a judicial lien, whether or not such a creditor exists;

(2) a creditor that extends credit to the debtor at the time of the commencement of the case, and obtains, at such time and with respect to such credit, an execution against the debtor that is returned unsatisfied at such time, whether or not such a creditor exists; or

(3) a bona fide purchaser of real property, other than fixtures, from the debtor, against whom applicable law permits such transfer to be perfected, that obtains the status of a bona fide purchaser and has perfected such transfer at the time of the commencement of the case, whether or not such a purchaser exists.

(b) The trustee may avoid any transfer of an interest of the debtor in property or any obligation incurred by the debtor that is voidable under applicable law by a creditor holding an unsecured claim that is allowable under section 502 of this title or that is not allowable only under section 502(e) of this title.

* * *

§ 547. Preferences

(a) In this section—

(1) "inventory" means personal property leased or furnished, held for sale or lease, or to be furnished under a contract for service, raw materials, work in process, or materials used or consumed in a business, including farm products such as crops or livestock, held for sale or lease;

(2) "new value" means money or money's worth in goods, services, or new credit, or release by a transferee of property previously transferred to such transferee in a transaction that is neither void nor voidable by the debtor or the trustee under any applicable law, including proceeds of such property, but does not include an obligation substituted for an existing obligation;

(3) "receivable" means right to payment, whether or not such right has been earned by performance; and

(4) a debt for a tax is incurred on the day when such tax is last payable without penalty, including any extension.

(b) Except as provided in subsection (c) of this section, the trustee may avoid any transfer of an interest of the debtor in property—

(1) to or for the benefit of a creditor;

(2) for or on account of an antecedent debt owed by the debtor before such transfer was made;

(3) made while the debtor was insolvent;

(4) made—

(A) on or within 90 days before the date of the filing of the petition; or

(B) between ninety days and one year before the date of the filing of the petition, if such creditor at the time of such transfer was an insider; and

(5) that enables such creditor to receive more than such creditor would receive if—

(A) the case were a case under chapter 7 of this title;

(B) the transfer had not been made; and

(C) such creditor received payment of such debt to the extent provided by the provisions of this title.

(c) The trustee may not avoid under this section a transfer—

(1) to the extent that such transfer was—

(A) intended by the debtor and the creditor to or for whose benefit such transfer was made to be a contemporaneous exchange for new value given to the debtor; and

(B) in fact a substantially contemporaneous exchange;

(2) to the extent that such transfer was—

(A) in payment of a debt incurred by the debtor in the ordinary course of business or financial affairs of the debtor and the transferee;

(B) made in the ordinary course of business or financial affairs of the debtor and the transferee; and

(C) made according to ordinary business terms;

(3) that creates a security interest in property acquired by the debtor—

(A) to the extent such security interest secures new value that was—

(i) given at or after the signing of a security agreement that contains a description of such property as collateral;

(ii) given by or on behalf of the secured party under such agreement;

(iii) given to enable the debtor to acquire such property; and

(iv) in fact used by the debtor to acquire such property; and

(B) that is perfected on or before 10 days after the debtor receives possession of such property;

(4) to or for the benefit of a creditor, to the extent that, after such transfer, such creditor gave new value to or for the benefit of the debtor—

(A) not secured by an otherwise unavoidable security interest; and

(B) on account of which new value the debtor did not make an otherwise unavoidable transfer to or for the benefit of such creditor;

(5) that creates a perfected security interest in inventory or a receivable or the proceeds of either, except to the extent that the aggregate of all such transfers to the transferee caused a reduction, as of the date of the filing of the petition and to the prejudice of other creditors holding unsecured claims, of any amount by which the debt secured by such security interest exceeded the value of all security interests for such debt on the later of—

(A)(i) with respect to a transfer to which subsection (b)(4)(A) of this section applies, 90 days before the date of the filing of the petition; or

(ii) with respect to a transfer to which subsection (b)(4)(B) of this section applies, one year before the date of the filing of the petition; or

(B) the date on which new value was first given under the security agreement creating such security interest;

(6)   that is the fixing of a statutory lien that is not avoidable under section 545 of this title; or

(7)   if, in a case filed by an individual debtor whose debts are primarily consumer debts, the aggregate value of all property that constitutes or is affected by such transfer is less than $600.

(d) The trustee may avoid a transfer of an interest in property of the debtor transferred to or for the benefit of a surety to secure reimbursement of such a surety that furnished a bond or other obligation to dissolve a judicial lien that would have been avoidable by the trustee under subsection (b) of this section. The liability of such surety under such bond or obligation shall be discharged to the extent of the value of such property recovered by the trustee or the amount paid to the trustee.

(e)(1) For the purposes of this section—

(A)   a transfer of real property other than fixtures, but including the interest of a seller or purchaser under a contract for the sale of real property, is perfected when a bona fide purchaser of such property from the debtor against whom applicable law permits such transfer to be perfected cannot acquire an interest that is superior to the interest of the transferee; and

(B)   a transfer of a fixture or property other than real property is perfected when a creditor on a simple contract cannot acquire a judicial lien that is superior to the interest of the transferee.

(2) For the purposes of this section, except as provided in paragraph (3) of this subsection, a transfer is made—

(A)   at the time such transfer takes effect between the transferor and the transferee, if such transfer is perfected at, or within 10 days after, such time;

(B)   at the time such transfer is perfected, if such transfer is perfected after such 10 days; or

(C)   immediately before the date of the filing of the petition, if such transfer is not perfected at the later of—

(i)   the commencement of the case; or

(ii)   10 days after such transfer takes effect between the transferor and the transferee.

(3) For the purposes of this section, a transfer is not made until the debtor has acquired rights in the property transferred.

(f) For the purposes of this section, the debtor is presumed to have been insolvent on and during the 90 days immediately preceding the date of the filing of the petition.

(g) For the purposes of this section, the trustee has the burden of proving the avoidability of a transfer under subsection (b) of this section, and the creditor or party in interest against whom recovery or avoidance is sought has the burden of proving the nonavoidability of a transfer under subsection (c) of this section.

* * *

§ 548. Fraudulent transfers and obligations

(a) The trustee may avoid any transfer of an interest of the debtor in property, or any obligation incurred by the debtor, that was made or incurred on or within one year before the date of the filing of the petition, if the debtor voluntarily or involuntarily—

(1) made such transfer or incurred such obligation with actual intent to hinder, delay, or defraud any entity to which the debtor was or became, on or after the date that such transfer was made or such obligation was incurred, indebted; or

(2)(A) received less than a reasonably equivalent value in exchange for such transfer or obligation; and

(B)(i) was insolvent on the date that such transfer was made or such obligation was incurred, or became insolvent as a result of such transfer or obligation;

(ii) was engaged in business or a transaction, or was about to engage in business or a transaction, for which any property remaining with the debtor was an unreasonably small capital; or

(iii) intended to incur, or believed that the debtor would incur, debts that would be beyond the debtor's ability to pay as such debts matured.

(b) The trustee of a partnership debtor may avoid any transfer of an interest of the debtor in property, or any obligation incurred by the debtor, that was made or incurred on or within one year before the date of the filing of the petition, to a general partner in the debtor, if the debtor was insolvent on the date such transfer was made or such obligation was incurred, or became insolvent as a result of such transfer or obligation.

(c) Except to the extent that a transfer or obligation voidable under this section is voidable under section 544, 545, or 547 of this title, a transferee or obligee of such a transfer or obligation that takes for value and in good faith has a lien on or may retain any interest transferred or may enforce any obligation incurred, as the case may be, to the extent that such transferee or obligee gave value to the debtor in exchange for such transfer or obligation.

(d)(1) For the purposes of this section, a transfer is made when such transfer is so perfected that a bona fide purchaser from the debtor against whom applicable law permits such transfer to be perfected cannot acquire an interest in the property transferred that is superior to the interest in such property of the transferee, but if such transfer is not so perfected before the commencement of the case, such transfer is made immediately before the date of the filing of the petition.

(2) In this section—

(A) "value" means property, or satisfaction or securing of a present or antecedent debt of the debtor, but does not include an unperformed promise to furnish support to the debtor or to a relative of the debtor;

(B) a commodity broker, forward contract merchant, stockbroker, financial institution, or securities clearing agency that receives a margin payment, as defined in section 101(34), 741(5) or 761(15) of this title, or settlement payment, as defined in section 101(35) or 741(8) of this title, takes for value to the extent of such payment;

(C) a repo participant that receives a margin payment, as defined in section 741(5) or 761(15) of this title, or settlement payment, as defined in section 741(8) of this title, in connection with a repurchase agreement, takes for value to the extent of such payment; and

(D) a swap participant that receives a transfer in connection with a swap agreement takes for value to the extent of such transfer.

* * *

§ 706. Conversion

(a) The debtor may convert a case under this chapter to a case under chapter 11, 12, or 13 of this title at any time, if the case has not been converted under section 1112, 1307, or 1208 of this title. Any waiver of the right to convert a case under this subsection is unenforceable.

(b) On request of a party in interest and after notice and a hearing, the court may convert a case under this chapter to a case under chapter 11 of this title at any time.

(c) The court may not convert a case under this chapter to a case under chapter 12 or 13 of this title unless the debtor requests such conversion.

(d) Notwithstanding any other provision of this section, a case may not be converted to a case under another chapter of this title unless the debtor may be a debtor under such chapter.

* * *

§ 707. Dismissal

(a) The court may dismiss a case under this chapter only after notice and a hearing and only for cause, including—

(1) unreasonable delay by the debtor that is prejudicial to creditors;

(2) nonpayment of any fees or charges required under chapter 123 of title 28; and

(3) failure of the debtor in a voluntary case to file, within fifteen days or such additional time as the court may allow after the filing of the petition commencing such case, the information required by paragraph (1) of section 521, but only on a motion by the United States trustee.

(b) After notice and a hearing, the court, on its own motion or on a motion by the United States Trustee, but not at the request or suggestion of any party in interest, may dismiss a case filed by an individual debtor under this chapter whose debts are primarily consumer debts if it finds that the granting of relief would be a substantial abuse of the provisions of this chapter. There shall be a presumption in favor of granting the relief requested by the debtor.

* * *

§ 726. Distribution of property of the estate

(a) Except as provided in section 510 of this title, property of the estate shall be distributed—

(1) first, in payment of claims of the kind specified in, and in the order specified in, section 507 of this title;

(2) second, in payment of any allowed unsecured claim, other than a claim of a kind specified in paragraph (1), (3), or (4) of this subsection, proof of which is—

(A) timely filed under section 501(a) of this title;

(B) timely filed under section 501(b) or 501(c) of this title; or

(C) tardily filed under section 501(a) of this title, if—

(i) the creditor that holds such claim did not have notice or actual knowledge of the case in time for timely filing of a proof of such claim under section 501(a) of this title; and

(ii) proof of such claim is filed in time to permit payment of such claim;

(3) third, in payment of any allowed unsecured claim proof of which is tardily filed under section 501(a) of this title, other than a claim of the kind specified in paragraph (2)(C) of this subsection;

(4) fourth, in payment of any allowed claim, whether secured or unsecured, for any fine, penalty, or forfeiture, or for multiple, exemplary, or punitive damages, arising before the earlier of the order for relief or the appointment of a trustee, to the extent that such fine, penalty, forfeiture, or damages are not compensation for actual pecuniary loss suffered by the holder of such claim;

(5) fifth, in payment of interest at the legal rate from the date of the filing of the petition, on any claim paid under paragraph (1), (2), (3), or (4) of this subsection; and

(6) sixth, to the debtor.

(b) Payment on claims of a kind specified in paragraph (1), (2), (3), (4), (5), (6) or (7) of section 507(a) of this title, or in paragraph (2), (3), (4), or (5) of subsection (a) of this section, shall be made pro rata among claims of the kind specified in each such particular paragraph, except that in a case that has been converted to this chapter under section 1112 1208, or 1307 of this title, a claim allowed under section 503(b) of this title incurred under this chapter after such conversion has priority over a claim allowed under section 503(b) of this title incurred under any other chapter of this title or under this chapter before such conversion and over any expenses of a custodian superseded under section 543 of this title.

(c) Notwithstanding subsections (a) and (b) of this section, if there is property of the kind specified in section 541(a)(2) of this title, or proceeds of such property, in the estate, such property or proceeds shall be segregated from other property of the estate, and such property or proceeds and other property of the estate shall be distributed as follows:

(1) Claims allowed under section 503 of this title shall be paid either from property of the kind specified in section 541(a)(2) of this title, or from other property of the estate, as the interest of justice requires.

(2) Allowed claims, other than claims allowed under section 503 of this title, shall be paid in the order specified in subsection (a) of this section, and, with respect to claims of a kind specified in a particular paragraph of section 507 of this title or subsection (a) of this section, in the following order and manner:

(A) First, community claims against the debtor or the debtor's spouse shall be paid from property of the kind specified in section 541(a)(2) of this title, except to the extent that such property is solely liable for debts of the debtor.

(B) Second, to the extent that community claims against the debtor are not paid under subparagraph (A) of this paragraph, such community claims shall be paid from property of the kind specified in section 541(a)(2) of this title that is solely liable for debts of the debtor.

(C) Third, to the extent that all claims against the debtor including community claims against the debtor are not paid under subparagraph (A) or (B) of this paragraph such claims shall be paid from property of the estate other than property of the kind specified in section 541(a)(2) of this title.

(D) Fourth, to the extent that community claims against the debtor or the debtor's spouse are not paid under subparagraph (A), (B), or (C) of this paragraph, such claims shall be paid from all remaining property of the estate.

* * *

§ 727. Discharge

(a) The court shall grant the debtor a discharge, unless—

(1) the debtor is not an individual;

(2) the debtor, with intent to hinder, delay, or defraud a creditor or an officer of the estate charged with custody of property under this title, has transferred, removed, destroyed, mutilated, or concealed, or has permitted to be transferred, removed, destroyed, mutilated, or concealed—

(A) property of the debtor, within one year before the date of the filing of the petition; or

(B) property of the estate, after the date of the filing of the petition;

(3) the debtor has concealed, destroyed, mutilated, falsified, or failed to keep or preserve any recorded information, including books, documents, records, and papers, from which the debtor's financial condition or business transactions might be ascertained, unless such act or failure to act was justified under all of the circumstances of the case;

(4) the debtor knowingly and fraudulently, in or in connection with the case—

(A) made a false oath or account;

(B) presented or used a false claim;

(C) gave, offered, received, or attempted to obtain money, property, or advantage, or a promise of money, property, or advantage, for acting or forbearing to act; or

(D) withheld from an officer of the estate entitled to possession under this title, any recorded information, including books, documents, records, and papers, relating to the debtor's property or financial affairs;

(5)   the debtor has failed to explain satisfactorily, before determination of denial of discharge under this paragraph, any loss of assets or deficiency of assets to meet the debtor's liabilities;

(6)   the debtor has refused, in the case—

(A) to obey any lawful order of the court, other than an order to respond to a material question or to testify;

(B) on the ground of privilege against self-incrimination, to respond to a material question approved by the court or to testify, after the debtor has been granted immunity with respect to the matter concerning which such privilege was invoked; or

(C) on a ground other than the properly invoked privilege against self-incrimination, to respond to a material question approved by the court or to testify;

(7)   the debtor has committed any act specified in paragraph (2), (3), (4), (5), or (6) of this subsection, on or within one year before the date of the filing of the petition, or during the case, in connection with another case, under this title or under the Bankruptcy Act, concerning an insider;

(8)   the debtor has been granted a discharge under this section, under section 1141 of this title, or under section 14, 371, or 476 of the Bankruptcy Act, in a case commenced within six years before the date of the filing of the petition;

(9)   the debtor has been granted a discharge under section 1228 or 1328 of this title, or under section 660 or 661 of the Bankruptcy Act, in a case commenced within six years before the date of the filing of the petition, unless payments under the plan in such case totaled at least—

(A) 100 percent of the allowed unsecured claims in such case; or

(B)(i) 70 percent of such claims; and

(ii) the plan was proposed by the debtor in good faith, and was the debtor's best effort; or

(10) the court approves a written waiver of discharge executed by the debtor after the order for relief under this chapter.

(b) Except as provided in section 523 of this title, a discharge under subsection (a) of this section discharges the debtor from all debts that arose before the date of the order for relief under this chapter, and any liability on a claim that is determined under section 502 of this title as if such claim had arisen before the commencement of the case, whether or not a proof of claim based on any such debt or liability is filed under section 501 of this title, and whether or not a claim based on any such debt or liability is allowed under section 502 of this title.

(c)(1) The trustee, a creditor, or the United States trustee may object to the granting of a discharge under subsection (a) of this section.

(2) On request of a party in interest, the court may order the trustee to examine the acts and conduct of the debtor to determine whether a ground exists for denial of discharge.

(d) On request of the trustee, a creditor, or the United States trustee, and after notice and a hearing, the court shall revoke a discharge granted under subsection (a) of this section if—

(1) such discharge was obtained through the fraud of the debtor, and the requesting party did not know of such fraud until after the granting of such discharge;

(2) the debtor acquired property that is property of the estate, or became entitled to acquire property that would be property of the estate, and knowingly and fraudulently failed to report the acquisition of or entitlement to such property, or to deliver or surrender such property to the trustee; or

(3) the debtor committed an act specified in subsection (a)(6) of this section.

(e) The trustee, a creditor, or the United States trustee may request a revocation of a discharge—

(1) under subsection (d)(1) of this section within one year after such discharge is granted; or

(2) under subsection (d)(2) or (d)(3) of this section before the later of—

(A) one year after the granting of such discharge; and

(B) the date the case is closed.

* * *

SELECTED RULES OF THE FEDERAL RULES OF BANKRUPTCY PROCEDURE

This appendix contains only some of the Federal Rules of Bankruptcy Procedure related to the issues discussed in the text. The applicability of other rules and the Bankruptcy Code must be considered before taking action in a bankruptcy matter. In addition, local bankruptcy rules must also be consulted.

* * *

Rule 1007. Lists, Schedules, and Statements; Time Limits

(a) LIST OF CREDITORS AND EQUITY SECURITY HOLDERS.

(1) Voluntary Case. In a voluntary case, the debtor shall file with the petition a list containing the name and address of each creditor unless the petition is accompanied by a schedule of liabilities.

(2) Involuntary Case. In an involuntary case, the debtor shall file within 15 days after entry of the order for relief, a list containing the name and address of each creditor unless a schedule of liabilities has been filed.

(3) Equity Security Holders. In a chapter 11 reorganization case, unless the court orders otherwise, the debtor shall file within 15 days after entry of the order for relief a list of the debtor's equity security holders of each class showing the number and kind of interests registered in the name of each holder, and the last known address or place of business of each holder.

(4) Extension of Time. Any extension of time for the filing of the lists required by this subdivision may be granted only on motion for cause shown and on notice to the United States trustee and to any trustee, committee elected pursuant to § 705 or appointed pursuant to § 1102 of the Code, or other party as the court may direct.

(b) SCHEDULES AND STATEMENTS REQUIRED.

(1) Except in a chapter 9 municipality case, the debtor, unless the court orders otherwise, shall file schedules of assets and liabilities, a schedule of current income and expenditures, a schedule of executory contracts and unexpired leases, and a statement of financial affairs, prepared as prescribed by the appropriate Official Forms.

(2) An individual debtor in a chapter 7 case shall file a statement of intention as required by § 521(2) of the Code, prepared as prescribed by the appropriate Official Form. A copy of the statement of intention shall be served on the trustee and the creditors named in the statement on or before the filing of the statement.

(c) TIME LIMITS. The schedules and statements, other than the statement of intention, shall be filed with the petition in a voluntary case, or if the petition is accompanied by a list of all the debtor's creditors and their addresses, within 15 days thereafter, except as otherwise provided in subdivisions (d), (e), and (h) of this rule. In an involuntary case the schedules and statements, other than the statement of intention, shall be filed by the debtor within 15 days after entry of the order for relief. Schedules and statements previously filed in a pending chapter 7 case shall be deemed filed in a superseding case unless the court directs otherwise. Any extension of time for the filing of the schedules and statements may be granted only on motion for cause shown and on notice to the United States trustee and to any committee elected pursuant to § 705 or appointed pursuant to § 1102 of the Code, trustee, examiner, or other party as the court may direct. Notice of an extension shall be given to the United States trustee and to any committee, trustee, or other party as the court may direct.

(d) LIST OF 20 LARGEST CREDITORS IN CHAPTER 9 MUNICIPALITY CASE OR CHAPTER 11 REORGANIZATION CASE. In addition to the list required by subdivision (a) of this rule, a debtor in a chapter 9 municipality case or a debtor in a voluntary chapter 11 reorganization case shall file with the petition a list containing the name, address and claim of the creditors that hold the 20 largest unsecured claims, excluding insiders, as prescribed by the appropriate Official Form. In an involuntary chapter 11 reorganization case, such list shall be filed by the debtor within 2 days after entry of the order for relief under § 303(h) of the Code.

(e) LIST IN CHAPTER 9 MUNICIPALITY CASES. The list required by subdivision (a) of this rule shall be filed by the debtor in a chapter 9 municipality case within such time as the court shall fix. If a proposed plan requires a revision of assessments so that the proportion of special assessments or special taxes to be assessed against some real property will be different from the proportion in effect at the date the petition is filed, the debtor shall also file a list showing the name and address of each known holder of title, legal or equitable, to real property adversely affected. On motion for cause shown, the court may modify the requirements of this subdivision and subdivision (a) of this rule.

(f) [Abrogated]

(g) PARTNERSHIP AND PARTNERS. The general partners of a debtor partnership shall prepare and file the schedules of the assets and liabilities, schedule of current income and expenditures, schedule of executory contracts and unexpired leases, and statement of financial affairs of the partnership. The court may order any general partner to file a statement of personal assets and liabilities within such time as the court may fix.

(h) INTERESTS ACQUIRED OR ARISING AFTER PETITION. If, as provided by § 541(a)(5) of the Code, the debtor acquires or becomes entitled to acquire any interest in property, the debtor shall within 10 days after the information comes to the debtor's knowledge or within such further time the court may allow, file a supplemental schedule in the chapter 7 liquidation case, chapter 11 reorganization case, chapter 12 family farmer's debt adjustment case, or chapter 13 individual debt adjustment case. If any of the property required to be reported under this subdivision is claimed by the debtor as exempt, the debtor shall claim the exemptions in the supplemental schedule. The duty to file a supplemental schedule in accordance with this subdivision continues notwithstanding the closing of the case, except that the schedule need not be filed in a chapter 11, chapter 12, or chapter 13 case with respect to property acquired after entry of the order confirming a chapter 11 plan or discharging the debtor in a chapter 12 or chapter 13 case.

(i) DISCLOSURE OF LIST OF SECURITY HOLDERS. After notice and hearing and for cause shown, the court may direct an entity other than the debtor or trustee to disclose any list of security holders of the debtor in its possession or under its control, indicating the name, address and security held by any of them. The entity possessing this list may be required either to produce the list or a true copy thereof, or permit inspection or copying, or otherwise disclose the information contained on the list.

(j) IMPOUNDING OF LISTS. On motion of a party in interest and for cause shown the court may direct the impounding of the lists filed under this rule, and may refuse to permit inspection by any entity. The court may permit inspection or use of the lists, however, by any party in interest on terms prescribed by the court.

(k) PREPARATION OF LIST, SCHEDULES, OR STATEMENTS ON DEFAULT OF DEBTOR. If a list, schedule, or statement, other than a statement of intention, is not prepared and filed as required by this rule, the court may order the trustee, a petitioning creditor, committee, or other party to prepare and file any of these papers within a time fixed by the court. The court may approve reimbursement of the cost incurred in complying with such an order as an administrative expense.

(l) TRANSMISSION TO UNITED STATES TRUSTEE. The clerk shall forthwith transmit to the United States trustee a copy of every list, schedule, and statement filed pursuant to subdivision (a)(1), (a)(2), (b), (d), or (h) of this rule.

* * *

Rule 3002. Filing Proof of Claim or Interest

(a) NECESSITY FOR FILING. An unsecured creditor or an equity security holder must file a proof of claim or interest in accordance with this rule for the claim or interest to be allowed, except as provided in Rules 1019(3), 3003, 3004 and 3005.

(b) PLACE OF FILING. A proof of claim or interest shall be filed in accordance with Rule 5005.

(c) TIME FOR FILING. In a chapter 7 liquidation, chapter 12 family farmer's debt adjustment, or chapter 13 individual's debt adjustment case, a proof of claim shall be filed within 90 days after the first date set for the meeting of creditors called pursuant to § 341(a) of the Code, except as follows:

(1) On motion of the United States, a state, or subdivision thereof before the expiration of such period and for cause shown, the court may extend the time for filing of a claim by the United States, a state, or subdivision thereof.

(2) In the interest of justice and if it will not unduly delay the administration of the case, the court may extend the time for filing a proof

of claim by an infant or incompetent person or the representative of either.

(3) An unsecured claim which arises in favor of an entity or becomes allowable as a result of a judgment may be filed within 30 days after the judgment becomes final if the judgment is for the recovery of money or property from that entity or denies or avoids the entity's interest in property. If the judgment imposes a liability which is not satisfied, or a duty which is not performed within such period or such further time as the court may permit, the claim shall not be allowed.

(4) A claim arising from the rejection of an executory contract or unexpired lease of the debtor may be filed within such time as the court may direct.

(5) If notice of insufficient assets to pay a dividend was given to creditors pursuant to Rule 2002(e), and subsequently the trustee notifies the court that payment of a dividend appears possible, the clerk shall notify the creditors of that fact and that they may file proofs of claim within 90 days after the mailing of the notice.

(6) In a chapter 7 liquidation case, if a surplus remains after all claims allowed have been paid in full, the court may grant an extension of time for the filing of claims against the surplus not filed within the time herein above prescribed.

* * *

Rule 4001. Relief from Automatic Stay; Prohibiting or Conditioning the Use, Sale, or Lease of Property; Use of Cash Collateral; Obtaining Credit; Agreements

(a) RELIEF FROM STAY; PROHIBITING OR CONDITIONING THE USE, SALE, OR LEASE OF PROPERTY.

(1) Motion. A motion for relief from an automatic stay provided by the Code or a motion to prohibit or condition the use, sale, or lease of property pursuant to § 363(e) shall be made in accordance with Rule 9014 and shall be served on any committee elected pursuant to § 705 or appointed pursuant to § 1102 of the Code or its authorized agent, or, if the case is a chapter 9 municipality case or a chapter 11 reorganization case and no committee of unsecured creditors has been appointed pursuant to § 1102, on the creditors included on the list filed pursuant to Rule 1007(d), and on such other entities as the court may direct.

(2) Ex Parte Relief. Relief from a stay under § 362(a) or a request to prohibit or condition the use, sale, or lease of property pursuant to § 363(e) may be granted without prior notice only if (A) it clearly appears from specific facts shown by affidavit or by a verified motion that immediate and irreparable injury, loss, or damage will result to the

movant before the adverse party or the attorney for the adverse party can be heard in opposition, and (B) the movant's attorney certifies to the court in writing the efforts, if any, which have been made to give notice and the reasons why notice should not be required. The party obtaining relief under this subdivision and § 362(f) or § 363(e) shall immediately give oral notice thereof to the trustee or debtor in possession and to the debtor and forthwith mail or otherwise transmit to such adverse party or parties a copy of the order granting relief. On two days notice to the party who obtained relief from the stay without notice or on shorter notice to that party as the court may prescribe, the adverse party may appear and move reinstatement of the stay or reconsideration of the order prohibiting or conditioning the use, sale, or lease of property. In that event, the court shall proceed expeditiously to hear and determine the motion.

* * *

Rule 4003. Exemptions

(a) CLAIM OF EXEMPTIONS. A debtor shall list the property claimed as exempt under § 522 of the Code on the schedule of assets required to be filed by Rule 1007. If the debtor fails to claim exemptions or file the schedule within the time specified in Rule 1007, a dependent of the debtor may file the list within 30 days thereafter.

(b) OBJECTIONS TO CLAIM OF EXEMPTIONS. The trustee or any creditor may file objections to the list of property claimed as exempt within 30 days after the conclusion of the meeting of creditors held pursuant to Rule 2003(a) or the filing of any amendment to the list or supplemental schedules unless, within such period, further time is granted by the court. Copies of the objections shall be delivered or mailed to the trustee and to the person filing the list and the attorney for such person.

(c) BURDEN OF PROOF. In any hearing under this rule, the objecting party has the burden of proving that the exemptions are not properly claimed. After hearing on notice, the court shall determine the issues presented by the objections.

(d) AVOIDANCE BY DEBTOR OF TRANSFERS OF EXEMPT PROPERTY. A proceeding by the debtor to avoid a lien or other transfer of property exempt under § 522(f) of the Code shall be by motion in accordance with Rule 9014.

Rule 4004. Grant or Denial of Discharge

(a) TIME FOR FILING COMPLAINT OBJECTING TO DISCHARGE; NOTICE OF TIME FIXED. In a chapter 7 liquidation case a complaint objecting to the debtor's discharge under § 727(a) of the Code shall be filed not later than 60 days following the first date set for the meeting of creditors held pursuant to § 341(a). In a chapter 11 reorganization case, such complaint shall be filed not later than the first date set for the hearing on confirmation. Not less than 25 days notice of the time so fixed shall be given to the United States trustee and all creditors as provided in Rule 2002(f) and (k) and to the trustee and the trustee's attorney.

(b) EXTENSION OF TIME. On motion of any party in interest, after hearing on notice, the court may extend for cause the time for filing a complaint objecting to discharge. The motion shall be made before such time has expired.

(c) GRANT OF DISCHARGE. In a chapter 7 case, on expiration of the time fixed for filing a complaint objecting to discharge and the time fixed for filing a motion to dismiss the case pursuant to Rule 1017(e), the court shall forthwith grant the discharge unless (1) the debtor is not an individual, (2) a complaint objecting to the discharge has been filed, (3) the debtor has filed a waiver under § 727(a)(10), or (4) a motion to dismiss the case under Rule 1017(e) is pending. Notwithstanding the foregoing, on motion of the debtor, the court may defer the entry of an order granting a discharge for 30 days and, on motion within such period, the court may defer entry of the order to a date certain.

(d) APPLICABILITY OF RULES IN PART VII. A proceeding commenced by a complaint objecting to discharge is governed by Part VII of these rules.

(e) ORDER OF DISCHARGE. An order of discharge shall conform to the appropriate Official Form.

(f) REGISTRATION IN OTHER DISTRICTS. An order of discharge that has become final may be registered in any other district by filing a certified copy of the order in the office of the clerk of that district. When so registered the order of discharge shall have the same effect as an order of the court of the district where registered.

(g) NOTICE OF DISCHARGE. The clerk shall promptly mail a copy of the final order of discharge to those specified in subdivision (a) of this rule.

Rule 4007. Determination of Dischargeability of a Debt

(a) PERSONS ENTITLED TO FILE COMPLAINT. A debtor or any creditor may file a complaint to obtain a determination of the dischargeability of any debt.

(b) TIME FOR COMMENCING PROCEEDING OTHER THAN UNDER § 523(c) OF THE CODE. A complaint other than under § 523(c) may be filed at any time. A case may be reopened without payment of an additional filing fee for the purpose of filing a complaint to obtain a determination under this rule.

(c) TIME FOR FILING COMPLAINT UNDER § 523(c) IN CHAPTER 7 LIQUIDATION, CHAPTER 11 REORGANIZATION, AND CHAPTER 12 FAMILY FARMER'S DEBT ADJUSTMENT CASES; NOTICE OF TIME FIXED. A complaint to determine the dischargeability of any debt pursuant to § 523(c) of the Code shall be filed not later than 60 days following the first date set for the meeting of creditors held pursuant to § 341(a). The court shall give all creditors not less than 30 days notice of the time so fixed in the manner provided in Rule 2002. On motion of any party in interest, after hearing on notice, the court may for cause extend the time fixed under this subdivision. The motion shall be made before the time has expired.

(d) TIME FOR FILING COMPLAINT UNDER § 523(c) IN CHAPTER 13 INDIVIDUAL'S DEBT ADJUSTMENT CASES; NOTICE OF TIME FIXED. On motion by a debtor for a discharge under § 1328(b), the court shall enter an order fixing a time for the filing of a complaint to determine the dischargeability of any debt pursuant to § 523(c) and shall give not less than 30 days notice of the time fixed to all creditors in the manner provided in Rule 2002. On motion of any party in interest after hearing on notice the court may for cause extend the time fixed under this subdivision. The motion shall be made before the time has expired.

(e) APPLICABILITY OF RULES IN PART VII. A proceeding commenced by a complaint filed under this rule is governed by Part VII of these rules.

* * *

Rule 5011. Withdrawal and Abstention from Hearing a Proceeding

(a) WITHDRAWAL. A motion for withdrawal of a case or proceeding shall be heard by a district judge.

(b) ABSTENTION FROM HEARING A PROCEEDING. A motion for abstention pursuant to 28 U.S.C. § 1334(c) shall be governed by Rule 9014 and shall be served on the parties to the proceeding.

(c) EFFECT OF FILING OF MOTION FOR WITHDRAWAL OR ABSTENTION. The filing of a motion for withdrawal of a case or proceeding or for abstention pursuant to 28 U.S.C. § 1334(c) shall not stay the administration of the case or any proceeding therein before the bankruptcy judge except that the bankruptcy judge may stay, on such terms and conditions as are proper, proceedings pending disposition of the motion. A motion for a stay ordinarily shall be presented first to the bankruptcy judge. A motion for a stay or relief from a stay filed in the district court shall state why it has not been presented to or obtained from the bankruptcy judge. Relief granted by the district judge shall be on such terms and conditions as the judge deems proper.

* * *

Rule 9020. Contempt Proceedings

(a) CONTEMPT COMMITTED IN PRESENCE OF BANKRUPTCY JUDGE. Contempt committed in the presence of a bankruptcy judge may be determined summarily by a bankruptcy judge. The order of contempt shall recite the facts and shall be signed by the bankruptcy judge and entered of record.

(b) OTHER CONTEMPT. Contempt committed in a case or proceeding pending before a bankruptcy judge, except when determined as provided in subdivision (a) of this rule, may be determined by the bankruptcy judge only after a hearing on notice. The notice shall be in writing, shall state the essential facts constituting the contempt charged and describe the contempt as criminal or civil and shall state the time and place of hearing, allowing a reasonable time for the preparation of the defense. The notice may be given on the court's own initiative or on application of the United States attorney or by an attorney appointed by the court for that purpose. If the contempt charged involves disrespect to or criticism of a bankruptcy judge, that judge is disqualified from presiding at the hearing except with the consent of the person charged.

(c) SERVICE AND EFFECTIVE DATE OF ORDER; REVIEW. The clerk shall serve forthwith a copy of the order of contempt on the entity named therein. The order shall be effective 10 days after service of the order and shall have the same force and effect as an order of contempt entered by the district court unless, within the 10 day period, the entity named therein serves and files objections prepared in the manner provided in Rule 9033(b). If timely objections are filed, the order shall be reviewed as provided in Rule 9033.

(d) RIGHT TO JURY TRIAL. Nothing in this rule shall be construed to impair the right to jury trial whenever it otherwise exists.

* * *

Rule 9029. Local Bankruptcy Rules

Each district court by action of a majority of the judges thereof may make and amend rules governing practice and procedure in all cases and proceedings within the district court's bankruptcy jurisdiction which are not inconsistent with these rules and which do not prohibit or limit the use of the Official Forms. Rule 83 F.R.Civ.P. governs the procedure for making local rules. A district court may authorize the bankruptcy judges of the district, subject to any limitation or condition it may prescribe and the requirements of 83 F.R.Civ.P., to make rules of practice and procedure which are not inconsistent with these rules and which do not prohibit or limit the use of the Official Forms. In all cases not provided for by rule, the court may regulate its practice in any manner not inconsistent with the Official Forms or with these rules or those of the district in which the court acts.

* * *

APPENDIX D

SELECTED SECTIONS OF TITLE 28 UNITED STATES CODE

§ 158   Appeals
§ 451   Definitions
§ 1334   Bankruptcy cases and proceedings

This appendix contains only some of the sections of Title 28 of the U.S. Code relevant to bankruptcy procedure. The applicability of other sections of Title 28, the Bankruptcy Code and the Federal Rules of Bankruptcy Procedure must be considered before taking action in a bankruptcy matter. In addition, local bankruptcy rules must also be consulted.

§ 158. Appeals

(a) The district courts of the United States shall have jurisdiction to hear appeals from final judgments, orders, and decrees, and, with leave of the court, from interlocutory orders and decrees, of bankruptcy judges entered in cases and proceedings referred to the bankruptcy judges under section 157 of this title. An appeal under this subsection shall be taken only to the district court for the judicial district in which the bankruptcy judge is serving.

(b)(1) The judicial council of a circuit may establish a bankruptcy appellate panel, comprised of bankruptcy judges from districts within the circuit, to hear and determine, upon the consent of all the parties, appeals under subsection (a) of this section.

(2) If authorized by the Judicial Conference of the United States, the judicial councils of 2 or more circuits may establish a joint bankruptcy appellate panel comprised of bankruptcy judges from the districts within the circuits for which such panel is established, to hear and determine, upon the consent of all the parties, appeals under subsection (a) of this section.

(3) No appeal may be referred to a panel under this subsection unless the district judges for the district, by majority vote, authorize such referral of appeals originating within the district.

(4) A panel established under this section shall consist of three bank-ruptcy judges, provided a bankruptcy judge may not hear an appeal origi-nating within a district for which the judge is appointed or designated under section 152 of this title.

(c) An appeal under subsections (a) and (b) of this section shall be taken in the same manner as appeals in civil proceedings generally are taken to the courts of appeals from the district courts and in the time pro-vided by Rule 8002 of the Bankruptcy Rules.

(d) The courts of appeals shall have jurisdiction of appeals from all fi-nal decisions, judgments, orders, and decrees entered under subsections (a) and (b) of this section.

*   *   *

§ 451. Definitions

As used in this title:

The term "court of the United States" includes the Supreme Court of the United States, courts of appeals, district courts constituted by chapter 5 of this title, including the Court of Claims, the Court of Customs and Patent Appeals, the Customs Court and any court created by Act of Con-gress the judges of which are entitled to hold office during good behavior.

The terms "district court" and "district court of the United States" mean the courts constituted by chapter 5 of this title.

The term "judge of the United States" includes judges of the courts of appeals, district courts, Court of Claims, Court of Customs and Patent Appeals, Customs Court and any court created by Act of Congress, the judges of which are entitled to hold office during good behavior.

The term "justice of the United States" includes the Chief Justice of the United States and the associate justices of the Supreme Court.

The term "district" and "judicial district" mean the districts enumer-ated in Chapter 5 of this title.

The term "department" means one of the executive departments enu-merated in section 1 of Title 5, unless the context shows that such term was intended to describe the executive, legislative, or judicial branches of the government.

The term "agency" includes any department, independent establish-ment, commission, administration, authority, board or bureau of the United States or any corporation in which the United States has a propri-etary interest, unless the context shows that such term was intended to be used in a more limited sense.

*   *   *

§ 1334. Bankruptcy cases and proceedings

(a) Except as provided in subsection (b) of this section, the district court shall have original and exclusive jurisdiction of all cases under title 11.

(b) Notwithstanding any Act of Congress that confers exclusive jurisdiction on a court or courts other than the district courts, the district courts shall have original but not exclusive jurisdiction of all civil proceedings arising under title 11, or arising in or related to cases under title 11.

(c)(1) Nothing in this section prevents a district court in the interest of justice, or in the interest of comity with State courts or respect for State law, from abstaining from hearing a particular proceeding arising under title 11 or arising in or related to a case under title 11.

(2) Upon timely motion of a party in a proceeding based upon a State law claim or State law cause of action, related to a case under title 11 but not arising under title 11 or arising in a case under title 11, with respect to which an action could not have been commenced in a court of the United States absent jurisdiction under this section, the district court shall abstain from hearing such proceeding if an action is commenced, and can be timely adjudicated, in a State forum of appropriate jurisdiction. Any decision to abstain or not to abstain made under this subsection is not reviewable by appeal or otherwise by the court of appeals under section 158(d), 1291, or 1292 of this title or by the Supreme Court of the United States under section 1254 of this title. This subsection shall not be construed to limit the applicability of the stay provided for by section 362 of title 11, United States Code, as such section applies to an action affecting the property of the estate in bankruptcy.

(d) The district court in which a case under title 11 is commenced or is pending shall have exclusive jurisdiction of all of the property, wherever located, of the debtor as of the commencement of such case and of property of the estate.

* * *

APPENDIX E
SAMPLE PLEADINGS

These sample pleadings are included to facilitate commentary or discussion. They are substantially similar to pleadings that actually were filed with a bankruptcy court in Chapter 7 cases. Similar issues can arise in cases under Chapters 11 or 13 and the pleading format would be similar in such cases. The requirements and ramifications of a plan of reorganization present additional issues under Chapters 11 and 13. These pleadings are not intended as examples to be followed or avoided.

Sample Pleading 1

IN THE UNITED STATES BANKRUPTCY COURT
FOR THE _____ DISTRICT OF _____

IN RE:	
Debtor	Bankr. No.
Movant	Motion No.
vs.	Chapter 7
Debtor/Respondent	

MOTION FOR RELIEF FROM AUTOMATIC STAY

AND NOW comes _____ by and through her attorneys, _____ and in support of her Motion for Relief from Automatic Stay, alleges as follows:

1. Debtor/Respondent filed a Petition pursuant to Chapter 7 of the United States Bankruptcy Code on January 17, 1990, at the above number.

2. Movant and Respondent were formerly married to each other, having been divorced pursuant to Decree entered on _____, in _____ County, State of _____ at Civil Action No. _____.

3. Thereafter, the Court entered an Order dated _____, providing for spousal maintenance. A copy of this Order is attached hereto, made a part hereof, and marked Exhibit "A".

4. The Order provides for regular support payments in the amount of _____ per month.

5. Respondent is in arrears with respect to the support payments and continues to be in violation of the support Order by virtue of his failure to make the payments set forth therein.

6. The monthly support payments are nondischargeable debts as set forth in the United States Bankruptcy Code, 523(a)(5).

7. Movant desires relief from the automatic stay in order to seek appropriate state court remedies to enforce the Order for support and maintenance.

WHEREFORE, Movant respectfully requests this Honorable Court enter an Order granting Movant relief from the automatic stay to enforce support and maintenance payments.

_____
Attorney's name
Address
Telephone number

Sample Pleading 2

IN THE UNITED STATES BANKRUPTCY COURT
FOR THE _____ DISTRICT OF _____

IN RE:	
Debtor	Bankr. No.
_____	Motion No.
Movant	Chapter 7
vs.	
Debtor/Respondent	

ANSWER TO REQUEST FOR RELIEF FROM STAY

AND NOW COMES _____ by his attorney _____ and files the following Answer and avers as follows:

1. Admitted.
2. Admitted.
3. Admitted.
4. Admitted.
5. The allegations contained in paragraph 5 are denied. On the contrary it is averred that although Respondent is in arrears, his earning capacity has significantly changed since the original order and Respondent is presently contacting counsel in order to petition the Court for a decrease. In any event the question of alimony is not before this Honorable Court for collection or for dispute and is not the province of this Court.
6. The allegations contained in paragraph 6 are denied. On the contrary it is averred that support payments are modifiable as circumstances warrant or as they change from time to time between the parties.
7. Requires no response.

WHEREFORE, the Respondent requests that the Motion be dismissed with respect to those items of which the Court has no jurisdiction and/or schedule a full hearing with respect to the dischargeability of the various items sought to be enforced if that which is sought to be enforced is more than the monthly _____ alimony payment.

Respectfully submitted,

_____
Attorney's name
Address
Telephone number

Authors' Comments: Some federal jurisdictions permit the bankruptcy courts to consider the debtor's changed financial circumstances in determining the question of dischargeability. Others, such as courts in the Third Circuit, do not. In either type of jurisdiction the question of whether this should be treated as an adversary proceeding under Bankruptcy Rule 7001 would arise because the answer challenges the alleged nondischargeability of the debt. The procedural requirements for adversary proceedings are different than for a motion for relief from stay. Relief from stay generally must await a determination of whether the debt is nondischargeable. If such a motion is used as the vehicle for determining dischargeability the court may treat it as a motion for purposes of the filing fee but invoke the adversary procedural rules at trial.

Sample Pleading 3

**IN THE UNITED STATES BANKRUPTCY COURT
FOR THE _____ DISTRICT OF _____**

IN RE:	
Debtor	Bankr. No.
_____	Motion No.
Debtor/Movant	Chapter 7
vs.	
Respondent	

**EMERGENCY MOTION REGARDING
VIOLATION OF AUTOMATIC STAY**

TO THE HONORABLE _____, BANKRUPTCY JUDGE:

The emergency motion of Debtor by and through his attorney, _____ Esquire, respectfully represents:

1. Debtor/Movant, filed a Chapter 7 bankruptcy on _____, which was docketed at the above number.

2. On _____, the Debtor/Movant received an automatic stay from the continuation of any judicial orders, pursuant to 11 U.S.C. Section 362.

3. The state court order, dated _____, requiring the Debtor/Movant to pay Respondent the sum of _____ by _____, was stayed pursuant to 11 U.S.C. § 362. A copy of said order is attached hereto, marked Exhibit "A".

4.   On _____, this court granted partial relief from the automatic stay, to pursue the action pending in the Family Court of the _____ County. Said order states: "No action may be taken in aid of execution on any judgment, however, without further order of this court." A copy of said order of _____, is attached hereto, marked Exhibit "B".

5.   On _____, the state court found the Debtor/Movant to be in contempt of court for violating the state court order of _____, and jailed the Debtor/Movant in the _____ County Jail, with the requirement that Debtor/Movant pay Respondent the sum of _____, in order to purge his contempt. The act of jailing the Debtor/Movant is an action taken in aid of execution of a judgment and is a violation of the bankruptcy court's order of _____. A copy of the contempt order of the state court is attached hereto, marked Exhibit "C".

6.   That Debtor/Movant has filed an application for stay and an appeal of the contempt order of the state court with the State Appellate Court. The State Appellate Court entered an order of court, dated _____, denying the request for stay, and referred the Debtor/Movant to this court for interpretation of any restrictions on the lifting of the automatic stay.

WHEREFORE, the Debtor/Movant, respectfully requests that this Honorable Court immediately schedule a hearing on this matter, and thereafter enter an order releasing the Debtor/Movant from the _____ County Jail, and staying the state contempt order as entered in violation of the automatic stay and the order of the bankruptcy court or grant other appropriate relief.

_____

Attorney's name
Address
Telephone number

Sample Pleading 4

IN THE UNITED STATES BANKRUPTCY COURT
FOR THE _____ DISTRICT OF _____

IN RE:
 	
       Debtor
 	
_____
 	
    Debtor/Movant
 	
vs.
 	
     Respondent
	Bankr. No.
	
	Motion No.
	
	Chapter 7

ANSWER TO EMERGENCY MOTION REGARDING
VIOLATION OF AUTOMATIC STAY

TO THE HONORABLE _____, BANKRUPTCY JUDGE:

Respondent hereby files the within Answer to the Debtor/Movant's Emergency Motion, as follows:

  1. Admitted
  2. Admitted
  3. It is denied that the state court Order was stayed pursuant to 11 U.S.C. Section 362 insofar as it is alleged that that Order awards to the Respondent, a certain sum of money which represents part of the marital estate between the parties. As such, the award is not really a debt owed to Respondent by the Debtor/Movant, but rather represents a portion of the marital estate over which the Debtor/Movant acts merely as bailee prior to the effectuation of equitable distribution. By way of further answer, it is alleged that the intention of the Bankruptcy Code is not to offer relief to debtors who intentionally attempt to avoid a distribution order of the state courts effectuating distribution of marital property to rightful owners as directed by the state court.
  4. Admitted.
  5. It is admitted that the State Court found that Debtor/Movant violated the state court Order when he willfully and deliberately filed an Action in Bankruptcy, and, as a result of such contemptuous conduct, placed the Debtor/Movant in the _____ County Jail with the directive that he could purge himself of such contempt by paying to Respondent the sum of _____. It is denied that the act of jailing the Debtor/Movant is an action taken in aid of execution of a judgment and thus in violation of the order of the bankruptcy court entered on _____. Rather, it is alleged that the state court had full authority to determine that the Debtor/Movant, by intentionally and expressly engaging in conduct to deliberately avoid an order issued by that court, was in contempt. It is further alleged that the requirement that the Defendant pay to the Plaintiff the sum of _____ so as to purge himself of such contempt was not an action taken by the state court in aid of execution of any prior judgment or a directive that necessitated encumbrance of any assets held by the bankruptcy trustee. Rather, it represents clearly and independently of any prior order, payment of such sum the court deems to be sufficient so as to have the Debtor/Movant purge himself of his contemptuous behavior directed toward the state court. In addition, the state court entered its Order after a hearing wherein the Debtor/Movant testified he could obtain funds from a source which is not a part of the bankruptcy estate. Further, the Debtor/Movant is free to withdraw his bankruptcy action. The fact that the amount directed by the court is identical to a portion of the prior order, in amount, is not tantamount to an act in aid of execution.
  6. It is admitted that the Debtor/Movant filed an Application for Stay with the State Appellate Court, and it is admitted that the State Appellate Court, after oral argument, denied the request for stay of the contempt order.

It is denied that such request was specifically referred for interpretation to this court, but rather it is alleged that the denial of the stay indicated that the parameters of the stay should properly be made by this court. Thus the State Appellate Court denied the request for stay without prejudice to seeking relief in this Court.

NEW MATTER

7. On _____, the Honorable _____ of the State Court conducted a hearing with regard to Respondent's Petition for Contempt.

8. At the time of that hearing, Debtor/Movant admitted he was aware of possible bankruptcy options before he entered into the first state court Order, he admitted that he fully and freely and voluntarily entered into the state court order and he further admitted that it was within ten minutes of the signing of that Order, as he was walking back to his attorney's office with his attorney, that he and his counsel decided to file the bankruptcy petition that was filed in this action. Further, the Debtor/Movant admitted that such action was taken deliberately to avoid distribution of marital assets to his spouse as directed in the state court Order.

9. The Debtor/Movant's failure to comply with the state court Order was not his first contemptuous action in the state courts insofar as the Debtor/Movant was also in contempt of a prior order to which he agreed and which was entered by the Honorable _____ on _____.

10. It is believed, and therefore averred, that it is contrary to law and not in the best interest of justice, for this Honorable Court to deprive the state court of jurisdiction to render a debtor in contempt of a state court Order when a debtor's action in filing for bankruptcy is done with the sole and deliberate purpose of avoiding a state court Order that has been entered after consultation, negotiation and with consent of the debtor. It is further alleged that to do so would be contrary to the intent and purpose of the Bankruptcy Code and that such action by this Court would substantially stand to abrogate any and all rights persons in this state have pursuant to the Divorce Code of this state to determine the nature and extent of marital property, which is not analogous to joint property.

11. As the Debtor/Movant has failed, on several occasions, to make payments of money as directed by the state court, the only action which the state court could take that was sufficient and appropriate with regard to his contempt, was to incarcerate him and to compel him to pay a substantial sum of money in order to avoid further incarceration.

12. It is believed, and therefore averred, that in the event this Court determines that such action was in violation of its order for relief from stay, and thus relieves the Debtor/Movant from incarceration, such action will also stand to abrogate various rights pursuant to the Divorce Code, and will serve to create remedies to state court action that are not provided for in state law nor intended by the Bankruptcy Code.

WHEREFORE, it is respectfully requested that the Debtor/Movant's request for a hearing on this matter be denied, and further requested that if a hearing is conducted, thereafter, this Court enter an Order denying the relief requested in the Debtor/Movant's Emergency Motion Regarding the Automatic Stay.

Respectfully submitted,

_____

Attorney's name
Address
Telephone number

Authors' Comments: One of the issues in this case was whether the money ordered to be paid to the non-debtor spouse as a condition of purging the contempt had to be paid from estate assets. The state court judge jailed the debtor for contempt for failure to pay after finding that the debtor had a source of funds to draw on which was not property of the bankruptcy estate. The debtor actually obtained the funds from nonestate assets, paid his former spouse and was released from jail.

Note that in paragraph three of her answer the non-debtor spouse/respondent alleged that the debtor's obligation represented a property division. Under the current state of the law such an assertion could almost guarantee a finding of dischargeability. On the other hand, by labelling the debtor as a bailee, the issue of the extent of the debtor's interest in the property is raised.

Counsel must be aware that there is no such thing as a "New Matter" in the federal system of pleading.

Sample Pleading 5

**IN THE UNITED STATES BANKRUPTCY COURT
FOR THE _____ DISTRICT OF _____**

IN RE:	
Debtor	Bankr. No.
	Motion No.
Movant	Chapter 7
vs.	
Debtor/Respondent	

MOTION FOR DETERMINATION THAT CERTAIN PAYMENTS ARE NOT SUBJECT TO AUTOMATIC STAY

To: The Honorable Bankruptcy Court:

AND NOW COMES Movant, by her attorneys and respectfully represents:

1. The Movant, resides at _____ and is the former wife of the Debtor.

2. On _____, Movant and Debtor were divorced from the bonds of matrimony by a decree issued by the State Court, Family Division.

3. Thereafter, Movant and Debtor entered into an Agreement, a copy of which is attached hereto and marked Exhibit "A".

4. Paragraph 3(A) of said Agreement provides that "Husband specifically agrees to assume and pay until satisfied the second mortgage" on the former marital residence located at _____.

5. The payments required of the Debtor under Paragraph 3(A) of the Agreement attached hereto as Exhibit "A" are in the nature of alimony, maintenance or support.

6. Pursuant to 11 U.S.C. Sec. 362(b)(2), the payment required of the Debtor under Paragraph 3(A) of said Agreement are therefore not subject to the automatic stay of 11 U.S.C. Sec. 362(a).

WHEREFORE, Petitioner prays that this Honorable Court designate the payments required of the Debtor under Paragraph 3(A) of the Agreement attached hereto as Exhibit "A" as being in the nature of alimony, maintenance and support. Petitioner further prays that this Honorable Court declare that, pursuant to 11 U.S.C. Sec. 362(b)(2), Petitioner is not precluded by 11 U.S.C. 362(a) from proceeding for collection of said payments from property that is not property of the estate.

Respectfully submitted,

_____
Attorney's name
Address
Telephone number

Sample Pleading 6

**IN THE UNITED STATES BANKRUPTCY COURT
FOR THE _____ DISTRICT OF _____**

IN RE:

              Debtor,   Case No.

              Movant   Motion No.

vs.   Chapter 7

        Debtor/Respondent.

**RESPONSE TO MOTION FOR DETERMINATION THAT
CERTAIN PAYMENTS ARE NOT SUBJECT TO AUTOMATIC STAY**

AND NOW comes the Debtor, by and through his attorney, and sets forth the following in support of his Response:

1. Admitted.
2. Admitted.
3. Admitted.
4. It is admitted that as a division of their respective property the husband contracted to convey the marital residence to his wife and to make payments to a second mortgage. The liability to the wife arises under husband's promise to hold wife harmless from this debt under Paragraph 3(a).
5. Denied. This averment in Paragraph 5 is a conclusion of law to which no responsive pleading is required. To the extent a pleading is required, Paragraph 15 of Exhibit A contains the exclusive alimony liability of the Debtor. The Debtor has fully discharged his obligation to pay alimony under that agreement. By way of further averment, the Debtor is current on all of his support obligations of his minor children.
6. Denied. 11 U.S.C. § 362(b)(2) does not determine what debts are in the nature of support or alimony. 11 U.S.C. § 362(b)(2) only dictates that once a debt is determined to be in the nature of support and alimony, it is not subject to the automatic stay. The determination of whether a debt is in the nature of alimony or support must be raised by an adversary action under 11 U.S.C. § 523(a)(5) and in accordance with Bankruptcy Rule 7001. Accordingly, this Motion is premature and not ripe. An action for Relief From Stay should not be brought until the nature of the debt has been determined.

WHEREFORE, your Respondent requests that this Honorable Court dismiss the Motion as premature, or in the alternative, dismiss the Motion because it attempts to adjudicate a dischargeability issue by Motion as if it were a contested matter in violation of the rules.

Respectfully submitted,

_____
Attorney's name
Address
Telephone number

Sample Pleading 7

IN THE UNITED STATES BANKRUPTCY COURT
FOR THE _____ DISTRICT OF _____

IN RE:	
Debtor	Bankr. No.
	Adv. No.
Plaintiff	Chapter 7
vs.	
Debtor/Defendant	

COMPLAINT FOR DETERMINATION OF
DISCHARGEABILITY OF A DEBT

AND NOW comes Plaintiff by her attorneys, and in support of her Complaint for determination of dischargeability of debt, alleges as follows:

1. This is a core proceeding under 11 U.S.C. § 523(a)(5).

2. Debtor/Defendant filed a Petition pursuant to Chapter 7 of the United States Bankruptcy Code on _____, at the above number.

3. Plaintiff and Defendant were formerly married to each other, having been divorced pursuant to Decree entered on _____, in _____ County at Civil Action No. _____.

4. Thereafter, the Court entered an Order dated _____, providing for spousal maintenance. A copy of said Order is attached hereto, made a part hereof, and marked Exhibit "A".

5. The aforesaid Order provides for spousal maintenance in the following particulars: payment by the Defendant on behalf of the Plaintiff of a charge card debt of _____, arrearages for temporary maintenance and automobile

payments in the amount of $_____, and attorney's fees due Plaintiff's attorney in the amount of $_____.

6. No payments have been made and the aforesaid obligations are listed on Schedule A-3 of Debtor's Petition.

7. Pursuant to the United States Bankruptcy Code, Section 523(a)(5), those obligations are maintenance and are, accordingly, nondischargeable.

WHEREFORE, Petitioner respectfully requests this Honorable Court enter an Order determining that the aforedescribed obligations are nondischargeable.

_____

Attorney's name
Address
Telephone number

Note: As of August 1, 1991, Schedule A-3 became Schedule F.

Sample Pleading 8

**IN THE UNITED STATES BANKRUPTCY COURT
FOR THE _____ DISTRICT OF _____**

IN RE:	
Debtor	Bankr. No.
Plaintiff	Adv. No.
vs.	Chapter 7
Defendant	

ANSWER TO COMPLAINT FOR DETERMINATION
OF DISCHARGEABILITY OF A DEBT

AND NOW COMES Debtor/Defendant by his attorney and files the following Answer and avers as follows:

1. Admitted.
2. Admitted.
3. Admitted.
4. The allegations contained in paragraph 4 are denied. To the contrary it is averred the Order referred to contains numerous provisions which are both spousal maintenance and alternative awards to the Plaintiff.
5. The allegations contained in paragraph 5 are denied. To the contrary it is averred that the Order referred to does not unequivocally provide for total

maintenance payments but has various forms of relief which must be brought before the Court to determine their dischargeability. It is further denied that payments for attorney's fees are alimony, support or maintenance.

    6. Admitted.

    7. Paragraph 7 requires no response as the allegations represent conclusions of law.

WHEREFORE, the Defendant requests that the complaint be dismissed and the obligations be discharged.

Respectfully submitted,

_____

Attorney's name
Address
Telephone number

Sample Pleading 9

UNITED STATES BANKRUPTCY COURT
FOR THE _____ DISTRICT OF _____

IN RE:	
Debtor	Bankr. No.
	Adv. No.
Plaintiff	Chapter 7
vs.	
Debtor/Defendant	

COMPLAINT TO DETERMINE DISCHARGEABILITY OF A DEBT

AND NOW, comes Plaintiff, by her attorney, and files the following Complaint:

    1. This is an adversary proceeding, a core matter, to determine the dischargeability of a debt of the Debtor pursuant to 11 U.S.C. § 523(a)(5) and Bankruptcy Rules 4007 and 7001.

    2. Plaintiff is an adult individual who is licensed to practice law in the Commonwealth of Pennsylvania.

    3. Plaintiff herein is counsel of record for _____ in a proceeding presently pending before the Family Division of the State Court in the case of _____ vs. _____ presently pending before that Court at No. _____.

4. On _____, the State Court _____ entered an Order in the aforementioned divorce and support case in which Debtor was ordered to pay _____ in counsel fees to Plaintiff for services rendered to in the support/ divorce case. A true and correct copy of the Court Order is attached hereto and marked as Exhibit "A".

5. Through the date of filing of this Complaint, Debtor owes Plaintiff _____.

6. The aforesaid debt is non-dischargeable pursuant to 11 USC § 523(a)(5) in that the debt is owed for the support and maintenance of Debtor's spouse.

WHEREFORE, Plaintiff requests that the Court determine the debt owed to Plaintiff is non dischargeable pursuant to 11 U.S.C. § 523(a)(5).

Respectfully submitted,

_____

Attorney's name
Address
Phone number

Sample Pleading 10

UNITED STATES BANKRUPTCY COURT
FOR THE _____ DISTRICT OF _____

IN RE:	
Debtor	Bankr. No.
	Adv. No.
Plaintiff	Chapter 7
vs.	
Debtor/Defendant.	

ANSWER TO COMPLAINT TO DETERMINE
DISCHARGEABILITY OF A DEBT

AND NOW, comes, Debtor/Defendant, by and through his attorneys, and responds to the Complaint of Plaintiff as follows:

DIRECT RESPONSE TO COMPLAINT (FIRST DEFENSE)

1. Paragraph No. 1 of the Complaint is admitted.
2. Paragraph No. 2 of the Complaint is admitted.

3. Paragraph No. 3 of the Complaint is admitted.

4. Paragraph No. 4 of the Complaint is admitted in part and denied in part. It is admitted that, the State Court Family Division ("the family Court") entered an Order dated _____ ("the Order") in a proceeding under the Divorce Code at No. _____ ("the divorce action"). It is also admitted that the Debtor was ordered to pay $_____ in "preliminary counsel fees" to Plaintiff in the divorce action. It is admitted that there has been a claim for spousal support in the divorce action. To the extent that Paragraph 4 of the Complaint implies that the divorce action relates to child support, it is denied. Debtor, is the custodial parent of three (3) teenage children/adults and is and has been their sole source of support. The remaining averments of Paragraph 4 of the Complaint are denied.

5. Paragraph 5 of the Complaint is denied as stated. The Debtor filed for Chapter 7 Bankruptcy relief on _____ and shortly thereafter filed a Schedule of liabilities wherein Plaintiff was listed as having an unsecured claim with an estimated, liquidated value of _____. Debtor believes and therefore avers that Plaintiff has performed legal services for Debtor's spouse in excess of _____ prior to the date the bankruptcy was filed, for which the Debtor is or may be liable but the fee for these legal services of the Plaintiff have not yet been liquidated by the family Court. The Debtor seeks discharge of these "unliquidated" fees of the Plaintiff, and to the extent deemed necessary, will amend his Schedule of Liabilities to reflect this contingent, unliquidated liability. Debtor paid to the Plaintiff the sum of $_____ on or about _____. To the extent that this payment was properly applied to the liquidated claim represented by the family Court Order, Plaintiff has a pre-petition, liquidated claim against the Debtor in the amount of $_____. The Debtor denies that this is a proper application of the funds paid.

6. Paragraph 6 of the Complaint is denied. It is specifically denied that any debt that Debtor owes or may owe to the Plaintiff is in the nature of support and maintenance of the Debtor's spouse. In the alternative, to the extent that a debt was owed by the Debtor to the Plaintiff which was in the nature of support and maintenance of the Debtor's spouse, Debtor paid that obligation on _____.

ADDITIONAL DEFENSES

7. Plaintiff performed services for Debtor's spouse prior to the date the bankruptcy was filed which were not related to the spousal support and maintenance of the Debtor's spouse including, but not limited to, seeking a divorce decree for the Debtor's spouse and seeking a determination of the equitable distribution of the Debtor's and Debtor's spouse's property.

8. Debtor has paid the Plaintiff all sums due and owing related to the Plaintiff performing legal services for the Debtor's spouse that relate to, or are in the nature of, support and maintenance of the Debtor's spouse. Any claim Plaintiff has against the Defendant is dischargeable under the Bankruptcy Code.

9.   The obligation of the Debtor to the Plaintiff, if any, is and/or should be avoidable under Section 548 of the Bankruptcy Code as it was an obligation incurred by the Debtor within one year before the filing of the Debtor's bankruptcy petition, the Debtor received less than reasonably equivalent value in exchange for such obligation, and the Debtor was insolvent on the date the obligation was incurred or intended to incur, or believed that the Debtor would incur, debts that would be beyond the debtors ability to pay as such debts matured.

10.   Plaintiff's Complaint fails to state a cause of action.

11.   Plaintiff's Complaint should be dismissed as Plaintiff has failed to join an indispensable party to this proceeding.

12.   Plaintiff is not a real party in interest, under the family Court order.

WHEREFORE, Defendant respectfully requests this Honorable Court to enter Judgment in favor of the Defendant, and against Plaintiff, and determine that any debt owed by the Debtor to Plaintiff is dischargeable under the Bankruptcy Code.

Respectfully submitted,

_____

Attorney's name
Address
Telephone number

Sample Pleading 11

FORM B10
(6/90)

FORM 10. PROOF OF CLAIM

United States Bankruptcy Court _____ District of _____	PROOF OF CLAIM
In re (Name of Debtor)	Case Number

NOTE: This form should not be used to make a claim for an administrative expense arising after the commencement of the case. A "request" for payment of an administrative expense may be filed pursuant to 11 U.S.C. § 503.

Name of Creditor *(The person or other entity to whom the debtor owes money or property)* **Name and Address Where Notices Should be Sent** Telephone No.	☐ Check box if you are aware that anyone else has filed a proof of claim relating to your claim. Attach copy of statement giving particulars. ☐ Check box if you have never received any notices from the bankruptcy court in this case. ☐ Check box if this address differs from the address on the envelope sent to you by the court. **THIS SPACE IS FOR COURT USE ONLY**

ACCOUNT OR OTHER NUMBER BY WHICH CREDITOR IDENTIFIES DEBTOR: Check here if this claim ☐ replaces / ☐ amends a previously filed claim, dated: _____

1. BASIS FOR CLAIM

☐ Goods sold
☐ Services performed
☐ Money loaned
☐ Personal injury/wrongful death
☐ Taxes
☐ Other (Describe briefly)

☐ Retiree benefits as defined in 11 U.S.C. § 1114(a)
☐ Wages, salaries, and compensations (Fill out below)
Your social security number _____
Unpaid compensation for services performed
from _____ to _____
             (date)   (date)

2. DATE DEBT WAS INCURRED	**3. IF COURT JUDGMENT, DATE OBTAINED:**

4. CLASSIFICATION OF CLAIM. Under the Bankruptcy Code all claims are classified as one or more of the following: (1) Unsecured nonpriority, (2) Unsecured Priority, (3) Secured. It is possible for part of a claim to be in one category and part in another.
CHECK THE APPROPRIATE BOX OR BOXES that best describe your claim and STATE THE AMOUNT OF THE CLAIM.

☐ **SECURED CLAIM** $ _____
Attach evidence of perfection of security interest
Brief Description of Collateral:
☐ Real Estate   ☐ Motor Vehicle   ☐ Other (Describe briefly)

Amount of arrearage and other charges included in secured claim above, if any $ _____

☐ **UNSECURED NONPRIORITY CLAIM** $ _____
A claim is unsecured if there is no collateral or lien on property of the debtor securing the claim or to the extent that the value of such property is less than the amount of the claim.

☐ **UNSECURED PRIORITY CLAIM** $ _____
Specify the priority of the claim.
☐ Wages, salaries, or commissions (up to $ 2000), earned not more than 90 days before filing of the bankruptcy petition or cessation of the debtor's business, whichever is earlier) - 11 U.S.C. § 507(a)(3)
☐ Contributions to an employee benefit plan - U.S.C. § 507(a)(4)
☐ Up to $ 900 of deposits toward purchase, lease, or rental of property or services for personal, family, or household use - 11 U.S.C. § 507(a)(6)
☐ Taxes or penalties of governmental units - 11 U.S.C. § 507(a)(7)
☐ Other - 11 U.S.C. §§ 507(a)(2), (a)(5) - (Describe briefly)

5. TOTAL AMOUNT OF CLAIM AT TIME CASE FILED: $ _____ (Unsecured) $ _____ (Secured) $ _____ (Priority) $ _____ (Total)

☐ Check this box if claim includes prepetition charges in addition to the principal amount of the claim. Attach itemized statement of all additional charges.

6. CREDITS AND SETOFFS: The amount of all payments on this claim has been credited and deducted for the purpose of making this proof of claim. In filing this claim, claimant has deducted all amounts that claimant owes to debtor. **7. SUPPORTING DOCUMENTS:** <u>Attach copies of supporting documents,</u> such as promissory notes, purchase orders, invoices, itemized statements of running accounts, contracts, court judgments, or evidence of security interests. If the documents are not available, explain. If the documents are voluminous, attach a summary. **8. TIME-STAMPED COPY:** To receive an acknowledgment of the filing of your claim, enclose a stamped, self-addressed envelope and copy of this proof of claim.	**THIS SPACE IS FOR COURT USE ONLY**

Date	Sign and print the name and title, if any, of the creditor or other person authorized to file this claim (attach copy of power of attorney, if any)

Penalty for presenting fraudulent claim: Fine of up to $500,000 or imprisonment for up to 5 years, or both. 18 U.S.C. §§ 152 and 3571.

Authors' Comments: As of August 1, 1991, this is the only Proof of Claim form to be used. Claimant must file the form with the clerk of the bankruptcy court in which the case is pending. The claim must be filed before the claims bar date. Creditors usually are notified of the bar date in the notice of the first meeting of creditors.

TABLE OF CASES

Case	Book §
In re Adams, 12 B.R. 540 (Bankr. D. Utah 1981)	§ 1.5
Addison v. Addison, 95 Ohio App. 191, 118 N.E.2d 225 (1953)	§ 6.5
Aetna Life Ins. Co. v. Bunt, 110 Wash. 2d 368, 754 P.2d 993 (1988)	§ 3.3
In re Albany Partners Ltd., 749 F.2d 670 (11th Cir. 1984)	§ 1.5
In re Allshouse, 34 B.R. 512 (Bankr. W.D. Pa. 1983)	§ 2.4
In re Altchek, 124 B.R. 944 (Bankr. S.D.N.Y. 1991)	§ 8.3
In re Arnold Print Works, Inc., 815 F.2d 165 (1st Cir. 1987)	§ 7.3
In re Ashe, 669 F.2d 105 (3d Cir.), *vacated and remanded,* 459 U.S. 1082 (1982), *aff'd,* 712 F.2d 864 (3d Cir. 1983), *cert. denied,* 465 U.S. 1024, *reh'g denied,* 466 U.S. 963 (1984)	§ 4.3
In re Atallah, 95 B.R. 910 (Bankr. E.D. Pa. 1989)	§ 6.3
In re Atlantic Business & Community Corp., 901 F.2d 325 (3d Cir. 1990)	§ 8.2
In re Babo, 81 B.R. 389 (Bankr. W.D. Pa. 1988)	§ 6.1
In re Baldwin United Corp., 52 B.R. 541 (Bankr. S.D. Ohio 1985)	§ 7.3
Barrett v. Barrett, 470 Pa. 253, 368 A.2d 616 (1977)	§ 8.1
Begier v. IRS, 878 F.2d 762 (3d Cir. 1989), *aff'd,* 110 S. Ct. 2258 (1990)	§ 3.2
Belisle v. Plunkett, 877 F.2d 512 (7th Cir.), *cert. denied,* 110 S. Ct. 241 (1989)	§§ 3.2, 4.6
Bellotti v. Baird, 428 U.S. 132 (1976)	§ 7.4
In re Bennett, 36 B.R. 893 (Bankr. W.D. Ky. 1984)	§ 1.3
In re Better Homes of Va., Inc., 804 F.2d 289 (4th Cir. 1986)	§ 8.2
Biegenwald v. Fauver, 882 F.2d 748 (3d Cir. 1989)	§§ 7.1, 7.4
In re Bland, 793 F.2d 1172 (11th Cir. 1986)	§ 4.2
In re Boggess, 105 B.R. 470 (Bankr. S.D. Ill. 1989)	§ 4.1
In re Borbidge, 90 B.R. 728 (Bankr. E.D. Pa. 1988), *aff'd* 114 B.R. 63 (E.D. Pa. 1990)	§ 6.5
Borman v. Leiker, 886 F.2d 273 (10th Cir. 1989)	§ 1.8
In re Boughton, 49 B.R. 312 (Bankr. N.D. Ill. 1985)	§ 7.3
Bowers v. Bailey, 237 Iowa 295, 21 N.W.2d 773 (1946)	§ 5.5
In re Boyd, 26 B.R. 772 (Bankr. D. Minn. 1982)	§ 1.8
Boyd v. Robinson, 741 F.2d 1112 (8th Cir. 1984)	§§ 1.8, 3.1, 4.1
Boyle v. Donovan, 724 F.2d 681 (8th Cir. 1984)	§§ 1.1, 2.5
In re Brock, 58 B.R. 797 (Bankr. S.D. Ohio 1986)	§ 8.2

TABLE OF UNITED STATES CODE CITATIONS

Code	Book §
10 U.S.C. § 848	§ 8.3
11 U.S.C. § 101 *et seq.*	§§ 1.2, 2.1, 3.1, 3.3, 4.1, 4.2, 4.4, 5.2
11 U.S.C. §§ 105, 706(b)	§ 1.9
11 U.S.C. § 301	§ 1.2
11 U.S.C. § 303	§ 1.2
11 U.S.C. § 304(c)	§ 7.4
11 U.S.C. § 305(a)	§§ 7.3, 7.4
11 U.S.C. § 305(c)	§ 7.2
11 U.S.C. § 362	§ 1.5
11 U.S.C. § 362	§ 7.4
11 U.S.C. § 362(b)(2)	§ 1.5
11 U.S.C. § 362(c)	§ 1.5
11 U.S.C. § 362(h)	§§ 8.1, 8.2
11 U.S.C. § 363	§§ 2.5, 4.4
11 U.S.C. § 506(d)	§§ 3.3, 4.1, 7.4
11 U.S.C. § 521	§§ 1.2, 1.3, 1.5
11 U.S.C. § 522(b)	§§ 1.4, 6.1
11 U.S.C. § 522(d)	§§ 5.7, 6.2
11 U.S.C. § 522(f)	§ 4.2
11 U.S.C. § 523(a)(4)	§ 3.2
11 U.S.C. § 523(a)(5)	§§ 1.5, 2.1, 2.3, 3.3, 5.1, 5.3, 5.8
11 U.S.C. §§ 524, 1141(d)(1)	§ 1.7
11 U.S.C. § 541	§§ 1.3, 3.3, 6.1
11 U.S.C. § 541(a)	§§ 1.3, 1.5, 2.5
11 U.S.C. § 544	§§ 3.2, 4.6
11 U.S.C. §§ 547, 548	§§ 1.6, 1.8
11 U.S.C. § 548(d)(1)	§ 4.6
11 U.S.C. § 548(d)(2)(A)	§ 4.5
11 U.S.C. § 706(c)	§ 1.9
11 U.S.C. § 707(a)	§ 1.8
11 U.S.C. § 726	§§ 1.9, 8.2
11 U.S.C. § 1328	§ 3.3
11 U.S.C. § 1334	§ 7.2
28 U.S.C. § 158(c)	§ 8.1
28 U.S.C. § 451	§ 8.3
28 U.S.C. § 1334(c)(2)	§ 7.3
28 U.S.C. § 1930	§ 1.2

INDEX